CIMA EXAMINATION TEXT

Intermediate Level

Paper 5

Business Taxation

Finance Act 2003

ISBN 1 84390 096 3

British Library Cataloguing-in-Publication data

A catalogue record for this book is available from the British Library.

We are grateful to the Chartered Institute of Management Accountants for permission to reproduce past assessment material. The solutions have been prepared by The Financial Training Company.

Published by

The Financial Training Company
22J Wincombe Business Park
Shaftesbury
Dorset
SP7 9QJ

Contents

Chapter

How to use this examination text

Objective

The aim of this Examination Text is a simple one: to give you the best possible chance of achieving the pass mark when you attempt the CIMA Business Taxation examination. To do this, we follow three main principles:

♦ The texts cover **all** areas of the syllabus with sufficient depth to ensure that you are fully prepared. However, we use our knowledge and experience to home in on the key syllabus areas and give these areas extra attention.

♦ We use our extensive experience of teaching CIMA students to assess how much the majority of students can assimilate. We do not make the mistake of overloading you with material that you will find worthless in the examination room.

♦ We believe that the best way to prepare for an examination is by practice. We intersperse explanatory text with frequent examples for you to try your hand at. Full solutions are provided in all cases.

Using the Examination Text

Each chapter begins with a section headed 'Exam Focus'. This reflects our key objective: we are interested above all in your examination success.

We set out CIMA's own Learning Outcomes and the main structural divisions into which the chapter is organised. This gives you a clear picture of what you should be aiming to achieve as you work through the text, and guidance on the steps to follow on the way.

The main body of each chapter consists of very full explanation of all syllabus areas. We concentrate on clear explanations of what really matters. We emphasise drills — standardised approaches that you can follow for typical questions. Never again need you ask: 'Where do I begin?'

Each chapter includes practice questions. These are graded: earlier questions involve material from the earlier sections of the chapter, while in later questions we progress to include more complex examples, including exam-standard questions. To get the best from the text you should make a serious attempt to tackle all the practice questions. Only then should you refer to our suggested solutions, which are contained in the final chapter of the text.

Each chapter ends by summarising the main points that you should have digested as you worked your way through.

Key features

The text is written in an interactive style:

- key terms and concepts are clearly defined

- 'pitfalls' and 'examination tips' help you avoid commonly made mistakes and help you focus on what is required to perform well in your examination

- frequent practice examples throughout the chapters ensure that what you have learnt is regularly reinforced

Icons

Throughout the text we use symbols to highlight the elements referred to above.

 Key facts

 Examination tips and techniques

 Pitfalls

 Practice questions

Syllabus

Syllabus aims

To test the student's ability to:

♦ Identify the rules imposed upon employers in relation to employee taxation
♦ Explain and apply the system of corporation tax self assessment, capital gains and VAT
♦ Identify and evaluate the impact of international aspects on a UK company's taxation
♦ Identify and evaluate the impact of different tax planning scenarios

Guidance introduction

The syllabus recognises that management accountants will not be expected to become experts in taxation, but rather that they will recognise the important role that taxation can have to play in the decision making process in business. It is expected that the management accountant should be able to raise relevant issues with their tax advisers from an informed point of view. For example, they should be able to prepare notes concerning taxation issues which are to be discussed at a meeting.

Having mastered the basic rules involved in each of the taxes included in the syllabus, candidates will be able to produce correct computations of the tax liabilities of the business on the basis of the information given. However, more than this will be required in the paper. In many cases, candidates will be required to compute the taxation liability in more than one scenario and to advise on the most tax-efficient course of action. In some cases, the question will contain a 'what if' element. In addition the scenario based question in the new examination paper will carry marks for demonstrating communication skills required in reporting information.

Candidates should be aware that commercial decisions are not driven by tax alone and that, at all times, the commercial considerations should take priority. The approach taken in this paper is that where more than one course of action can be used to achieve a desired commercial objective, then management should be aware of the respective taxation implications of the alternatives.

The examination paper

The three hour paper will be divided into three sections.

Section A consists of **ten** objective test questions (of the multiple-choice type (MCQs) worth two marks each. These questions will examine any knowledge based topic within the syllabus.

Section B comprises a **compulsory** scenario based question which could include any elements of the syllabus including planning and compliance aspects. This question will be worth a total of **40 marks** with six marks available for style, presentation and communication skills. The format of the required answer will be specified – report, memo, letter, etc, and it is important to produce your answer in the format specified.

Section C will require **two** technical questions to be answered from a choice of four questions, with each question carrying 20 marks. While these questions could test any part of the syllabus, they are more likely to come from sections (ii), (iii), (iv) and (v). It is not envisaged that a full 20 mark question on section (vi) – VAT – would be asked although VAT could be a significant part of a Section C question. Questions in this section could contain a planning element. Any administration aspects would be incorporated into a larger question.

The weightings in the syllabus are a guide to the level of study required. They do not necessarily represent the spread of the marks in any single examination paper.

A taxation information sheet showing tax rates, etc will be included with the examination paper. To reduce the need to remember standard information, the information sheet will give details of capital allowances rates and the size of qualifying companies.

Syllabus content

Note: For each section of the syllabus the published content is shown first. This is followed by a commentary which expands this content, showing specific areas which are examinable. There are also notes identifying those topics which are excluded from the syllabus.

Chapter

5(i)   Tax administration – (study weighting 5%)

Learning outcomes

On completion of their studies students should be able to:

◆	Describe the system of Corporation Tax Self Assessment (CTSA)	13
◆	Identify the key dates for submission of returns	13
◆	Describe the Inland Revenue's powers of enquiry	13
◆	Identify the various penalties and interest charges in CTSA	13
◆	Identify the minimum record-keeping requirements	13
◆	Identify the compliance requirements imposed on employers in relation to employee taxation	16
◆	Identify the VAT registration/de-registration requirements and the rules and penalties in relation to VAT returns	14

Syllabus content

◆	Corporation Tax Self Assessment – all compliance aspects: returns; interest and penalties	13
◆	Returns required by employers in connection with employees' tax and NICs	16
◆	VAT administration	14

Commentary

In relation to CTSA, candidates would be expected to learn about deadlines for submission of Form CT600; appeals and time limits for making appeals and other claims; the nature of Revenue enquiries.

In relation to the VAT element, candidates would be expected to know about registration matters and the timing of returns.

Given a weighting of only 5%, there is little opportunity for asking a full question on this area. It is more likely that elements of this section will be incorporated in a larger question – for example, the date by which the Revenue may instigate an enquiry into a CT600 CTSA Return; the impact of EC regulations on VAT.

Questions on this area will tend to require a narrative response.

Chapter

5(ii)   Employees' taxation – (study weighting 10%)

Learning outcomes

On completion of their studies students should be able to:

◆	Apply knowledge of the Benefits in Kind (BIK) system for employees	15
◆	Identify the rules for different types of employees	15
◆	Calculate the total assessable benefits of an employee and explain the effect on code numbers	15, 16
◆	Evaluate the relative tax efficiency of different methods of rewarding employees	16

Syllabus content

◆	All aspects of the system of benefits in kind	15
◆	Contrast salaries with dividends	16
◆	Efficient methods of rewarding employees	16

Commentary

The only income tax questions in the paper could cover employee taxation under the Employment Income Rules (formerly called Schedule E) and the related employer's duties and responsibilities. Note that the relevant legislation is now contained in the Income Tax (Earnings and Pensions) Act 2003 (ITEPA 2003). Tax efficient methods of rewarding staff will be an important aspect. The syllabus is taken to include the following topics:

♦ Quantification of assessable benefits in kind for an employee. Including the new rules for motor car benefits and mileage allowances introduced from 6 April 2002.

♦ The treatment of employees' expenses under SS328-331 ITEPA 2003 together with relevant case law.

♦ The operation of the PAYE system including the operation of code numbers.

♦ Knowledge of the employers' compliance duties in respect of the PAYE system.

♦ Alternative tax efficient methods of rewarding employees, including dividends vs salaries for staff who are shareholders.

♦ Employee share option schemes (including SIPs and EMI).

♦ Status issues and an awareness only of the consequences for IR35 type 'employees'.

In relation to National Insurance contributions (NIC), knowledge will be required of employer's class 1, class 1A and class 1B (on PSAs) only. The new rules for the application of class 1A to certain benefits will be required knowledge. There will be no questions on non-standard earnings or on the special arrangements for directors.

Chapter

5(iii) Corporation tax – (study weighting 25%)

Learning outcomes

On completion of their studies students should be able to:

	Chapter
♦ Calculate the Schedule DI profit for taxation purposes, showing knowledge of case law and statute	3
♦ Calculate the total profits of a company for CT purposes	1
♦ Calculate the capital allowances entitlement of a company	4, 5
♦ Calculate the CT liability of a company (including that of small and intermediate companies)	2, 11
♦ Prepare a schedule of CT payments of a large company covering a two year period under the quarterly payment system	13
♦ Identify the effect of all forms of loss relief on a company's, group's or a consortium's CT liability	9, 10
♦ Explain the effect of the loan relationships rules on a company's CT liability	1
♦ Explain the operation of shadow advance corporation tax (ACT). No computation of ACT will be required	2

Syllabus content

	Chapter
♦ Adjustment of trading profits for taxation purposes - underlying principles and legislation	3
♦ Computation of total income and CT liability	2, 11
♦ Quarterly payment rules	2, 13
♦ All forms of relief for losses including Groups, Consortia and joint ventures	9, 10
♦ Capital Allowances	4, 5
♦ Loan Relationships	1
♦ Shadow ACT – an awareness only	2

Commentary

This is the largest single topic within the syllabus, reflecting the fact that most chartered management accountants will be employed by limited companies. The knowledge required is extensive and it is the area to which most study time should be devoted.

The FA 1996 introduced new rules for dealing with interest paid and received by companies under the generic heading 'loan relationships'. This area will be examined in every future corporation tax question and it must be learned.

It is important to distinguish between trade and non-trade loans and to be able to show how non-trade deficits can be relieved.

The syllabus is taken to include knowledge of the following topics:

♦ The method of computing the chargeable income and total income of a company (most frequently the adjusted profit figure will be given). Note that the total income determines the status of the company (large, small or intermediate – note that from 1 April 2000 there are two new categories: very small and small intermediate). If the company is large – taking into account associated companies – it may be required to pay its CT under the quarterly arrangements.

♦ Candidates should be aware of the effect of any brought forward surplus ACT on dividend policy. No ACT calculations will be required. Note that surplus shadow ACT will not be examined nor will any group aspects of shadow ACT.

♦ Full knowledge of accounting periods for CT purposes including the treatment of long periods of account.

♦ The detailed schedule of payment dates and amounts of CT under the quarterly payment arrangements – bearing in mind that the system is being phased in over a four year period.

♦ Full knowledge of the treatment of loan interest receivable and payable and of the treatment of corporate debt under the loan relationships rules. Be able to deal with non-trading deficits in the most tax efficient manner.

♦ Full knowledge of the treatment of patent royalties from 1 April 2002 under the FA 2002 legislation dealing with intangible assets. Note that, apart from rollover reliefs, no other aspect of the intangible assets rules will be examined in 2004.

♦ Detailed knowledge of the reliefs available for trading losses under present legislation and of the interaction between charges and trading losses. No questions will be set on the effect of a loss carried back to 1999 which creates surplus ACT prior to 6 April 1999.

♦ Detailed knowledge of all aspects of group and consortium reliefs, including the treatment of capital gains, including the treatment of pre-entry losses. Knowledge of the FA 2000 rules involving the role of non-UK resident companies in groups is required. No questions will be set involving 'link companies'. 'Group consortium' companies are examinable from 2004. Occasionally, narrative questions on group situations may be set.

♦ Knowledge of close companies and close investment-holding companies. Generally narrative questions will be set, although examination questions could involve calculating shareholdings to establish whether a company is close. Be aware of the principal members' rule. The consequences of close company status should be understood, including loans and benefits in kind to participators and the arrangements for paying any resulting tax.

♦ The method of calculating a company's Schedule A assessment under the FA 1998 rules and how to deal with Schedule A losses.

♦ Knowledge of the capital allowances system relating to plant (including short life assets and motor cars with low CO_2 emissions) and industrial buildings only. (Knowledge is not required concerning long life assets nor such items as patents and agricultural buildings.) The new relief for research and development expenditure in both FA 2000 and 2002 is examinable from May 2004 onwards.

Chapter

5(iv) International aspects – (study weighting 20%)

Learning outcomes

On completion of their studies students should be able to:

◆ Evaluate the taxation implications of alternative methods of running an overseas operation	12
◆ Identify the significance of company residences for tax purposes	12
◆ Calculate the CT liability of a UK company which has overseas income, using the rules of double tax relief (but excluding knowledge of Treaties)	12
◆ Identify transfer pricing problems, calculating any adjustment required and state how this will be reported in its CTSA return	12
◆ Identify a controlled foreign company (CFC)	12
◆ Calculate the CT liability arising as a result of the presence of a CFC	12

Syllabus content

◆ Foreign operations – Subsidiary vs Branch	12
◆ Company Residence	12
◆ Double Taxation relief (DTR)	12
◆ Transfer Pricing	12
◆ Controlled Foreign Companies (CFC)	12
◆ International Trading	12

Commentary

The present syllabus for IBTX is the first to include a separate section on overseas matters. However, since this is a first level tax paper, a number of the complex matters involved are not examinable. A list of these exclusions is shown at the end of this section.

The syllabus is taken to include knowledge of the following topics:

◆ Identifying the residence of a company for UK tax purposes. The effect of location of management on residence status.

◆ The taxation in the UK of overseas income received by a UK resident company.

◆ The alternative methods that a UK company may adopt in running an overseas operation.

◆ Basic double tax relief (DTR) – unilateral relief only – not treaty reliefs.

◆ The treatment of excess foreign tax credits under the FA 2000 rules (but not involving 'on-shore pooling' – see below).

◆ Identification of controlled foreign companies (CFC) and the consequences for UK companies.

◆ Fundamental aspects only of transfer pricing (no APAs).

◆ The role of non-UK resident companies in forming groups or consortia.

It is equally important to be aware of those aspects which are not in the IBTX syllabus and which will not be examined and are:

◆ Foreign companies trading in the UK.

◆ The use of 'mixer' companies.

◆ 'Capping' of the rates of DTR.

◆ 'On-shore pooling' of foreign dividends and the calculation of 'eligible unrelieved foreign tax' (EUFT) involving on-shore pooling.

◆ The calculation of 'exit charges' where a company ceases to be UK resident.

Questions could be set in any of the following areas:

♦ The completion of a CT computation involving double tax relief (DTR). Minor aspects of DTR may appear in the compulsory sections of the paper, including the scenario-based question (Section B), but any full question on this topic would be an optional question in Section C of the paper.

♦ Candidates should be able to identify a CFC from information supplied; know the consequences of this status for CTSA purposes; compute any CT due on CFC income and be aware of any exemptions.

♦ An awareness only of the fundamental aspects of transfer pricing as required under the CTSA reporting rules. No questions will be set on advance pricing agreements (APA).

♦ The important taxation differences under the different methods by which a UK company could run an overseas operation. Branch or subsidiary. Candidates would be expected to give advice on the choice.

Chapter

5(v) Capital gains (for companies only) – (study weighting 10%)

Learning outcomes

On completion of their studies students should be able to:

♦ Identify chargeable assets for taxation as capital gains	6
♦ Apply rollover and holdover reliefs for tangible and intangible business assets	3, 8
♦ Identify the CGT reliefs available in a group situation and the anti-avoidance rules relating to pre-entry assets	10
♦ Calculate the gain arising on the disposal of quoted securities using the pooling system	7
♦ Apply the substantial shareholding exemption rules (SSE)	7

Syllabus content

♦ Scope	6
♦ Reliefs for Business Assets	8
♦ Groups of Companies	10
♦ Shares and securities	7
♦ The substantial shareholding exemption (SSE)	7

Commentary

In this topic, computations of chargeable gains will always be required and the topic could be examined in the scenario-based question in Section B of the paper. ONE of the questions in Section C will always be wholly on CGT issues.

The syllabus is taken to include the following topics:

♦ Detailed knowledge of rollover relief and hold over relief on tangible business assets, including deferred gains on assets sold between 1985 and 1988.

♦ Knowledge of the new form of reinvestment rollover relief for intangible assets introduced in the FA 2002.

♦ Full knowledge of the reliefs for investments in Venture Capital Trusts (VCT) and in enterprise investment schemes (EIS). (See note below.)

♦ A knowledge of the new Corporate Venturing scheme introduced in the FA 2000 is required.

♦ A knowledge of basic planning in capital gains tax, for example which asset to sell; identification of planning opportunities within a group structure.

♦ Full knowledge of such areas as indexation allowance, re-basing at 31 March 1982 and the pooling of quoted shares.

♦ The anti-avoidance legislation on pre-entry capital losses in groups.

♦ Re-allocation relief in respect of a gain arising on a company leaving a group (within 6 years of an asset transfer). FA 2002. 'De-merging gains'.

♦ Relief for disposals of substantial shareholdings. Conditions for qualifying.

While no questions involving the calculation of a CGT liability for an individual will be asked, EIS and VCTs are examinable. The context of questions on these areas would be that a company was trying to raise finance and would require to explain to potential shareholders the taxation benefits (and disadvantages) of EIS and VCTs.

The following items are not examinable:

♦ Disposals by individuals in any circumstances.
♦ Disposals of agricultural quotas.

Chapter

5(vi) Value Added Tax – (study weighting 10%)

Learning outcomes

On completion of their studies students should be able to:

♦ Identify the significance of Standard rate, Zero rate and exempt supplies and those supplies outwith the scope of VAT	14
♦ Identify the correct tax point of a supply and understand its significance	14
♦ Identify the significance of EU and non-EU countries when dealing with VAT	14
♦ Discuss the problems and opportunities inherent in a VAT group registration	14

Syllabus content

♦ Scope	14
♦ Zero rating; exemption; partial exemption	14
♦ Tax point; payment and refunds	14
♦ The concept of a group registration and the consequent VAT regulations	14
♦ Transactions with foreign companies	14
♦ Groups of companies	14
♦ VAT treatment of basic transactions in property	14

Commentary

This section has a 10% weighting and a full 20 mark question in the optional Section C is unlikely. However, VAT will be examined in some form in every paper; either as an element within the scenario-based question or in the MCQs in Section A.

The syllabus is taken to include the following topics:

♦ The registration/de-registration rules; penalties; default surcharges.

♦ Knowledge of VAT in relation to basic property transactions – 'opting to tax' elections.

♦ Knowledge of the VAT regulations in connection with exports and imports, including trading with EU and non-EU countries.

♦ The planning opportunities available in a group context. Separate registrations.

♦ An understanding of VAT in property transactions.

♦ An understanding of the partial exemption rules.

The following items are not examinable:

♦ Fully computational questions on VAT, although occasionally some computation may be required as a minor aspect of a question, including compulsory ones.

♦ No questions will be set on any anti-avoidance provisions relating to groups of companies.

Chapter

5(vii) Tax planning – (study weighting 20%)

Learning outcomes

Students are reminded that 'Tax Planning' is not a discrete area of taxation. It is the application of the knowledge you gain while studying each section of the syllabus. Try to grasp the planning opportunities when studying each section.

On completion of their studies students should be able to:

♦	Calculate the form of loss relief which will minimise the CT liability in either a single company or in a group or consortium	9, 10
♦	Evaluate the tax efficiency of alternative methods of acquiring other businesses	10
♦	Contrast the tax implications of financing a company by debt or equity	11
♦	Demonstrate the planning aspects of maximising the use of surplus ACT existing at 6 April 1999 for a company	2
♦	Demonstrate the most efficient method of disposing of assets to third parties by a group of companies	10
♦	Discuss the most efficient method of arranging VAT registrations for groups of companies	14
♦	Demonstrate how to maximise DTR	12
♦	Demonstrate the importance of timing in tax planning	3, 4, 5, 7, 8, 9, 10

Syllabus content

♦	Optimum use of trading losses	9, 10
♦	Capital allowances and R&D expenditure	3, 4, 5
♦	Company acquisitions – assets or shares?	10
♦	Alternative methods of financing a company	11
♦	Shadow ACT	2
♦	Sales of Group assets	10
♦	VAT – Groups	14
♦	Charges and losses in DTR computations	12
♦	Loan relationships	1

Commentary

Although this subject has been allocated a separate section of the syllabus, it must be treated as an integral part of all areas covered in the syllabus. Within each section of the syllabus there have been references made to planning approaches.

All of the tax planning aspects inherent in any situation should be considered when candidates are studying a particular topic. For example:

♦ Whether to acquire other companies and the methods of acquisition; consider when studying groups and associated companies.

♦ Whether (or not) to have a group VAT registration; consider when studying VAT.

♦ When to buy an asset; consider when studying capital allowances.

♦ Whether to finance a company by debt or equity; consider when studying loan relationships.

♦ Whether or not to pay a dividend; consider when studying shadow ACT.

♦ Whether to provide employees with motor cars or let them buy their own.

Planning aspects will always be a feature of the scenario-based question in Section B. Every report asked for will contain some requirement to give advice on taxation matters. In Section C some planning could be examined in any question, often as a second requirement. Planning questions often require candidates to perform a computation and then to give advice based on the computation. It is therefore important to master the basic computational rules.

TAX RATES

TAX TABLE

The following table of tax rates should be used in answering this paper. The capital gains tax indexation factors for use with question 5 are given in the question.

Corporation tax

| | *Financial years* | |
| | 2002 | 2003 |
	Year ended 31/3/2003	*Year ended 31/3/2004*
Upper threshold	£1,500,000	£1,500,000
Standard rate of tax	30%	30%
Lower threshold	£300,000	£300,000
Small company rate	19%	19%
Taper relief fraction	11/400	11/400
Upper threshold for starting rate	£50,000	£50,000
Lower threshold for starting rate	£10,000	£10,000
Starting rate	Nil%	Nil%
Taper fraction for starting rate	19/400	19/400
Shadow ACT rate	20%	20%
FII tax credit rate (for calculating shadow ACT)	20%	20%
Rate for grossing up net dividends received for small company threshold purposes	100/90	100/90
Rate of income tax suffered/retained on receiving/paying debenture or loan interest	20%	20%

Rates of income tax to be used in dealing with UFII and charges   22% for 2003/04
(22% for 2002/03)

Income tax and NIC

Income Tax rates:

First £1,960	10%
Next £28,540	22%
Balance	40%
Employer's NIC, Classes 1A and 1B NIC	12.8%

VAT

Registration threshold from April 2003	£56,000

Meaning of CIMA's examination requirements

CIMA use precise words in the requirements of their questions. In the schedule below we reproduce the precise meanings of these words from the CIMA syllabus. You must learn these definitions and make sure that in the exam you do precisely what CIMA requires you to do.

Learning objective	Verbs used	Definition
1 Knowledge What you are expected to know	List	Make a list of
	State	Express, fully or clearly, the details of/facts of
	Define	Give the exact meaning of
2 Comprehension What you are expected to understand	Describe	Communicate the key features of
	Distinguish	Highlight the differences between
	Explain	Make clear or intelligible/state the meaning of
	Identify	Recognise, establish or select after consideration
	Illustrate	Use an example to describe or explain something
3 Application Can you apply your knowledge?	Apply	To put to practical use
	Calculate/compute	To ascertain or reckon mathematically
	Demonstrate	To prove with certainty or to exhibit by practical means
	Prepare	To make or get ready for use
	Reconcile	To make or prove consistent/compatible
	Solve	Find an answer to
	Tabulate	Arrange in a table
4 Analysis Can you analyse the detail of what you have learned?	Analyse	Examine in detail the structure of
	Categorise	Place into a defined class or division
	Compare and contrast	Show the similarities and/or differences between
	Construct	To build up or compile
	Discuss	To examine in detail by argument
	Interpret	To translate into intelligible or familiar terms
	Produce	To create or bring into existence
5 Evaluation Can you use your learning to evaluate, make decisions or recommendations?	Advise	To counsel, inform or notify
	Evaluate	To appraise or assess the value of
	Recommend	To advise on a course of action

Objective test questions

The objective test questions will comprise a question with four possible answers. For example,

1   What is the world's tallest mountain?

    A   Ben Nevis

    B   K2

    C   Mount Everest

    D   Mount Snowdon

You have to select the correct answer (which in the above example is of course **C**).

In the examination, however, the incorrect answers, called distractors, may be quite plausible and are sometimes designed if not exactly to mislead you, they may nevertheless be the result of fairly common mistakes.

The following is a suggested technique for answering these questions, but as you practice for the examination you have to work out a method which suits you.

Step 1

Read all the questions, but not necessarily the answers. Select the ones which you think are the most straightforward and do them first.

Step 2

For more awkward questions, some people prefer to work the question without reference to the answers which increases your confidence if your answer then matches one of the options. However some people prefer to view the question with the four answers as this may assist them in formulating their answer.

This is a matter of personal preference and you should perhaps practise each to see which you find most effective.

Step 3

If your answer does not match one of the options you must:

(a)   Re-read the question carefully to make sure you have not missed some important point.

(b)   Re-work your solution eliminating any mistakes.

(c)   Beware the plausible distractors but do not become paranoid. The examiner is not trying to trip you up and the answer should be a straightforward calculation from the question.

Step 4

Time allocation. As with all questions you must not overrun your time. The questions are technically worth only two marks each which is about three to four minutes per question. It is very easy to get bogged down. If you cannot get one of the right answers then move on to the next question.

Step 5

When you have finished all the questions go back to the ones you have not answered.

Keep an eye on the clock – don't overrun the time allocation.

If you really cannot do it, **have a guess**. You are not penalised for wrong answers. **Never leave any questions unanswered.**

CHAPTER 1

Introduction to corporation tax

EXAM FOCUS

This chapter is the first of several dealing with corporation tax. It explains how to calculate a company's taxable profits. This is a key area of the syllabus and according to the guidance notes questions on various aspects of CT could appear in any or all of the examination paper sections.

Corporation tax accounts for 25% of the new syllabus. This makes it the largest topic in the syllabus. The pilot paper for the new syllabus has a compulsory question on corporation tax. It is worth 46 marks, although nine of these marks are for presentation. We think that you can expect a major question on corporation tax in every examination.

LEARNING OUTCOMES

This chapter covers the following learning outcomes of the CIMA syllabus:

> Calculate the total profits of a company for CT purposes
> Explain the effect of the Loan Relationship rules on a company's CT liability.

In order to cover these learning outcomes the following topics are included:

> The structure of a corporation tax computation
> The relevance of accounting periods
> Profits chargeable to corporation tax (PCTCT).

1 The structure of a corporation tax computation

A proforma for a typical corporation tax computation is shown below. The main sections of this chapter and Chapter 2 will then build on this framework.

Company name	
Corporation tax computation for XX months ending	
	£
Schedule D Case I	X
Schedule D Case III	X
Other income	X
Schedule A	X
Chargeable gains	X
Less: Charges on income (Gift Aid)	(X)
Profits chargeable to corporation tax	X
Corporation tax liability at relevant rate	X
Less: Income tax suffered	(X)
Mainstream corporation tax (MCT) payable (repayable)	X

2 The relevance of accounting periods

2.1 Length of accounting period

A company prepares a computation of 'profits' for an *accounting period*, usually known as a *chargeable accounting period* (CAP). 'Profits' include income and gains (covered in Section 3 below). From the outset, you need to be aware of the length of the 'period of account' and the impact this has on a company's 'chargeable accounting period'.

A CAP can be any length up to 12 months, but cannot exceed 12 months. In a normal situation, a company prepares a 12 month set of accounts and has a matching CAP. Where the period of account is shorter (eg 9 months) then there is a shorter CAP. This does not affect how profits are computed, but does affect the computation of the liability.

A CAP can never exceed 12 months. Therefore, where the period of account exceeds 12 months, there is a CAP for 12 months and then a separate CAP for the balance. No other combination is acceptable. This is illustrated in Figure 1.1.

Figure 1.1   Financial period of account of 18 months

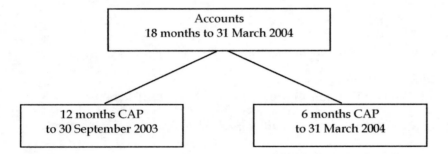

The method of allocating profits from the accounts between the two periods is covered later.

A CAP normally *starts* when the previous CAP *ends* and runs for *12 months*, but there are special situations which can trigger a start or end.

A CAP starts in any of the following circumstances.

♦   A company begins to trade.
♦   A company first acquires a source of chargeable income.
♦   A previous CAP ends.

A CAP ends on the *earliest* date indicated by the following rules.

♦   The 12 month rule
♦   The date 'accounts' are made up to
♦   The date the company ceases or begins to trade
♦   The start of the winding up of the company
♦   The date when the company begins or ceases to be UK resident

2.2 Example

A Ltd was incorporated on 1 September 2002 and opened a deposit account on 1 October 2002. It commenced to trade on 1 March 2003, and makes up accounts to 31 December starting in 2002.

Required

State the first four CAPs of the company.

2.3   Solution

1 October 2002 – 31 December 2002	(CAP ends, to coincide with accounts)
1 January 2003 – 28 February 2003	(CAP ends, company starts to trade)
1 March 2003 – 31 December 2003	(CAP ends, to coincide with accounts)
1 January 2004 – 31 December 2004	(12 months – 'normal' rule applies)

2.4   Financial years

The rates of corporation tax are set for financial years. A financial year (FY) runs from 1 April to the following 31 March and is known by the calendar year in which it starts – eg FY 2003 (or FY03) is the year from 1 April 2003 to 31 March 2004.

In Figure 1.1 above the CAP of 12 months to 30 September 2003 falls six months in FY 2002 and six months in FY 2003. Half the profits are therefore taxed using FY 2002 rates and half are taxed at the FY 2003 rates. In fact the rates for FY 2002 and FY 2003 are exactly the same but there were differences in the rates between FY 2001 and FY 2002 so you may need to understand the calculation techniques to apply when differences arise. This is covered in detail in Chapter 2.

Financial years are only relevant to *corporation tax*. As we see later, individuals and partnerships pay *income tax* on a *fiscal year* basis. A fiscal year runs from 6 April to the following 5 April, eg '2003/04' is the fiscal year (or 'tax year' or 'year of assessment') from 6 April 2003 to 5 April 2004.

3   Profits chargeable to corporation tax (PCTCT)

3.1   Introduction

The first stage of a single company computation is to ascertain the PCTCT. This comprises income and gains, less charges on income. There are a variety of topics which could be examined, but key elements frequently recur, and the procedures below should ensure that you have a sound base. We start with an overview of Schedule D Case I – the tax heading which applies to trading profits.

3.2   Schedule D Case I

Schedule D Case I comprises the following elements.

		Notes	£
Adjusted accounting profit of trading		1	X
Less	*Capital allowances*		
	Plant and machinery	2	(X)
	Industrial building allowances	2	(X)
Add	*Balancing charges*	2	X
Schedule D Case I			X
Deduct DI trading loss brought forward from earlier CAP		3	(X)
			X

Notes

(1)   The adjusted accounting profit of trading is the net profit before taxation, as adjusted for tax purposes, as will be explained in detail in Chapter 3. A common adjustment is for disallowed expenses such as entertaining and depreciation. Such items are 'added back' to profit. Similarly non-trading income has to be excluded so, for example, rental income included in the published trading profit would have to be deducted.

(2)   Calculations are often required in these areas (see Chapters 4 and 5).

(3)   Losses will be explained in detail in Chapter 9.

Dividends paid by a company are not an allowable deduction in calculating Schedule DI profits being an appropriation of profit, not an expense of earning the profit. In any event, these should not have been deducted in arriving at the net accounting profit.

3.3 Loan relationship rules

We consider the loan relationship rules at this point because of their potential relevance to Schedule D Case I.

 The importance of the loan relationship rules to your studies is emphasised in the syllabus guidance notes. The rules apply to all monetary loans

♦ made by a company on which it receives interest and
♦ received by a company on which it pays interest.

The legislation distinguishes between loans for *trading* purposes and loans for *non-trading* purposes.

 For examination purposes, if a company *receives* a loan you can normally assume that it is for *trading* purposes. For example, a company may borrow money in order to finance the purchase of new assets for use in its trade. If a company *makes* a loan, you can normally assume that this is for a *non-trading* purpose.

 You will, however, need to read the question carefully to make sure that these assumptions are not contradicted.

Net or gross?

Prior to 1 April 2001 certain types of interest were paid or received net of 20% income tax. From 1 April 2001 most interest is paid or received gross (with the exception of interest paid to individuals).

You must always include the gross amounts in the corporation tax computation.

Trading loans

Interest paid - All interest charged in the profit and loss account will be an allowable deduction for Schedule DI purposes. The normal accruals basis applies. This means you will not need to make any adjustments in converting the accounting profit into the Schedule DI profit.

Interest received - You are unlikely to see any interest received for trading purposes. However, if you do, such interest will be included in the trading profit on an accruals basis and therefore needs no adjustment.

Capital value - The capital value of a loan may change, for example due to exchange rate variations. Any such changes are treated as trading income (or trading expenses, if applicable). Note that changes in the capital value of a loan due to repayments are ignored.

Non-trading loans

Examples of non-trading loans are loans to suppliers, customers or employees. Non-trading loans are dealt with under Schedule D Case III rather than Schedule D Case I.

Both interest paid and interest received are dealt with on an accruals basis. They are netted off against each other to produce one overall Schedule DIII figure. Any non-trading loans written off are deducted from the Schedule DIII figure.

If the net result is a positive figure, it is included in the corporation tax computation as Schedule DIII income. If the net result is a negative figure, it is a Schedule DIII deficit. This is a type of loss. Its treatment is explained in Chapter 9.

3.4   Patent royalties

From 1 April 2002 patent royalties paid or received are dealt with for tax purposes on a normal accruals basis. Prior to 1 April 2002 they were recognised for tax purposes on a paid or received basis – ie, not an accruals basis.

You are not likely to be tested in any detail on the rules applying before 1 April 2002.

Royalties payable

Since 1 April 2002 royalties are relieved as a trading expense against Schedule D Case I income on a normal accruals basis. So if they have been correctly charged through the accounts no adjustment should be needed.

Patent royalties paid before 1 April 2002 are relieved on a paid basis as a charge on income.

Royalties receivable

Since 1 April 2002, royalties receivable on patents are taxed under Schedule D Case I as trading income. Again if the income has been correctly shown on an accruals basis no adjustment should be needed.

Depreciation of patent rights

Any write off of the capital cost of a patent made on properly applied accounting principles is allowable for Schedule D Case I purposes and therefore will not require adjustment. Note that this contrasts with the tax treatment of depreciation charges in general (such as on plant and machinery) which are **not** allowable as a Schedule D Case I expense – see Chapter 3.

Royalties subject to income tax deductions

From 1 April 2001 patent royalties are usually received gross, except that patent royalties received from individuals are received net of basic rate tax. Similarly, all patent royalties are usually paid gross, except that patent royalties paid to individuals are paid net of basic rate tax.

Companies account for income tax deductions on a quarterly basis – see Chapter 13.

Non-trading situations

Where patent royalties are payable or receivable for a non-trading purpose (eg, patent rights acquired as an investment) they are dealt with under Schedule D Case VI.

3.5   Other profits and charges

 In ascertaining Schedule D Case I for a company, various items are adjusted for as they do not represent trading expenses or income.

Item	*Reason for adjustment*
♦ Gift Aid donation	Non-trade charge
♦ Rental income	Investment income
♦ Interest on bank or building society account	Investment income
♦ Dividends received	Investment income
♦ Profit on sale of fixed asset	Capital gain

For example, any rental income included in trading profits would have to be deducted (reducing profits) and any Gift Aid payment deducted from trading profits should be added back (increasing profits).

The treatment of these items in finding PCTCT will now be outlined.

3.6 Schedule D Case III

The loan relationship rules were covered earlier in this section to explain their relevance for Schedule D Case I. To recap, various types of *interest receivable* will be included under the heading Schedule D Case III, not Case I.

This includes:

♦ interest from banks, building societies, UK government stock,
♦ loan stock and debentures.

After 1 April 2001 the only source of interest received net by a UK company was Local Authority stock interest. This was received net of 20% tax and had to be grossed up at 100/80. From 1 October 2002 even Local Authority stock interest paid to a company is payable gross so from then all interest received by a company is received gross.

 In all cases, it is the *accrued* amount for the accounting period which should be used. This should be the same as the amount shown in the profit and loss account.

Schedule DIII also includes interest *payable* on a loan taken out for a non-trading purpose such as to acquire or improve property used for commercial letting. This is known as non-trading interest payable. It is deducted from Schedule D Case III, on an accruals basis. If the interest payable exceeds interest receivable, there will be a DIII deficit. Relief for the deficit is explained in Chapter 9.

3.7 Other income

 Dividend income from UK resident companies is not chargeable to corporation tax. If it is included in the profit and loss account, it must be deducted for DI purposes. This is because dividend income is paid out of after-tax profits of another company (ie the profits generating the dividend have already been subject to UK corporation tax). Dividend income is, of course, chargeable to tax when received by individuals.

This only applies to dividends from UK resident companies. Overseas dividends are still assessable (under Schedule D Case V) – see Chapter 12.

3.8 Schedule A

Rental income is included under the heading Schedule A, and comprises the following.

		Notes	£
(a)	*Rental income* (furnished or unfurnished)	1	X
	Less Expenses (excluding loan interest payable)	1	(X)
(b)	*Income element of premium on any short lease (less than 50 years)*	2	X
			X

Notes

(1) This is the accrued income and expenses for the accounting period. Expenses are allowed (or disallowed) as if the letting business was a trade (see Chapter 3).

(2) This is premium *received* $\times \dfrac{51-n}{50}$ where n = number of years of lease.

If the property is let furnished the landlord can claim a 'wear and tear' allowance equal to 10% of the rent receivable net of any council tax and water rates (if these are paid by the landlord).

Schedule A losses are covered in Chapter 9.

3.9 Capital gains

A company's PCTCT includes capital gains as well as income. The calculation of the capital gain or loss on individual transactions is covered in Chapters 6-8. For the purpose of this chapter, all individual gains and losses are already computed. You will, however, need to be able to produce a summary of the position for PCTCT.

This is formulated as follows.

		£
Gain (transaction 1)		X
Gain (transaction 2)		X
Loss (transaction 3)		(X)
		X
Less	Capital losses brought forward	(X)
Net chargeable gains		X

Current period gains and losses are netted off automatically.

Any excess capital losses can *only* be carried forward for relief against future capital gains.

3.10 Charges

The final component in finding PCTCT is to deduct from the total profits (income and gains) any allowable payments known as *charges on income*.

Prior to 1 April 2002, patent royalties paid were relieved as a charge on income and were the only form of trading charge you were likely to encounter. As royalties paid are now relieved as a DI expense, trading charges are now irrelevant for exam purposes.

The only form of charge you will meet in periods commencing on or after 1 April 2002 is the non-trade charge of Gift Aid payments. These are paid gross by companies.

The gross amount deductible for a CAP is the amount *paid*. This may be different from the amount accrued in the accounts.

A Gift Aid donation is basically any donation by a company to a charity unless the payment already qualifies as a business expense. Only donations that are 'small' and 'local in effect' will normally be allowed as a DI expense.

There is an example below on computing PCTCT, which will also be used to start developing good habits on exam technique in your approach to CT questions.

3.11 Example

Laserjet Ltd provides you with the following information for its year to 31 March 2004.

	Note	£
Adjusted trading profit		500,600
Capital allowances		16,000
Rental income (net of expenses)		12,000
Bank loan interest accrued and paid to purchase rental property		4,000
Building society interest (accrued)	1	20,000
10% Debenture interest accrued and received on £60,000 nominal value		6,000
Agency commissions receivable	2	20,000
Gift Aid payment made		14,000

Notes

(1) The amount actually received was £15,000.
(2) The agency commissions were not received as part of the company's trading activities and are therefore assessable under DVI.
(3) There were capital losses brought forward of £2,000.

Compute the PCTCT for the year ended 31 March 2004, assuming all reliefs are claimed as early as possible.

Approach to the example

It is essential to develop a methodical approach from the outset in computing PCTCT, to enable you to tackle examination level questions later.

Step 1

Set up a skeleton CT computation proforma. Keep this on a separate sheet of paper.

	£
Schedule D Case I (W1)	
Schedule D Case III (W2)	
Schedule A	
Schedule D Case VI	
Chargeable gains	
Less Charges on income	_____
PCTCT	_____

The headings are not required to be in any particular order, but it is accepted best practice to put DI first.

Step 2

Set up a *separate* working sheet for any necessary workings and work through the information *methodically*. Schedule D Case I often (though not in this example) requires more than one working for the component parts of:

♦ adjusted profit
♦ capital allowances on plant and machinery, etc.

As you complete each working slot the result into the proforma.

Step 3

Show clearly the *use* of any available losses brought forward and, where available, the carrying forward position in compiling step 2.

3.12 Solution

Laserjet Ltd

CT computation for the year ended 31 March 2004

	£
Schedule D Case I (W1)	484,600
Schedule D Case III (W2)	22,000
Schedule A	12,000
Schedule D Case VI	20,000
Gains (W3)	Nil
	_____
	538,600
Less Charges on income – Gift Aid	(14,000)
	_____
PCTCT	524,600
	_____

Marks may be awarded for presentation and a clear structured answer creates a good impression with a marker!

Workings

(W1)   Schedule D Case I

	£
Adjusted trading profit	500,600
Less Capital allowances	(16,000)
	484,600

In exam questions take great care not to adjust a profit which has already been adjusted for.

(W2)   Schedule D Case III

	Notes	£
Building society interest	1	20,000
Debenture interest (10% × £60,000 = £6,000 gross per annum)		6,000
		26,000
Less Loan interest payable – rental property	2	(4,000)
		22,000

Notes

(1)   The *accrued* figure is the assessable amount, not the *paid* figure.

(2)   This is not a Schedule A deduction but has to be dealt with as a 'non-trading' loan.

(W3)   Chargeable gains

There are no gains to utilise losses brought forward of £2,000, therefore carry forward.

4   Summary

Calculating PCTCT is an essential part of every corporation tax question. In the next chapter you will learn how to calculate a company's corporation tax liability.

Multiple choice questions 1 - 5 *(The answers are in the final chapter of this book)*

Each of the questions below has only one correct answer.

1   Moore Ltd owned a number of shops and prepares accounts to 31 March each year. On 1 June 2003 the company granted a lease to Ramsden Ltd for a period of 15 years at an annual rent of £6,000 payable half yearly in advance on 1 June and 1 December. Ramsden Ltd also paid a once-and-for-all premium of £20,000 in consideration of granting the lease.

Moore Ltd's Schedule A assessment for the year to 31 March 2004 will be

A   £14,400

B   £18,900

C   £19,400

D   £20,400

2   Jamboree Ltd received rental income in respect of the following two properties in its year to 31 March 2004.

    (1)   A house that was first let furnished on 1 August 2003. Rent of £4,200 accrued in the period to 31 March 2004. Expenses of £649 were paid in the period. Jamboree Ltd claims an allowance for wear and tear of furnishings calculated as 10% of rent receivable.

    (2)   A house that had been let unfurnished for several years at a rent of £6,000 per annum. £800 was spent on repairing the property in October 2003.

What amount is assessed under Schedule A in the year to 31 March 2004?

    A   £3,131

    B   £5,200

    C   £8,331

    D   £8,751

3   Bull Ltd disposed of three properties in its year to 31 March 2004 resulting respectively in a gain of £10,000, a loss of £18,000 and a gain of £22,000. In the previous period it had made a capital loss of £15,000. Which of the following statements is true?

    A   Net gains: £14,000; loss b/f and c/f £15,000

    B   Net gains: nil; loss to carry forward £1,000

    C   Net gains: nil; loss to set against other income £1,000

    D   Net gains: £17,000; loss to carry forward £18,000

4   Markby Ltd was incorporated on 1 November 2003. The company commenced to trade on 1 January 2004 and will prepare the first accounts to 31 March 2005.

When will the first accounting period end for corporation tax purposes?

    A   5 April 2004

    B   31 October 2004

    C   31 December 2004

    D   31 March 2005

5   Kitten Ltd drew up accounts for the six month period to 31 March 2004. Interest on its £10,000 12% debenture stock is paid annually on 1 December.

What amount will be allowed for tax purposes for the period to 31 March 2004?

    A   £600

    B   £800

    C   £1,200

    D   £1,800

CHAPTER 2

Calculation of corporation tax liability

EXAM FOCUS

In Chapter 1 you learned how to calculate a company's PCTCT. The calculation of PCTCT is the starting point for every corporation tax computation. In this chapter you will learn how to calculate a company's corporation tax liability. This is likely to form part of every examination question concerning corporation tax.

LEARNING OUTCOMES

This chapter covers the following learning outcomes of the CIMA syllabus:

> Calculate the CT liability of a company (including that of small and intermediate companies)

> Explain the operation of shadow advance corporation tax (ACT). No computation of ACT will be required

> Demonstrate the planning aspects of maximising the use of surplus ACT existing at 6 April 1999 for a company.

In order to cover these learning outcomes the following topics are included:

> The corporation tax liability
> Advance corporation tax
> The income tax set-off
> Quarterly administration of income tax

1 The corporation tax liability

1.1 Introduction

 Once you have computed a company's PCTCT, the next stage of the computation is to calculate the corporation tax liability. This is essentially divided into two steps.

♦ Determining PCTCT and 'profits' (P), a term which is used to determine the tax rates that will apply.

♦ Applying relevant tax rates to calculate the liability.

Step 1

	£	
PCTCT	X	'I'
Add Current FII	X	
Profits for determination of liability	X	'P'

FII is franked investment income. Current FII is the term used to describe UK dividends received in the current period, grossed up by the tax credit of 100/90.

 PCTCT (sometimes labelled 'I' for short) is the profit which is charged to tax, but 'P' is used to determine the rate of tax.

Step 2

The tax calculation is based on two main factors.

♦ 'Profits' P
♦ The financial year (FY) which matches the CAP.

For each FY (ie 1 April to following 31 March) the following information is provided.

	FY03
Lower limit	300,000
Upper limit	1,500,000
Fraction	$\frac{11}{400}$
Small company rate	19%
Ordinary rate	30%

For FY00 onwards a starting rate of corporation tax applies to companies with profits below £10,000. The rules on the starting rate are covered later in this chapter.

 Ignoring the starting rate for the moment, there are three situations that can apply.

♦ Where 'profits' (P) do not exceed the lower limit the small company rate applies to PCTCT.
♦ Where 'profits' (P) are at or above the upper limit, the ordinary rate applies to PCTCT.
♦ Where 'profits' (P) are between the limits then the following calculation is needed.

PCTCT at ordinary rate	X
Less Marginal relief	(X)
	X

Marginal relief is found by using the formula (likely to be provided in the examination).

$$\text{Fraction} \times (M - \text{'P'}) \times \frac{I}{P} \quad \text{where I = PCTCT, M = upper limit}$$

The following examples illustrate the calculation of CT liability.

1.2 Example

Small Ltd has the following PCTCT for the year ended 31 March 2004.

	£
Schedule D Case I	260,000
Schedule A	40,000
	300,000
Less Gift Aid paid	(10,000)
PCTCT	290,000

Required

What is the corporation tax liability if:

(a)   no dividends are received from UK companies
(b)   £9,000 of dividends are received from UK companies
(c)   £45,000 of dividends are received from UK companies?

1.3   Solution

(a)   *Step 1*

		£
PCTCT		290,000
FII		Nil
'P'		290,000

Step 2

Identify the financial year(s) which applies and determine the tax rate.

FY03 applies to the year ended 31 March 2004, and therefore to the whole of the accounting period.

'P' is below the lower limit so: CT = £290,000 × 19% = £55,100.

(b)   *Step 1*

		£
PCTCT		290,000
FII ($£9,000 \times \frac{100}{90}$)		10,000
'P'		300,000

Step 2

FY03 applies and 'P' is equal to the lower limit

Therefore CT = £290,000 × 19% = £55,100, as before. The 'profits' level has not altered the decision.

(c)   *Step 1*

		£
PCTCT		290,000
FII ($£45,000 \times \frac{100}{90}$)		50,000
'P'		340,000

Step 2

FY03 applies

'P is above £300,000 but below £1,500,000; marginal relief applies.

		£
£290,000 × 30%		87,000
Less Marginal relief		
$^{11}/_{400}$ × (£1,500,000 – £340,000) × $\frac{290,000}{340,000}$ =		(27,209)
CT		59,791

Practice question 1 *(The answer is in the final chapter of this book)*

Walton

Walton Ltd's profit and loss account for the year ended 31 March 2004 was as follows.

	£	£
Sales		486,280
Debenture interest receivable		2,900
UK dividends received (net of tax credit)		13,365
Profit on the sale of an investment		1,054
		503,599
Allowable trading expenses	109,756	
Disallowable trading expenses	6,344	
Debenture interest payable	6,000	
		122,100
Net profit		381,499

Capital allowances have been calculated at £4,800. All dividends were received in July 2003. The capital gain on the sale of the investment has been calculated at £1,538.

Required

Calculate Walton Ltd's corporation tax liability for the year ended 31 March 2004.

1.4 Short accounting periods

Short accounting periods – ie less than 12 months – can have an impact on the calculation of the CT liability as the lower and upper limits are annual limits and have to be time apportioned to fit the length of the accounting period.

1.5 Example

If Small Ltd (1.2 above) had a nine month accounting period to 31 March 2004 what would be the result assuming the dividend received was £9,000?

1.6 Solution

Step 1

	£
PCTCT	290,000
FII	10,000
'P'	300,000

Step 2

FY03 applies but to a nine month period therefore:

Lower limit = $\frac{9}{12} \times 300,000 =$ 225,000

Upper limit = $\frac{9}{12} \times 1,500,000 =$ 1,125,000

'P' is now *between* the limits so:

	£
PCTCT £290,000 × 30%	87,000
Less Marginal relief $^{11}\!/_{400}$ (£1,125,000 – £300,000) $\times \dfrac{290,000}{300,000}$	(21,931)
	65,069

Make sure you calculate tax on PCTCT not on 'P' – an easy mistake to make.

1.7 Non 31 March year ends

Many companies do not have CAPs which fall neatly into a financial year.

A company with a year end of 31 December 2002 is affected as follows.

	FY01 *1 January 2002 – 31 March 2002*	*FY02* *1 April 2002 – 31 December 2002*
Small company rate	20%	19%
Ordinary rate	30%	30%
Fraction	$\frac{1}{40}$	$^{11}\!/_{400}$
Lower limit	300,000	300,000
Upper limit	1,500,000	1,500,000

As the CT rates change from FY01 to FY02, it is necessary to time apportion the PCTCT and 'P' and compute the CT for each FY separately as follows.

Step 1

Determine 'P' as before and decide the level of tax (ie small, ordinary, marginal).

Step 2

Time apportion PCTCT between the financial years, and proceed as before, taking the number of months into account. If profits for the year to 31 December 2002 are below £300,000:

PCTCT $\times$ 20% $\times \frac{3}{12}$ FY01

PCTCT $\times$ 19% $\times \frac{9}{12}$ FY02

Note that for the year to 31 December 2003 (ie falling in FY02 and FY03) there would be no need to time apportion as the rates and limits remained the same.

 If that situation arises in an exam question (ie FY 'straddle' without a change of rates) you should explain briefly why you have not split up the calculation.

1.8 Example

Marginal Ltd had PCTCT of £290,000 for the year ended 30 September 2002 and received a dividend of £45,000 on 15 May 2002.

Required

Calculate the company's corporation tax liability.

1.9 Solution

Step 1

	Year ended 30 September 2002 £
PCTCT	290,000
FII $45,000 \times {}^{100}\!/_{90}$	50,000
'P'	340,000

Therefore we have a marginal company.

Step 2

	6m FY01 £	6m FY02 £	Total £
PCTCT	145,000	145,000	
@ 30%	43,500	43,500	87,000
FY01 $\frac{1}{40} \times (£1,500,000 - £340,000) \times \dfrac{290,000}{340,000} \times {}^{6}\!/_{12}$	(12,368)		(12,368)
FY02 ${}^{11}\!/_{400} \times (£1,500,000 - £340,000) \times \dfrac{290,000}{340,000} \times {}^{6}\!/_{12}$		(13,604)	(13,604)
	31,132	29,896	61,028

Note

The full rate of corporation tax is the same for both financial years so that part of the calculation could therefore be done in one step (ie, 30% × £290,000 = £87,000).

1.10 The starting rate of corporation tax

For FY 2003 (and FY 2002) there is a starting rate of Nil% applying to companies with profits not exceeding £10,000. If profits fall between £10,000 and £50,000 the small company rate of 19% applies but there is a form of marginal relief calculated using the formula ${}^{19}\!/_{400} \times (£50,000 - P) \times I/P$.

 A 10% starting rate of corporation tax was introduced with effect from 1 April 2000 and applied to FY 2000 and FY 2001. It applied to companies with profits not exceeding £10,000.

For FY 2000 and FY 2001 companies with profits between £10,000 and £50,000 were taxed at the small company rate of 20%, but their tax liability was then reduced by a form of marginal relief. This was calculated using the fraction of $\frac{1}{40}$ in the relief formula in place of the $\frac{19}{400}$ fraction used above.

These rates can be summarised as follows:

FY	Starting rate	Fraction	Lower limit	Upper limit
2000	10%	$\frac{1}{40}$	£10,000	£50,000
2001	10%	$\frac{1}{40}$	£10,000	£50,000
2002	Nil%	$\frac{19}{400}$	£10,000	£50,000
2003	Nil%	$\frac{19}{400}$	£10,000	£50,000

1.11 Example

Tiny Ltd has PCTCT of £9,000 for the year ended 31 March 2004.

Required

Calculate Tiny Ltd's corporation tax liability assuming that:

(a)   it received no dividends
(b)   it received dividends of £1,800.

1.12 Solution

(a)   Tiny Ltd's profits will be subjected to tax at the starting rate of Nil% as they are below £10,000. The corporation tax liability will therefore be Nil.

(b)   Tiny Ltd's profits are as follows.

	£
PCTCT	9,000
FII (£1,800 × 100/90)	2,000
P	11,000

As Tiny Ltd's profits fall between £10,000 and £50,000 it will be subjected to corporation tax at the rate of 19%. However, its liability will be reduced by marginal relief as shown.

	£
PCTCT (£9,000 × 19%)	1,710
$(£50,000 - £11,000) \times \dfrac{9,000}{11,000} \times \frac{19}{400}$	(1,516)
Corporation tax liability	194

1.13 Marginal tax rates

It is important to appreciate how the marginal corporation tax rates change as profit increases or decreases.

For example, the average tax rate has to move smoothly from 19% at £300,000 of profits to 30% at £1.5 million. To achieve this the marginal rate in the £300,000 to £1.5 million band has to exceed 30%. In fact it is 32.75% as the following calculation proves:

	Profit £	CT rate %	Corporation tax £
FY 2003	300,000	19	57,000
	1,500,000	30	450,000
Marginal effect	1,200,000		393,000

Extra profit of £1,200,000 attracts additional tax of £393,000 – a tax rate of 32.75%.

Similarly, it can be shown that as profits of £10,000 attract no tax and profits of £50,000 are taxed at 19% - ie, £9,500 – the marginal tax rate for the additional £40,000 of profit is 23.75% (£9,500/£40,000 × 100%).

It is a basic corporation tax planning tactic to avoid profits falling into these high marginal rate bands perhaps by paying director's bonuses or bringing forward revenue expenditure.

2 Advance Corporation Tax

2.1 Introduction

Although the examiner has stated that no computation of ACT will be required, this section uses calculations to show how surplus ACT arose, and how relief can be obtained by ACT set-off. The student should concentrate on understanding the impact of the payment of dividends on the set-off of surplus ACT.

Prior to 6 April 1999, when a company paid a dividend to its shareholders it had to account for Advance Corporation Tax (ACT). This was an early payment of the company's corporation tax liability.

The amount of ACT was calculated as follows:

Dividend paid × 20/80 = ACT

If the company received a dividend, this was taken into account in computing the amount of ACT payable as follows:

(Dividend paid - dividend received) × 20/80 = ACT

The amount of ACT paid by a company during its accounting period was deducted from its corporation tax liability. The balance of CT which still remained was known as mainstream CT.

The deduction of ACT was limited to a maximum of PCTCT × 20%. Any payments of ACT which exceeded the maximum set-off were known as surplus ACT. Surplus ACT could be carried back six years (subject to the maximum set-off in those earlier years) or carried forward indefinitely.

2.2 Example

Active Ltd had PCTCT of £100,000 for its year ended 31 March 1999. During the year the company paid a dividend of £40,000 and received a dividend of £8,000.

Required

Show the amount of mainstream corporation tax payable by Active Ltd for its year ended 31 March 1999. (For FY 1998 the CT rate was 21% if P < £300,000.)

2.3 Solution

Active Ltd would have had to pay ACT of (£40,000 - £8,000) × 20/80 = £8,000.

The maximum set-off of ACT was £100,000 × 20% = £20,000.

As Active Ltd's payment of ACT is within the maximum set-off, it can all be deducted in calculating the mainstream CT as follows:

	£
PCTCT £100,000 × 21% =	21,000
Less ACT	(8,000)
Mainstream CT	13,000

2.4   Shadow ACT

ACT was abolished with effect from 6 April 1999. This means that companies no longer have to account for ACT when they pay a dividend. However, some companies still have surplus ACT brought forward from earlier periods. To enable relief for that surplus ACT to be given, a system of shadow ACT was introduced. Shadow ACT is the ACT that would have been paid by a company if ACT had not been abolished.

The system of shadow ACT works as follows.

Step 1

Calculate the maximum set-off:

$$PCTCT \times 20\% = \qquad\qquad A$$

Step 2

Calculate the shadow ACT:

$$(\text{Dividend paid - dividends received}) \times 20/80 = \quad B$$

Step 3

The amount of surplus ACT that can be set off is   A - B

Step 4

Any unrelieved surplus ACT continues to be carried forward indefinitely.

2.5   Example

Surplus Ltd has PCTCT of £216,000 for its year ended 31 March 2004. During the year it paid a dividend of £65,000. It had surplus ACT of £45,000 brought forward at 1 April 2003.

Required

Calculate the corporation tax payable by Surplus Ltd for the year ended 31 March 2004 and state the amount of surplus ACT still unrelieved.

2.6   Solution

	£	£
PCTCT £216,000 × 19%		41,040
Maximum set-off £216,000 × 20% =	43,200	
Shadow ACT £65,000 × 20/80 =	(16,250)	
Surplus ACT set-off		(26,950)
Mainstream CT		14,090

The amount of surplus ACT still unrelieved is £18,050 (£45,000 - £26,950).

You can see from the above example, that the payment of a dividend restricts the amount of surplus ACT that a company can relieve. If Surplus Ltd had not paid a dividend, it would have been able to relieve £41,040 of its surplus ACT brought forward (set-off cannot reduce MCT below nil). Companies may therefore wish to minimise their dividend payments until they have relieved their surplus ACT.

Practice question 2 *(The answer is in the final chapter of this book)*

Shadow Ltd

Shadow Ltd has the following results for the two years ended 31 March 2000.

Year ended	31/3/99	31/3/00
	£	£
PCTCT	190,000	110,000
Dividends paid	180,000	90,000
Dividends received	18,000	27,000

Calculate the mainstream corporation tax payable by Shadow Ltd for the two years ended 31 March 2000.

Note the small company rates for FY 1998 and FY 1999 were 21% and 20% respectively.

Approach to the question

The first accounting period is prior to the abolition of ACT. Shadow Ltd would have paid ACT based on the formula (dividends paid - dividends received) × 20/80. You should find that the amount of ACT paid exceeds the maximum set-off. Make sure that you identify which financial year applies when calculating the CT liability.

The second accounting period is after the abolition of ACT. You need to calculate shadow ACT in order to work out how much of the surplus ACT can be deducted.

3 The income tax set-off

3.1 Overview

The final stage of the corporation tax computation involves reducing the corporation tax liability by any income tax which the company has paid, following the procedures outlined below.

♦ A company suffers income tax (IT) at source on certain income, but charges the 'gross' income to corporation tax.

♦ Similarly it deducts income tax at source from certain payments, but is allowed to take the 'gross payment' into account when calculating corporation tax.

♦ The excess suffered over the amounts deducted is set off in finding MCT payable.

The procedure which follows identifies the correct amount of IT set-off, which must take account of the fact that there are different IT rates for different types of income or payments. This is an easy point to overlook.

To calculate the IT set-off, first identify 'interest' receipts or payments in the CAP, which have 20% tax deducted or suffered.

	£		Income tax deducted (suffered)
(Gross)			
Local Authority stock interest received (before 1 October 2002)	(X)		
(Gross)			
Debenture interest paid	X		
	X/(X)	× 20%	X/(X) (A)

It is important to realise that there are now very few situations where interest receipts or payments have IT deducted or suffered.

From 1 April 2001 companies only received interest net on Local Authority loan stock. Prior to 1 April 2001 interest paid between non-group companies had to be paid under deduction of 20% income tax but that requirement was abolished. All other sources of interest – banks, building societies, UK government stocks and individuals – continue to be received gross. Since 1 October 2002 Local Authority stock interest has also been payable gross.

Since 1 April 2001 companies only deduct 20% income tax on debenture interest paid to individuals.

Secondly, identify other sources of income or payments in the CAP which have basic rate income tax deducted or suffered. The rate is 22%.

This applies to:

	£		
Patent royalties received (gross amount)	(X)		
Patent royalties paid (gross amount)	X		
	X/(X)	× 22%	X/(X) (B)

Again the rules have been relaxed from 1 April 2001. Income tax is only deducted on patent royalties paid to or received from individuals. Company-to-company payments are now always paid gross. Although the taxation of patent royalties changed on 1 April 2002 this did not change the requirement for deduction of basic rate income in appropriate circumstances.

Finally, summarise the position.

	£	
Result from first step	(X)/X	
Result from second step	(X)/X	
If excess IT suffered	(X)	IT set-off
If excess IT deducted	X	No set-off

3.2 Example

Enjoy Ltd has the following results for the year ended 31 March 2004.

	£
Schedule D Case I (Note)	210,000
Patent royalties received (gross) (received on 30 September and 31 March in two instalments)	50,000
	260,000
Less Gift Aid donation (gross)	(1,800)
Profits chargeable to corporation tax	258,200

Note

The patent royalties were received from individuals in respect of patent rights held by the company as an investment.

The Schedule D Case I figure is stated after deducting gross debenture interest, accrued and paid, of £40,000 (paid in two instalments on 31 May and 30 November each year). All the debenture holders were individuals and hence 20% tax is deducted at source.

Required

Compute Enjoy Ltd's MCT payable.

3.3 Solution

Using the procedure for IT set-off:

		£		Income tax deducted or (suffered) £
(1)	Debenture interest paid	40,000	× 20%	8,000
(2)	Patent royalties received (gross)	(50,000)	× 22%	(11,000)
IT set-off				(3,000)

This is then slotted into the corporation tax computation as follows.

	£
PCTCT	258,200
FII	–
'P'	258,200
Corporation tax (£258,200 × 19%)	49,058
Less IT set-off	(3,000)
MCT payable	46,058

Note that the Gift Aid donation is not taken into account in working out the IT set-off as it is paid gross.

4 Quarterly administration of income tax

4.1 Background

You may be asked to prepare the entries for income tax as they would appear on the quarterly form CT61. This is the administrative form used to return the information to the Inland Revenue Accounts Office about IT suffered and deducted.

It is prepared using the following proforma.

Return period	IT suffered (income)	IT deducted (payments)	Cumulative IT	Pay/(repay)	Due date
Qtr to 31.3.04	(X)	X	X	X	14.4.04

In preparing the return these rules are followed.

♦ The returns are prepared quarterly to 31 March, 30 June, 30 September and 31 December. Where the accounting period of a company ends on an alternative date, an additional return is prepared.

♦ Any payments of IT are due 14 days after the quarter end. There is no specific date for repayments.

♦ A payment of IT is required where IT deducted exceeds IT suffered.

♦ A repayment of IT is obtained where IT suffered exceeds IT deducted. However, this repayment cannot exceed IT already paid in the same accounting period. Where there is excess IT suffered in an accounting period, this is relieved through IT set off as explained above.

♦ If there is no receipt/payment subject to income tax there is no return required.

It is good exam technique to indicate when no return is needed stating the reason.

4.2 Example

Using the example Enjoy Ltd detailed above, the information would have been returned as follows.

Enjoy Ltd - Year ended 31 March 2004
Quarterly returns

Return	IT deducted (payments) £	IT suffered (receipts) £	Cumulative IT £	Pay/(repay) £	Due date
30.6.03	4,000*		4,000	4,000 pay	14.7.03
30.9.03		(5,500)**	(5,500)		
			(1,500)	(4,000) repay	Note
31.12.03	4,000***		4,000		
			2,500	2,500 pay	14.1.04
31.3.04		(5,500)	(5,500)	(2,500) repay	Note
			(3,000)		

*	£40,000 annual debenture interest ÷ 2 × 20% = £4,000
**	£50,000 annual patent royalty receipts ÷ 2 × 22% = £5,500
***	£4,000 on debenture interest

Note. At 30 September 2003, £1,500 is owed to the company. This cannot be repaid as there is no IT deducted to cover it, so it is used to relieve the next IT payment. Similarly only £2,500 can be repaid from the last quarter as there is only IT paid to cover that amount. There is no set date for repayment. The excess IT suffered of £3,000 as seen earlier is set off against the CT liability.

5 Summary

If a CAP straddles 31 March, PCTCT and FII are time apportioned into the two FYs for calculating the tax. There is, however, only one amount of CT payable – it is merely calculated in two parts.

Note that as 'P' increases the **'average'** rate of CT on all the PCTCT moves from Nil% to 30%. The **marginal** rates of 23.75% and 32.75% arise to smooth out the increases so, for example, a company does not pay 30% on all its PCTCT when it passes from P = £300,000 to P = £300,001.

Surplus ACT is an additional hazard. It is deducted from CT liability but limited by the shadow ACT rules – ie PCTCT × 20% but reduced by the ACT that would have been payable on any dividends paid.

An exam question may require the information to complete a CT61. Alternatively you may have to find the IT suffered on taxed income not yet recovered under quarterly accounting. Such IT is deductible against CT liability and can even lead to a repayment.

Multiple choice questions 1 - 5 *(The answers are in the final chapter of this book)*

Each of the questions below has only one correct answer.

1   Rufus Ltd has produced the following results for the year ended 31 March 2004.

	£
Adjusted trading profit	490,000
Capital gains	60,000
Local Authority stock interest accrued and received (gross)	90,000
Patent royalties paid to individuals (gross)	30,000

The interest is received half yearly on 30 September and 31 March each year without tax being deducted at source.

The patent royalties were paid for a trading purpose and have not been taken into account in the adjusted trading profit figure. The amount accrued for the year was £35,000.

What is the amount of corporation tax payable by Rufus Ltd on 1 January 2005?

A   £154,488

B   £156,888

C   £170,500

D   £177,000

2   Bone Machine Limited prepares accounts to 30 April. As at 1 May 2003 it has surplus ACT brought forward of £18,000. During the year ended 30 April 2004 it pays a dividend of £22,000. It has profits chargeable to corporation tax of £102,500 for the year. It will have surplus ACT to carry forward as at 30 April 2004 of

A   Nil

B   £1,900

C   £3,000

D   £18,000

3   Flan Ltd has the following corporation tax computation for the year ended 31 December 2003.

	£
Schedule D Case I	23,500
Schedule D Case III	17,500
Chargeable gain	8,000
	49,000
Less: Gift Aid	(2,500)
Profits chargeable to corporation tax	46,500

The Schedule D Case III income comprises Local Authority loan stock interest accrued and received during the period.

The company paid dividends of £31,000 on 1 September 2003.

What is the corporation tax payable?

A   £8,669

B   £8,835

C   £9,213

D   £9,310

4   Daniel Ltd received the following patent royalty income (net) from individuals during the year ended 30 September 2003.

	£
31 March 2003	780
30 June 2003	390
30 September 2003	780

The company paid patent royalties to individuals of £1,950 on 31 August 2003.

All the amounts stated are the actual amounts received or paid.

How much income tax was payable on 14 October 2003?

A   £Nil

B   £150

C   £200

D   £350

5   Kale Ltd commenced trading in 1970. Its accounts showed accrued debenture interest payable of £25,000 in respect of the year ended 31 January 2004, which was paid on 29 February 2004. The debenture holders were all individuals.

Income tax on this interest must be paid by

A   14 February 2004

B   14 March 2004

C   14 April 2004

D   14 May 2004

CHAPTER 3

Schedule D Case I

EXAM FOCUS

The Taxes Acts are divided into a number of different Schedules. Each Schedule deals with income from a different source. This chapter focuses on the computation of the Schedule DI profits of a company. Schedule DI refers to trading profits.

Under the old syllabus this topic tended to feature as an optional question. It remains to be seen whether it will continue to do so regularly under the new syllabus. It does, however, lend itself easily to assessment by multiple choice.

LEARNING OUTCOMES

This chapter covers the following learning outcome of the CIMA syllabus:

> Calculate the Schedule DI profit for taxation purposes, showing knowledge of case law and statute.

> Apply rollover and holdover reliefs for tangible and intangible business assets.

> Demonstrate the importance of timing in tax planning.

In order to cover this learning outcome the following topics are included:

> Overview
> Disallowable expenditure
> Other adjustments to accounting profits.

---

1 Overview

1.1 Definition of trade

 The profits of a trade are assessed under Schedule D Case I. The statute (S.832(1) ICTA 1988) defines 'trade' as including every trade, manufacture, adventure or concern in the nature of trade. This is not particularly helpful and it has been necessary for the Courts to decide whether an activity is or is not a trade.

In 1954 a Royal Commission summarised the existing case law relevant to 'trade' by identifying six attributes or 'badges' of trade:

♦ *Subject matter.* A company will usually acquire an asset either as an investment or as stock in trade or as a fixed asset.

♦ *Length of ownership.* A brief period of ownership is indicative of a trade.

♦ *Frequency of similar transactions.* The more frequent a transaction the more likely a trade is being conducted.

♦ *Supplementary work.* An asset bought and enhanced in some way before sale is more likely to be a trading asset than a similar asset simply bought and sold without improvement.

♦ *Circumstances of realisation.* It can be argued that the forced sale of an asset to relieve a cash flow crisis is less likely to be a disposal in the course of a trade.

♦ *Motive.* The presence of a profit motive is indicative of a trade.

A company will normally be subject to Schedule D Case I on the proceeds of any disposals but this may not always hold true.

In borderline cases it is necessary to look at all the 'badges' together and not give undue weight to any particular test.

1.2 Example

(a) Bartlett Ltd disposes of a factory which it has used in its trade for manufacturing brickbats.

- This is an isolated disposal of a fixed asset and will be taxed as a capital gain, not a trading profit.

(b) Calcott Ltd also manufactures brickbats but its directors have been buying and selling factories renovating and refitting them into smaller industrial units as they have noticed a local shortage in such accommodation.

- Several of the above 'badges' apply and it is likely that Calcott Ltd is conducting a trade of property development in addition to its manufacturing trade.

1.3 Implications of trading

The profits of a trade and the capital gains realised by a company are both subject to corporation tax as part of the company's chargeable profits.

It is important, however, to decide whether the Schedule D Case I rules or the capital gains rules apply as there are significant differences.

The Schedule D Case I rules are explained in Chapters 3, 4 and 5 and the capital gains rules are explained in Chapters 6, 7 and 8.

1.4 Measuring Schedule D Case I profits

The trading profits made by a company are taxed under Schedule D Case I. The starting point in determining the amount of profit assessable under Schedule D Case I is the net profit as shown in the accounts. However, the accounts may contain expenditure items which are not allowable under Schedule DI. There may also be income which is assessable under a different Schedule or not assessable at all. Therefore the company's net accounting profit must be adjusted for tax purposes.

Schedule D Case I comprises adjusted profits less capital allowances for plant and machinery (Chapter 4), less industrial buildings allowances (Chapter 5) for an accounting period.

The net profit shown in the accounts of a company must be adjusted to comply with the rules of taxable income and allowable expenditure for Schedule D Case I. The profit as adjusted for tax is referred to as the *adjusted profit*.

Outline proforma for adjustment of profits computation

		£	£
Net profit per accounts			X
Add	Disallowable expenditure	X	
			X
Less	Amounts credited in the accounts but not taxable under Case I	X	
	Amounts not charged in the accounts but deductible under Case I (for example, capital allowances)	X	
			X
Adjusted profit			X

The proforma shows three categories of adjustments. The first one – disallowable expenditure – is extensive enough to justify separate treatment in Section 2 of this Chapter. In Section 3 we will deal with the other categories of adjustment.

2 Disallowable expenditure

2.1 The general principle

Expenditure is only allowable as a deduction in calculating Schedule D Case I profits if it has been incurred *wholly and exclusively for the purposes of the trade* (S74 Income and Corporation Taxes Act (ICTA) 1988). This means that the expense must have been incurred in earning the profits of that particular business. Certain expenses, such as those which follow, fail this wholly and exclusively test.

Fines. Fines on the business should be disallowed as the business is expected to operate within the law. Typical examples are penalties for late payment of VAT or for infringing health and safety regulations. In practice, the Inland Revenue usually allow a deduction for parking fines incurred by employees while on company business. This concession does not, however, apply to directors' parking fines.

Fraud. Fraud undertaken by directors is disallowed, *Bamford v ATA Advertising Ltd (1972)*. This is because the loss does not relate to the company's trading activities. However, petty theft by non–senior employees which is not covered by insurance is generally allowable.

Donations. Donations to charity usually fail the *wholly and exclusively* test. In practice, this means that there is no deduction for donations to national charities or political parties, unless there is some clear benefit to the trade. However, small donations to local charities are allowable. Donations under the Gift Aid scheme (including those made under deed of covenant) are classed as charges on income.

Charges on income. Charges on income are payments such as deeds of covenant payments to charity or donations under the Gift Aid scheme. Charges are not allowable under Schedule D Case I but are deducted in arriving at PCTCT.

Note that since 1 April 2002 patent royalties are treated as trading expenses and not charges on income. They would only be disallowed under Schedule D Case I if they were incurred for a non-trading purpose.

Other major items of expenditure which are *not* allowed in an adjustment of profits computation are discussed below.

Note that we use a statutory reference above – S74 ICTA 1988. Unless indicated otherwise, any statutory reference in this text is to ICTA 1988. However, you do not have to memorise statutory references. They are usually shown in the text as useful labels which save writing out the rules – we see this in particular in Chapter 9 on losses.

2.2 Capital expenditure

As a rule, capital expenditure charged to the profit and loss account (eg depreciation) is not an allowable expense for tax purposes. For this reason, 'repairs' expenditure requires careful review, as it often contains items of a capital nature.

In general, repairs and redecoration are considered to be revenue expenditure and are therefore allowable. *Improvements*, however, are disallowable. In practice, the distinction between a repair and an improvement is not clear-cut. Repairs usually involve restoring an asset to its original condition or replacing part of an asset with a modern equivalent. Improvements usually involve enhancing the asset in some way.

An illustration of the dividing line can be seen where single glazed windows in a building are replaced with double glazing units. Originally the Revenue disallowed the cost as an improvement but they reversed their practice in June 2002 recognising that this is a common type of modernising.

If an asset is purchased in a dilapidated state, and the purchase price reflects this, then initial 'repairs' expenditure to bring the asset to a fit state for use in the business will not be deductible. Two cases illustrate the difficulty of applying this rule in practice.

In *Law Shipping Co Ltd v CIR (1923)* the company purchased a ship which was not in a seaworthy condition. Expenditure on making the ship seaworthy was held to be capital and therefore disallowed.

The *Law Shipping* case can be contrasted with *Odeon Associated Theatres Ltd v Jones (1971)*. In that case, the company purchased some cinemas which were in a run-down condition. Expenditure incurred in renovating the cinemas was held to be revenue and therefore allowable.

These two cases can be distinguished. In the *Law Shipping* case, the ship was not usable until the repairs were undertaken and the purchase price reflected the condition it was in. By contrast, in the *Odeon* case, the cinemas were capable of being used for the purpose of the trade prior to their renovation. In addition, the repairs were to remedy normal wear and tear.

Legal expenses of a capital nature. The general rule to determine whether legal expenses are allowable is to look at what they relate to. If they relate to a capital item, such as the purchase of a building, then the expenses will be disallowed. If they relate to a revenue item, such as the collection of trade debts or employee issues such as drawing up contracts of employment, then they will be allowable.

There are some exceptions to the capital rule. The following expenses are allowable.

♦ The legal costs of *renewing* a short lease (50 years or less)
♦ The legal costs of defending title to a fixed asset (eg disputes over land boundaries)

Depreciation. Depreciation, together with any profits or losses on the sale of fixed assets, is disallowed. Instead of depreciation, capital allowances may be given.

Lease amortisation. This is another form of depreciation whereby the premium paid on the acquisition of a lease is written off to the profit and loss account over the life of the lease. The amount deducted in the profit and loss account must be added back.

If the lease is a *short* lease (50 years or less) for trading premises, a deduction is given for part of the premium. The formula is as follows.

$$\frac{\text{Schedule A charge on landlord}}{n}$$

where n = number of complete years of lease

The part assessable on the landlord under Schedule A is $\frac{51-n}{50}$.

The balance is taxed on the landlord under the capital gains rules. In effect, 2% of the premium is treated as capital for every complete year (except the first) for which the lease can last.

2.3 Example

TM Ltd has traded for many years, making up accounts to 30 September. On 1 October 1995, it was granted a lease of business premises for 15 years, paying a premium of £6,000. TM Ltd's accounts for the year to 30 September 2003 include lease amortisation of £400.

Required

Show the adjustment for Schedule D Case I purposes, for the year to 30 September 2003.

2.4 Solution

The first stage is to add back the lease amortisation in the adjustment of profits computation.

	£
Net profit per accounts	X
Add lease amortisation	400

A working is then required to calculate the allowable deduction for the lease premium.

◆ First calculate the Schedule A charge on the landlord.

$$\text{Premium} \times \frac{51 - n}{50} = £6,000 \times \frac{51 - 15}{50} = £4,320$$

◆ Then the allowable deduction is $\dfrac{£4,320}{15 \text{ years}} = £288$

The completed adjustment is therefore as follows.

	£
Net profit per accounts	X
Add lease amortisation	400
Less: Allowable lease premium	(288)

You should show both adjustments rather than just the net result.

2.5 Provisions and appropriations

Dividends. Dividends are appropriations. They are paid out of profits **after** they have been subjected to tax. They are not expenses incurred in earning those profits.

Bad debts. Movements in the *general* bad debt provision and non–trade debts written off are not allowable. Movements in *specific* provisions and trade debts written off can be deducted.

2.6 Example

The bad debts account of Greenidge Ltd for the year ended 30 April 2004 appears as follows.

	£		£
Written off		Balance brought down	
Trade	274	Specific provision	185
Former employee	80	General provision	260
Balance carried down		Recoveries – trade	23
Specific provision	194	Profit and loss account	305
General provision	225		
	773		773

Required

Show the adjustment for Schedule D Case I purposes.

2.7 Solution

In this example, the information is presented in the form of a 'T' account. The first stage is to establish a breakdown of the profit and loss account charge of £305. Remember that this figure comprises amounts written off and recovered, and *movements* in provisions.

Profit and loss account charge	£	Allowable?
Increase in specific provision (£194 – £185)	9	✔
Decrease in general provision (£225 – £260)	(35)	✗
Amounts written off		
Trade debt	274	✔
Former employee	80	✗
Recoveries – trade	(23)	✔
	305	

The movement in the general provision and the amount owed by the former employee are both disallowed. In this case, the movement in the general provision is a *decrease*, so the adjustment made is to *deduct* it from the profit per the accounts.

The adjustment for Schedule D Case I purposes is therefore as follows.

	£
Add Former employee, debt written off	80
Less Decrease in general provision	(35)

 Write-offs of non-trading loans (such as here to the former employee) are allowed as a Schedule D Case III expense – easy to overlook.

Note that movements in any other *general* provisions charged to the profit and loss account should also be disallowed, for example stock provisions.

2.8 Interest

All aspects of borrowing and lending money are dealt with under the *loan relationship* rules. These were covered more fully in Chapter 1.

For the purpose of computing a company's Schedule DI profits you need to distinguish between trading and non-trading receipts and payments.

Interest payable on trading loans is an allowable expense for Schedule DI purposes. The accruals basis applies. As the accruals basis should have been used for drawing up the accounts, you should not need to make any adjustments in respect of, for example, interest payable on bank overdrafts or debentures used for trading purposes.

Receipts and payments in respect of non-trading loans need adjustment when calculating Schedule DI profits, as such items do not relate to trading. So, for example, interest payable on a loan to purchase a property for renting out must be added back. Interest received on a deposit with a building society or bank will be deducted. Such items are dealt with instead under Schedule D III.

2.9 Other miscellaneous adjustments

Pre-trading expenditure. Expenditure incurred up to seven years before a trade commences is allowed as an expense of the first CAP of trading provided it would have been allowable had the trade existed at the time the expenditure was incurred.

Entertaining. The cost of entertaining customers and suppliers is disallowed. However, the cost of entertaining staff is allowable.

Gifts. Gifts are only allowable if they fulfil the following three conditions.

♦ They incorporate a conspicuous advertisement for the business.
♦ The total cost per donee is not more than £50 per annum.
♦ The gift is not food, drink (alcoholic or otherwise) or tobacco or a voucher for such items.

Note that if the cost exceeds the £50 limit, the whole amount is disallowed.

Therefore desk diaries or biros embossed with the company name usually qualify but a bottle of whisky carrying an advert for the company would not!

Trade samples (not for resale) are allowable.

Hire or lease charges (expensive cars). If a car costing more than £12,000 is leased or hired, part of the rental cost is disallowed. The disallowable amount is calculated using the following formula.

$$\text{Disallowed amount} = \frac{\tfrac{1}{2}(\text{retail price when new} - £12,000)}{\text{Retail price when new}} \times \text{hire charge}$$

2.10 Example

HNN Ltd incurs annual rental expenditure of £1,960 on leasing a car with a retail price of £14,200. The car was first leased on 1 January 2003. HNN Ltd prepares accounts to 31 December.

Required

Show the amount disallowed for Schedule D Case I purposes in the year ended 31 December 2003.

2.11 Solution

The following amount is disallowed.

$$\frac{\tfrac{1}{2}(£14,200 - £12,000)}{£14,200} \times £1,960 = £152$$

2.12 Treatment of goodwill and other intangible fixed assets

The term 'intangible fixed assets' covers goodwill, patents, copyrights and similar assets which are not 'tangible' (unlike plant and buildings).

Patent royalties paid or received for trading purposes are allowed or taxed under Schedule D Case I on an accruals basis as discussed in Chapter 1.

The write-off of goodwill, patent rights etc acquired on or after 1 April 2002 for a trading purpose by a company is allowable for tax purposes and requires no adjustment in computing Schedule D Case I profits. Similarly expenses of registering patents, trademarks etc used for the company's trade are allowable under Schedule D Case I.

If a company disposes of goodwill, patent rights etc acquired on or after 1 April 2002 for its trade, any profit or loss compared to its written down value will be taxable or allowable under Schedule D Case I.

If goodwill had been acquired before 1 April 2002 – eg where it results from a trade that commences before that date – the asset is treated as a chargeable asset. Any profit or loss on disposal is dealt with as a capital gain.

A form of rollover relief is available if a profit arises on the disposal of goodwill, patent rights etc on or after 1 April 2002.

The excess of proceeds over cost on the disposal of an intangible asset which would otherwise be chargeable under Schedule D Case I can be deferred by acquiring replacement intangible assets. The rules briefly are as follows:

♦ The replacement must be acquired in the period starting 12 months before the disposal and ending three years after. Although the Revenue can extend these deadlines, they will only do so if there are good reasons. Failure to plan for the replacement is not sufficient.

♦ Provided the expenditure on the new asset equals or exceeds the proceeds of the old asset the gain (proceeds over cost) is deducted from the proceeds of the old asset and the cost of the new asset.

♦ The part of the gain equal to any amount written off under Schedule D Case I (cost less written down value) cannot be rolled over.

♦ If part of the proceeds are not reinvested the deferred amount is reduced by the unreinvested proceeds.

The reinvestment can be in any form of intangible asset, not necessarily of the same type as was sold.

Goodwill is no longer a qualifying asset for the capital gains rollover relief (see Chapter 8). However, where a gain arises on the disposal of 'old' goodwill, it can be rolled over under the new rules against the acquisition of 'new' goodwill.

If, however, the intangible fixed asset is held for investment purposes, then any profits and losses are dealt with under Schedule D Case VI. The computational rules are the same (including rollover relief), but the Schedule D Case I profit must be adjusted accordingly.

2.13 Example

Coates Ltd sold patent rights in 2006 for £100,000 having purchased them for £40,000 four years earlier for use in its trade and written their value down to £24,000. Six months later it acquired goodwill for £130,000.

How much of the gain can be rolled over and how would your answer differ if only £90,000 had been reinvested?

2.14 Solution

Gain on the patent rights – liable as a credit under Schedule D Case I –	
£100,000 - £24,000	£76,000
Gain that can be rolled over –	
£100,000 - £40,000	£60,000
Gain remaining chargeable under DI	£16,000
(this effectively reverses the write-offs of the four years of use)	
Tax cost of replacement asset –	
£130,000 - £60,000	£70,000
If the reinvestment had been £90,000 instead	
Gain that can be rolled over –	
£90,000 - £40,000	£50,000
Gain remaining chargeable under DI	£26,000
Tax cost of replacement asset	
£90,000 - £50,000	£40,000

2.15 Research and development expenditure

If a small or medium sized company incurs qualifying research and development (R and D) expenditure it is entitled to deduct 150% of the expenditure as a trading expense.

To meet the size criteria the company should have less than 250 employees and either:

(a)   a turnover below ∈ 40 million (about £25 million); or

(b)   total assets not exceeding ∈ 27 million (about £17 million).

The company is only entitled to the 50% uplift if it has spent at least £10,000 in a 12 month AP (scaled down if AP is less than 12 months). The R and D expenditure must be in respect of staff costs and consumables to qualify and must relate to the company's trade.

To the extent that the 150% of R and D expenditure generates a trading loss it can be surrendered in exchange for a tax credit equal to the lower of:

(a)   16% of the loss; or

(b)   the PAYE and NIC due for the tax months ending in the AP.

This tax credit will either be repaid to the company or set against any CT liability due.

The incentive scheme is extended to large companies from 1 April 2002 but only to allow a 25% uplift (not a 50% uplift) and does not allow the tax credit option of surrendering an R and D 'loss'.

3   Other adjustments to accounting profits

3.1 Amounts credited in the accounts but not taxable

 The following are examples of amounts which may be credited to the profit and loss account, but which are not taxable under Schedule D Case I.

♦   Income taxed in another way, for example rent (Schedule A), interest receivable (Schedule D Case III).

♦   Profits on sales of fixed assets (a chargeable gain may arise – see Chapter 6).

3.2 Amounts not charged in the accounts but deductible

Examples of expenditure not charged in the profit and loss account, but for which a deduction can be claimed, are as follows.

♦   Capital allowances (see Chapters 4 and 5).

♦   Deduction for part of the lease premium paid on the granting of a short lease (see under Section 2.2 above).

Now that the separate types of adjustments have been considered, it is appropriate to show you how a typical question on this area might be constructed.

Here is a comprehensive example based on a past examination question, which it is recommended you attempt using the typical proforma included below to guide you before considering the detailed solution. Please note that the proforma is *not* intended to cover every possible adjustment but reflects common adjustments only.

A typical proforma for adjustment of profits

		+ £	– £
Net profit per accounts		X	
Add: Items charged in accounts but not allowable for Schedule D Case I purposes:			
Depreciation and amortisation		X	
Loss on sale of fixed assets		X	
Capital expenditure		X	
Legal expenses of capital nature		X	
Fines and penalties		X	
Donations		X	
Entertaining (other than staff)		X	
Gifts to customers		X	
Increase in general bad debt provision		X	
Proportion of expensive car leasing costs		X	
Less: Items credited in accounts but not chargeable under Schedule D Case I:			
Rental income			X
Profit on sale of fixed assets			X
Interest receivable			X
Dividend income			X
Less: Expenditure not charged in accounts but deductible under Schedule D Case I:			
Proportion of lease premium paid			X
		X	X
		(X)	
Schedule D Case I profit before capital allowances		X	

3.3 Example

The profit and loss account of STD Ltd for the year ended 31 March 2004 showed a loss of £42,000 after accounting for the under-noted items:

Note	Expenditure	£		Income	£
(1)	Premium on lease	2,000		Discount received	3,200
	Depreciation	9,500		Insurance recovery re flood damage to stock	6,500
	Patent registration fees	4,000		Rents received	8,400
	Debenture interest	8,000		Interest on tax refund	1,600
	Loss on sale of lorry	6,000		Gain on sale of plant	7,400

Bad debts

		£	
Amounts written off	4,000		
Increase specific provision	2,000		
	6,000		
Decrease in general provision	1,000		
		5,000	

Note	Expenditure	£
(2)	Entertainment expenses	2,600
	Legal fees	
	Re new lease	3,200
	Re recovery of employee loan	1,200
	Re employees' service contracts	600
(3)	General expenses	4,000
(4)	Repairs and renewals	6,400

Capital allowances for the accounting period were calculated at £7,160 but have not been taken into account in the above loss figure.

Notes

(1)   This represents the amount written off in respect of a premium of £20,000 paid by the company on being granted a 10-year lease on its premises on 1 April 2003.

(2)   Entertainment consists of expenditure on:

	£
Entertaining customers	1,200
Staff dance (40 people)	800
Gifts to customers of food hampers	600

(3)   General expenses comprises:

	£
Penalty for late VAT return	2,200
Parking fines on company cars	300
Fees for employees attending courses	1,500

(4)   Included in the figure for repairs is an amount of £5,000 incurred in installing new windows in a recently-acquired second-hand warehouse. This building had suffered fire damage resulting in all of its windows being blown out shortly before being acquired by STD Ltd. Other repairs were of a routine nature.

Required

Compute the adjusted Schedule D Case I figure for the above period.

Your answer should show clearly your reasons for your treatment of *each* of the above items *including* those items not adjusted for in your computation.

3.4   Solution

Start your solution with the company's net profit or loss.

	+ £	- £
Net loss		(42,000)

In this question, the company has a loss. This does not affect the way you should approach the computation. You should still add back any disallowable items of expenditure. These add backs may turn an accounting loss into a Schedule D I profit.

Disallowable expenditure. Go through each expense in turn and decide whether or not it needs to be added back. If it does require adding back, add the figure to the + column of your proforma. If you do not know how to treat a particular item - guess. You have a good chance of getting the right answer. You might find it helpful to tick off each item as you deal with it. This ensures you do not miss any items.

You also need to explain the reason for your chosen treatment. This is probably best done on a separate page.

Income credited but not chargeable under Schedule DI. Deal with any credits in the order in which they appear in the accounts. For each credit, ask yourself whether it relates to the company's trade. If it does, no action is required. If it does not, include the figure in the - column.

Expenditure not charged in the accounts but deductible under Schedule DI. The two most likely items under this category are capital allowances and the deduction in respect of any lease premium. Include these items in the - column.

Finish by totalling the proforma.

Note that it is not essential for you to put headings such as 'disallowable expenditure' on your proforma. You could simply state 'add' and 'less'. You do, however, need to list each adjusted item in words as well as figures.

The finished answer is as follows:

STD Ltd - Adjustment of profit for the year ended 31 March 2004.

	+ £	- £
Net loss		(42,000)
Premium on lease	2,000	
Depreciation	9,500	
Loss on sale of lorry	6,000	
Entertainment expenses	1,800	
Legal fees	4,400	
General expenses	2,200	
Repairs and renewals	5,000	
Bad debts		(1,000)
Rents received		(8,400)
Interest on tax refund		(1,600)
Gain on sale of plant		(7,400)
Premium on lease		(1,640)
Capital allowances		(7,160)
	30,900	(69,200)
		30,900
Adjusted Schedule DI loss		(38,300)

3.5 Explanation

1   The lease premium is a capital item. A deduction is available for part of the premium, calculated as follows.

Assessable on landlord: $£20,000 \times \dfrac{51-10}{50} = £16,400$

Deduction £16,400/10 years = £1,640 per annum.

2   Depreciation is not an allowable deduction. Capital allowances are given instead.

3   The costs of registering patents are allowed as a trading expense.

4   Debenture interest is allowable (assuming the debenture proceeds were used for trading purposes).

5   Losses on the sale of fixed assets are treated in the same way as depreciation - they are added back as capital allowances are given instead. Conversely, profits on the sale of fixed assets are deducted.

6   The decrease in the general bad debts provision is not taxable. Write-offs of trade debts and specific provisions are allowable.

7   Expenditure on entertaining customers is not allowable. Expenditure on entertaining staff is. The cost of the hampers is not allowable as they contain food.

8   The legal fees in respect of the new lease are a capital item and are therefore not allowable. Employee loans are not for trading purposes, therefore the legal costs are also not allowable. Legal fees in connection with the service contracts are an allowable business expense.

9   VAT penalties are not allowable. Parking fines incurred by employees will generally be allowed. Course fees are also allowable, assuming the course relates to the company's trade.

10   The cost of new windows is not allowable. It is capital expenditure required to put a new asset into a usable state. (*Law Shipping*).

11   The discount received is taxable under Schedule DI as it is a trading item.

12   The insurance recovery is in respect of trading stock. It is therefore taxable under Schedule DI.

13   Rents received are taxable under Schedule A, not Schedule DI.

14   The interest received on the tax refund is taxable under Schedule DIII (see Chapter 1).

In an exam you should try to work methodically through the profit and loss account, making sure that if you break off to deal with a note you come back to the same point on the profit and loss account. Ticking off items as you use them should help.

Here is an additional question in an alternative style.

Practice question 1 *(The answer is in the final chapter of this book)*

Uranus

The following items are charged against profit in the accounts of Uranus Ltd, for the year ended 31 March 2004:

1   Running expenses of the managing director's BMW totalling £10,000 (including depreciation of £6,000). His total mileage in the year was 12,000 of which 6,000 was private. The car was owned by Uranus Ltd.

2   Entertainment expenditure totalling £25,000 of which £10,000 was incurred on overseas customers, £11,000 on UK customers and £4,000 on the annual company dinner for 200 employees.

3   £2,500 being the costs of registering a patent to protect a process developed by the company.

4   Lease rental of £6,000 on sales director's car costing £20,000.

5   A payment of £616 to the Royal National Lifeboat Institution under the Gift Aid rules.

6   A payment for £30,000 for the granting of a six year lease on a factory.

7   Debenture interest of £27,000 of which £3,000 was a closing accrual. The loan was used for a trading purpose.

8   A provision of £8,000 against a trade debt of the company, being 80% of the debt. The liquidator of the debtor company had advised Uranus Ltd of this figure but in the event £5,000 of the debt was paid in May 2004.

9   Repairs to a ship purchased on 1 April 2003 totalling £160,000 to make it seaworthy. The annual maintenance cost of the ship was £40,000.

10   Canteen subsidy costs of £100,000. This figure included the cost of providing subsidised meals to directors of £7,500. The meals of all other employees were subsidised at 50% of the cost of a director's meal.

11   Permanent repairs to the roof of a warehouse which was purchased on 1 August 2003 for £25,000. The warehouse, which was used to store raw materials, had a leaking roof when purchased but pending the permanent repairs this was covered by plastic sheeting to enable it to be used from the date of purchase.

Required

State how you would deal with each of the above items when preparing the company's Schedule D Case I computation for the year ended 31 March 2004.

Approach to the question

This question requires a written answer rather than a full calculation. For each of the items listed there are three possibilities.

♦   If the item is an *expense* which is *disallowable* for Schedule DI purposes, it must be *added back* to the net profit.

♦   If the item is a *credit* which is *not taxable* under Schedule DI, it must be *deducted* from the net profit.

♦   If the accounting treatment of the item is the same as the tax treatment, no adjustment is required. In other words, trading expenditure within the profit and loss account which satisfies the wholly and exclusively test requires no adjustment.

Make sure you explain the reason for your chosen treatment.

(Note that you may use the terms 'deductible' and 'non deductible' in place of 'allowable' and disallowable').

4   Summary

You should now be able to successfully attempt questions requiring you to calculate the Schedule DI profit for taxation purposes, showing knowledge of case law and statute.

The starting point for computing profits assessable under Schedule DI is the net profit shown in the company's accounts. This must be adjusted in respect of the following items.

♦   Expenditure charged in the accounts but not allowable for tax purposes. The main types of disallowable expenditure are

-   expenditure not wholly and exclusively for the purpose of the trade
-   capital expenditure
-   appropriations and general provisions
-   charges.

♦   Amounts credited in the accounts but not taxable under Schedule DI. For example

-   investment income
-   profits on the sale of fixed assets.

♦   Amounts not charged in the accounts but deductible under Schedule DI. For example

-   deductions for lease premiums
-   capital allowances.

For an exam question, it is advisable to use a '+' and '-' column and deal with each adjustment as you work methodically through the question. There is no need to arrange your answer into the three types of adjustment shown above.

The computation of capital allowances is shown in the next two chapters.
Here is an additional question in an alternative style.

Multiple choice questions 1 - 5 *(The answers are in the final chapter of this book)*

Each of the questions below has only one correct answer.

1   The following is an analysis of the entertaining expenditure incurred by AB Ltd.

	£
Entertaining customers	300
Entertaining suppliers	200
Staff Christmas party	500
	1,000

What is the total amount of entertaining expenditure that will be disallowed in arriving at AB Ltd's Schedule DI profit?

A   £300

B   £500

C   £700

D   £1,000

2   Which of the following items are **not** deductible in computing Schedule DI profits?

(i)   A contribution to the Labour party

(ii)   A donation to the Red Cross

(iii)   A donation of £20 to the local church

(iv)   Christmas gifts of bottles of wine, costing £12 each and bearing the company's name.

A   Items (i) and (ii)

B   Items (i), (ii) and (iv)

C   Items (i) and (iv)

D   All four items

3   The bad debts account of EF Ltd included the following amounts.

	£
Trade debts written off	400
Increase in general bad debt provision	700
Decrease in specific bad debt provision	(90)
Loan to customer written off	150

What is the total amount that must be added back in calculating EF Ltd's Schedule DI profits.

A   £610

B   £700

C   £850

D   £1,160

4   Harvey Kides Ltd's accounts for the year ended 31 March 2004 included a deduction in the profit and loss account for legal expenses of £4,816.

These comprised the following.

	£
Renewal of an existing short lease	424
Unsuccessful application for planning permission	3,720
Debt collection	672
	4,816

The legal fees allowable for tax purposes are

A   £672

B   £1,096

C   £4,392

D   £4,816

5   Weft & Co Ltd, weavers, spent £13,000 on repairs during the year ended 30 September 2003. The repairs comprised the following.

	£
Replacing the leaking slate roof on the office buildings with a new tiled roof	4,450
Overhauling a second-hand weaving machine purchased during the year but requiring repair before it could be used	2,600
Demolishing an out-house and building new ladies' toilets	5,950
	13,000

The repairs allowable for tax purposes in the Schedule D Case I computation are

A   £4,450

B   £7,050

C   £10,400

D   £13,000

CHAPTER 4

Capital allowances on plant and machinery

EXAM FOCUS

There are over a dozen categories of capital items for which a system of capital allowances is available. For the CIMA syllabus we are only concerned with the two main forms – plant and machinery allowances (covered in this chapter) and industrial buildings allowances (covered in the next chapter).

Plant and machinery capital allowances have frequently been examined under the old syllabus in both the compulsory and the optional sections of the paper. In the compulsory section, these allowances tend to form part of a longer corporation tax question. In the optional section, they may be examined in isolation.

LEARNING OUTCOMES

This chapter covers the following learning outcome of the CIMA syllabus:

> Calculate the capital allowances entitlement of a company (in respect of plant and machinery).

> Demonstrate the importance of timing in tax planning.

In order to cover this learning outcome the following topics are included:

> Qualifying expenditure
> Calculating the allowances
> Classifying plant and machinery
> Basis periods for capital allowances.

---

1 Qualifying expenditure

1.1 Introduction

In Chapter 3 you learned that capital expenditure is not an allowable deduction when calculating Schedule DI profits. Any depreciation charged in the accounts must be added back, as its calculation is highly subjective. Capital allowances may be given in place of depreciation. They give a standardised amount of tax relief for capital expenditure. They are effectively the taxation version of depreciation.

There is no automatic right to tax relief for capital expenditure. In order to qualify for capital allowances, expenditure must usually be in respect of plant or machinery.

1.2 What qualifies as plant and machinery?

There is no statutory definition of the words *machinery* and *plant*. Although the identification of *machinery* causes few problems, in deciding whether an item can be considered to be *plant*, case law has dictated that the following factors should be considered.

♦ The degree of *permanence* – there should be some degree of durability of the item.

♦ The *function* of the item – plant is an item *with which* the trade is carried on, as opposed to being part of the setting *in which* the taxpayer carries on his trade.

The Courts' interpretation of these factors has led to the following items being classed as plant.

Movable partitions

It was held in *Jarrold v John Good and Sons Ltd* that movable partitioning in an office building was plant. Fixed partitioning, however, would be deemed to be part of the setting in which the business was carried on, and would not qualify as plant.

Items that create atmosphere

Chattels used by an hotelier as part of the setting to create atmosphere and make the interior attractive to customers were held to be plant in *CIR v Scottish and Newcastle Breweries Ltd*. Thus the terms *setting* and *plant* are not mutually exclusive.

Dry dock for repairing ships

A dry dock built for repairing ships was held in *CIR v Barclay, Curle & Co Ltd* to be plant, and this included not only the cost of the concrete lining but also the cost of excavating the earth to form the basis.

Swimming and paddling pool at a caravan park

A swimming pool and paddling pool at a caravan park had to be considered as a single unit. The apparatus for purifying and heating the water, and the water which the pools were designed to contain, could not be divorced from the structure of the pools and their apparatus. Accordingly, they were held to be plant in *Cooke v Beach Station Caravans Ltd*.

Specialist lighting for window displays

In *Cole Brothers Ltd v Phillips* it was held that the provision of specialist lighting for window displays, and certain other items such as transformers, played an active role in the carrying on of the business, and qualified as plant.

Movable decorative screens

In the case of *Leeds Permanent Building Society v Proctor*, movable decorative screens which were displayed in the windows of building societies with the intention of attracting passers–by were plant. Part of the reasoning was that they were not part of or inseparably annexed to the structure of the office. They were not capable of use without considerable modification for any business but that of the Society. Indeed, some of them were of such a character that they were really only of use in the particular branch.

Dockside concrete silos

Even though an item performs more than one function, including a function which is not 'plant like', this does not prevent it from being plant. Thus in *Schofield v R & H Hall Ltd* the dockside concrete silos of a grain importer were held to be plant on the grounds that their *primary* function was to hold grain in a position from which it would be conveniently delivered to the purchasers and not to store it.

The following items have been held *not* to be plant.

General lighting

In *Cole Brothers Ltd v Phillips* (as discussed above) it was decided that, although specialist lighting qualified as plant, general lighting formed part of the setting, and was not plant.

This is a common examinable point. The question should make it clear what part of the electrical equipment, wiring etc is just part of a normal building and which part has a special application and qualifies as plant, eg high current wiring for electrical machinery.

False ceilings

The physical attachment of an item to something accepted as plant does not make that item plant, as demonstrated in *Hampton v Fortes Autogrill Ltd*. In this case, a catering company installed false ceilings in the premises from which it traded. The ceilings were a permanent installation and provided cladding and support for pipes carrying refreshments, ventilation trunking and lighting apparatus. It was held that the ceilings were not necessary for the functioning of any apparatus used for the purposes of the company's trade and were not part of the means by which the trade was carried on. Accordingly, they were not plant.

Canopy over a petrol station

In *Dixon v Fitch's Garage Ltd* it was held that a canopy over a petrol station did not perform a function in serving petrol to customers, and must be considered to be part of the setting. Accordingly, it did not qualify as plant.

Football stand

The case of *Brown v Burnley Football & Athletic Co Ltd* again demonstrated that the physical attachment of plant to another item does not make that other item plant. In this case, whilst it was agreed that the seats in a football stand were plant, the stand itself formed part of the stadium within which the football matches took place, and therefore did not qualify as plant.

1.3   *Statutory regulations*

Certain items have been deemed to be plant by *statute*.

♦ Thermal insulation in industrial buildings (see Chapter 5).

♦ Expenditure on compliance with fire safety requirements of the business premises.

♦ Expenditure necessary to obtain sports stadium safety certificates.

♦ Computer software even where acquired electronically or where the company merely acquires a licence to use software.

The status of items installed in a building has been a frequent problem which has resulted in disputes resolved through the Courts (see above). In the Finance Act 1994 rules were introduced to draw the dividing line but respecting existing case law decisions.

The following items are 'building' (not plant).

♦ Walls, floors, ceilings, doors, gates, windows and stairs.
♦ Mains services and systems of water, electricity and gas.
♦ Waste disposal, sewerage and drainage systems.

The following items may be 'building' but are nevertheless normally treated as 'plant'.

♦ Electrical, cold water and gas systems provided mainly to meet the particular requirements of the trade, or to serve particular machinery used for the purposes of the trade.

- Space or water heating systems, systems of ventilation and air cooling, and any ceiling or floor comprised in such systems.

- Manufacturing or processing equipment, storage equipment including cold rooms, display equipment, counters, check outs and similar equipment.

- Cookers, washing machines, dishwashers, refrigerators and similar equipment.

- Wash basins, sinks, baths, showers, sanitary ware and similar equipment.

- Furniture and furnishings.

- Lifts, escalators and moving walkways.

- Sound insulation to meet the particular requirements of the trade.

- Computer, telecommunication and surveillance systems (and their wiring).

- Sprinkler equipment and fire alarm systems.

- Burglar alarm systems and strong rooms.

- Movable partition walls where intended to be moved in the course of the trade.

- Decorative assets provided for the enjoyment of the public in a hotel, restaurant or similar trade.

- Advertising hoardings, signs and similar displays.

2 Calculating the allowances

2.1 The objective of capital allowances

The aim of capital allowances is to give tax relief for the net cost of an asset. That is the difference between the cost of an asset and its disposal value. Allowances are calculated for accounting periods and are given as a deduction in calculating Schedule D Case I profits.

As it is not known at the outset what the disposal value will be, a first year allowance (FYA) of 40% is normally given in the year of purchase. For each following year an annual writing down allowance (WDA) of 25% is given. This is calculated using the reducing balance method. A balancing adjustment may be given when the asset is disposed of: a balancing allowance gives any additional allowances due, whereas a balancing charge recovers any allowances in excess of the net cost.

The principle can be illustrated as follows.

		Asset
Cost		10,000
Year 1 Allowance 40% (FYA)		(4,000)
		6,000
Year 2 Allowance 25% (WDA)		(1,500)
		4,500
Year 3 Disposal		(6,300)
Balancing charge		(1,800)

Net cost	= £10,000 – £6,300	=	£3,700
Allowances	= £4,000 + £1,500 – £1,800	=	£3,700

Instead of calculating capital allowances for each individual asset, most types of expenditure are pooled.

The proforma below shows the layout which you should ideally use to present your answer. The examiner will certainly expect to see the use of an orderly layout. The various entries will be explained later in the chapter.

Layout of computation for capital allowances on plant and machinery

	General pool		Expensive car (1)	Expensive car (2)	Total allowances
	£	£	£	£	£
WDV b/f		X	X	X	
Additions *not* qualifying for FYAs*		X			
Disposals – lower of cost/sale proceeds		(X)	(X)		
		X	X	X	
BA/(BC)			X/(X)		X/(X)
WDA at 25%		(X)			X
WDA restricted				(X)	X
		X		X	
Additions qualifying for FYA	X				
FYA at 40%	(X)				X
		X			
WDV c/f		X	-	X	X

*FYA can only exceptionally be claimed on cars.

Note the following abbreviations.

♦ WDV = tax written down value (the amount of expenditure not yet written off by means of capital allowances)

♦ FYA = first year allowance

♦ BA/BC = balancing allowance/balancing charge

 Be sure not to confuse the order of the steps. For example, additions qualifying for FYA do **not** attract WDA in the same year so they are dealt with **after** calculating WDA.

3 Classifying plant and machinery

3.1 Introduction

 As companies may have many assets, it would be extremely time-consuming to calculate allowances separately for each asset. Therefore, all qualifying expenditure is pooled, apart from:

♦ *expensive cars*, (that is cars costing more than £12,000)
♦ assets for which a *short life* election has been made.

Each of the above categories will now be considered in detail below.

3.2 General pool

Most items of plant and machinery go into the general pool. Once an asset enters the pool, it loses its identity. This means that the writing down allowance (WDA) is calculated on the balance of the pool, rather than on the individual assets.

Allowances are given for accounting periods. Allowances commence in the year in which the expenditure is incurred. A full WDA is given in the year of purchase (unless FYA is claimed) irrespective of the date of purchase.

First year allowances

Plant and machinery (excluding cars) bought on or after 1 July 1998 by *small and medium–sized* businesses qualify for a first year allowance (FYA) of 40%. For items bought between 2 July 1997 and 1 July 1998, the FYA available was 50%. The FYA is given *instead of* the WDA in the period of the expenditure, after which the balance is added to the pool, so that a WDA of 25% can be given in subsequent periods. For a business to qualify for first year allowances as a small or medium-sized business it must meet at least two of the following three conditions.

♦ Turnover not exceeding £11.2 million
♦ Assets not exceeding £5.6 million in value
♦ No more than 250 employees.

Small businesses that invest in information and communication technology equipment between 1 April 2000 and 31 March 2004 can claim a 100% FYA. This FYA covers expenditure on

♦ computers, including peripherals and cabling
♦ software
♦ WAP and 3rd generation mobile phones.

A business is classed as small for the purpose of claiming the 100% FYA if it satisfies at least two out of the following conditions.

♦ Turnover not exceeding £2.8 million
♦ Assets not exceeding £1.4 million in value
♦ No more than 50 employees.

When reading an exam question on CAs look for any indication of business size, ie 'small' or 'medium'. The examiner should tell you or it should be obvious from other details such as turnover.

The above definitions of small and medium sized enterprises (SMEs) are due to be relaxed from a date to be announced during 2003/04 in line with changes under EU law.

The rates of capital allowances and the sizes of qualifying companies will be given to you in the exam.

Businesses of *any size* qualify for 100% first year allowance on cars registered on or after 17 April 2002 provided that either the carbon dioxide emissions are not more than 120 grams per kilometre travelled or the car is electrically propelled. This is to encourage the take up of technology that minimises atmospheric pollution. All new cars registered in the EU show their emission figure on their registration document. The emission yardstick also applies to calculating company car benefits for employees (see Chapter 15). However, very few cars are currently able to claim an emission rate not exceeding the threshold of 120 gm/km. Cars should only be treated as 'low emission' if the exam question specifically describes them as such.

From 1 April 2001 businesses of any size can claim 100% FYAs for capital expenditure on new energy-saving plant and machinery designed to reduce global warming. The precise items of plant qualifying are specified in government Energy Technology lists. For exam purposes you would have to be advised in the question as to whether the boilers and insulation equipment etc were 'listed'.

From 1 April 2003 businesses of any size can claim 100% FYAs for expenditure on plant on the Water Technology List covering equipment to reduce water use and improve water quality. Again the examiner would have to indicate whether plant in an exam question qualified for the relief.

Disposals

When a pool item is sold, the *sale proceeds* are deducted from the pool. This deduction cannot exceed the asset's original cost.

 If the deduction of the disposal proceeds causes the pool to become *negative*, the difference is a balancing charge. Otherwise the pool continues to be written down until cessation. This means that there will not usually be a balancing allowance on the general pool.

The following example illustrates the working of the general pool.

3.3   Example

Apple Ltd prepares accounts to 30 April each year.

On 1 May 2002 Apple Ltd incurred expenditure of £6,000 on the purchase of shop fittings and machinery. On 1 June 2002 the company sold some machinery for £600 (cost £400) and on 1 June 2003 purchased more plant for £1,000.

On 5 May 2003 the company sold equipment for £9,395 which had cost £11,200 in May 2000. The tax written down value of the pool at 1 May 2002 was £8,260.

Required

Compute the capital allowances for the years ended 30 April 2003 and 30 April 2004, assuming that Apple Ltd is a small company.

3.4   Solution

 The first step is to identify the balance brought forward at the beginning of the accounting period. This is called the *tax written down value* (tax WDV or TWDV).

	Pool
Year ended 30 April 2003	£
Tax WDV brought forward	8,260

 The next step is to identify the accounting periods in which the additions and disposals occur. In the year ended 30 April 2003, Apple Ltd acquired plant costing £6,000 and sold plant for £600. All other additions and disposals occur in the second accounting period.

 Identify any additions for which a FYA can be claimed. For example, the plant acquired on 1 May 2002 qualifies for a 40% FYA. Deal with this addition *after* calculating the WDA for that year on the other items in the general pool.

The working can then be completed, as shown below, dealing with one accounting period at a time.

	£	Pool £	Allowances £
Year ended 30 April 2003			
Tax WDV b/f		8,260	
Additions without FYA		-	
Disposals			
1 June 2002 (proceeds restricted to cost)		(400)	
		7,860	
WDA at 25%		(1,965)	1,965
Additions (FYA)			
1 May 2002	6,000		
FYA at 40%	(2,400)		2,400
Balance added to pool		3,600	
Tax WDV c/f		9,495	4,365

Year ended 30 April 2004			
Additions (no FYA)		-	
Disposals			
5 May 2003		(9,395)	
		100	
WDA at 25%		(25)	25
Additions (FYA)			
1 June 2003	1,000		
FYA at 40%	(400)		400
Balance added to pool		600	
Tax WDV c/f		675	425

If the exam question requires you to **maximise** capital allowances you might have to consider disclaiming part or all of the FYAs available. For example, if the disposal proceeds in the above question were £10,000 on 5 May 2003, this would have resulted in a balancing charge of £505 (10,000 – 9,495). The technique for avoiding this would be to split the additions of £1,000 on 1 June 2003 into £505 without FYA and £495 with FYA. The first part goes 'above the line' to cover the balancing charge and the £495 attracts 40% FYA 'below the line'. In effect the £505 is relieved at 100% (instead of 40%) as it covers the BC £1 for £1.

3.5 Expensive cars

Each car costing more than £12,000 is given a separate column in the capital allowances working. A 25% WDA is calculated for each individual car, but the maximum allowance that can be claimed is £3,000 per annum per car.

As each car has a separate column, there will be a balancing adjustment (either a balancing allowance or a balancing charge) on disposal. The balancing adjustment is not restricted to £3,000.

The expensive car rules do not apply to low emission cars (ie, not exceeding 120 gms of carbon dioxide per kilometre) or electric cars registered since 16 April 2002.

The examples below illustrate the working of capital allowances for both cheap and expensive cars.

3.6 Example

Grin Ltd prepares accounts to 31 December each year. No capital expenditure had been incurred prior to 1 January 2002. In the year to 31 December 2002 the following expenditure is incurred.

		Cost £
31 January 2002	Motor car	6,000
12 February 2002	Motor car	14,000
17 June 2002	Motor car	10,000

Required

Calculate Grin Ltd's capital allowances for the years ended 31 December 2002 and 31 December 2003.

3.7 Solution

In this example, there is no tax WDV brought forward, so the first task is to decide which cars will be brought into the general pool, and which need their own separate columns. A proforma can then be set up as below.

	General pool	Expensive car	Allowances
Year ended 31 December 2002	£	£	£

Now the additions can be put into the appropriate columns, and the allowances calculated, remembering that the allowance for the expensive car must be restricted to £3,000. The full working is as follows.

	General pool £	Expensive car £	Allowances £
Year ended 31 December 2002			
Additions			
31 January 2002	6,000		
12 February 2002		14,000	
17 June 2002	10,000		
	16,000		
WDA at 25% (restricted)	(4,000)	(3,000)	7,000
Tax WDV c/f	12,000	11,000	
Year ended 31 December 2003			
WDA at 25%	(3,000)	(2,750)	5,750
Tax WDV c/f	9,000	8,250	

Note that the 25% WDA allowance for the expensive car is not restricted for the year ended 31 December 2003, as it is less than £3,000. The separate column is, however, retained.

3.8 Example

Grin Ltd (see previous example) sells the car, bought in February 2002, in August 2004.

Required

Calculate the balancing adjustment on the car on the alternative assumptions:

(a)   that the car is sold for £7,000
(b)   that the car is sold for £9,200.

3.9 Solution

In this example, the expensive car is sold, so there will be a balancing adjustment.

First, the proceeds (restricted to original cost) are deducted from the written down value.

Then, if the remaining balance is positive, a balancing *allowance* will be given, but if the balance is negative a balancing *charge* will arise. This is like a negative allowance. Instead of being deducted from Schedule D Case I profits, it will be added back. In both cases, the tax WDV carried forward will be nil.

The solutions to the two different scenarios are as follows.

(a)   *Proceeds £7,000*

	General pool £	Expensive car £	Allowances £
Year ended 31 December 2004			
Tax WDV brought forward	9,000	8,250	
Disposal proceeds		(7,000)	
	9,000	1,250	
Balancing allowance		(1,250)	1,250
WDA at 25%	(2,250)		2,250
Tax WDV carried forward	6,750	–	3,500

(b) Proceeds £9,200

Year ended 31 December 2004	General pool £	Expensive car £	Allowances £
Tax WDV brought forward	9,000	8,250	
Disposal proceeds		(9,200)	
	9,000	(950)	
Balancing charge		950	(950)
WDA at 25%	(2,250)	–	2,250
Tax WDV carried forward	6,750	–	1,300

Note that a balancing allowance is usually pooled with WDA/FYA and a balancing charge is usually offset against WDA/FYA. Technically, however, balancing adjustments should be kept separate. The allowance is deducted in calculating the Schedule D Case I profits and the charge is added back.

The example below demonstrates the full capital allowances working.

3.10 Example

JNN Ltd, a small company, has been trading since 1 June 2001, making up accounts to 31 May each year.

The following assets have recently been purchased.

Date of purchase	Asset	Cost £
1 May 2001	Plant and machinery	11,616
9 November 2001	Used car	1,472
10 February 2002	Used car	928
8 June 2002	New car	19,500
2 July 2002	Equipment	1,720
2 June 2003	Computer equipment	982
10 July 2003	Typewriter	876
20 October 2003	New car	18,071

The new car acquired on 20 October 2003 was electric powered.

Required

Calculate the capital allowances due for the three years ending 31 May 2004.

3.11 Solution

The approach is as follows.

♦ Allocate additions and disposals to the relevant accounting periods. Any acquisitions made prior to the commencement of trading are treated as if made on the first day of trading.

♦ Identify which additions qualify for FYA and which rate of FYA applies.

The solution is then as follows.

Capital allowances computation

	£	Pool £	Expensive car £	Allowances £
Year ending 31 May 2002				
Additions (no FYA)				
9 November 2001		1,472		
10 February 2002		928		
		2,400		
WDA at 25%		(600)		600
Addition (FYA)				
1 May 2001	11,616			
40% FYA	(4,646)	6,970		4,646
		8,770		5,246
Year ending 31 May 2003				
Additions – not qualifying for FYA				
8 June 2002			19,500	
WDA 25%/restricted		(2,192)	(3,000)	5,192
Addition qualifying for FYA				
2 July 2002	1,720			
40% FYA	(688)			688
		1,032		
		7,610	16,500	5,880
Year ending 31 May 2004				
WDA 25%/ restricted		(1,902)	(3,000)	4,902
Additions qualifying for FYA at 100%				
2 June 2003	982			
20 October 2003	18,071			
100% FYA	19,053			19,053
Additions qualifying for FYA at 40%				
10 July 2003	876			
40% FYA	(350)			350
		526		
		6,234	13,500	24,305

Practice question 1 *(The answer is in the final chapter of this book)*

ENT Ltd

ENT Ltd prepares accounts to 31 December annually. On 1 January 2002 the balance of plant and machinery brought forward was £24,000. The following transactions took place in the year to 31 December 2002.

15 April 2002	Purchased car for £12,600
30 April 2002	Sold plant for £3,200 (original cost £4,800)
16 July 2002	Purchased car for £9,200
17 August 2002	Purchased car for £9,400

In the following year to 31 December 2003 ENT Ltd sold for £7,900 the car originally purchased on 17 August 2002. The car originally purchased on 15 April 2002 was sold for £9,400 on 9 March 2003. There were no other transactions.

Required

Compute the capital allowances and balancing adjustments for the years ended 31 December 2002 and 31 December 2003. (Ignore VAT).

3.12 Short–life assets (SLA)

Where an asset is expected to have a short life, approximately four years or less, and to decrease in value substantially, it may be beneficial to remove it from the general pool and treat it as a *short–life asset*. In doing this, a balancing allowance can be claimed when the asset is disposed of. (Remember that a balancing allowance can only be claimed on the general pool on cessation of the business.)

Each asset treated as a short–life asset should have a separate column in the capital allowances computation.

The following conditions apply.

♦ Short–life asset treatment is *not* available for cars.

♦ If a short–life asset is not sold within four years of the end of the accounting period in which it was purchased, its tax WDV will be transferred back into the general pool.

♦ A short-life asset election must be made within two years of the end of the accounting period in which the expenditure was incurred.

The following illustration demonstrates how short–life asset treatment accelerates the allowances claimed.

Illustration

Purchase (for £10,000) and sale (for £1,000) of a short-life asset.

Without election			*With election*		
	General pool			General pool	SLA
Year 1	£		*Year 1*	£	£
WDV b/f, say	50,000		WDV b/f, say	50,000	
WDA	(12,500)		Purchase		10,000
Purchase	10,000			50,000	10,000
FYA	(4,000)		WDA/FYA	(12,500)	(4,000)
Year 2			*Year 2*		
WDV b/f	43,500		WDV b/f	37,500	6,000
Disposal	(1,000)		Disposal	–	(1,000)
	42,500			37,500	5,000
BA	–		BA		(5,000)
WDA	(10,625)		WDA	(9,375)	
WDV c/f	31,875		WDV c/f	28,125	–
Total allowances given (£12,500 + £4,000 + £10,625)	27,125		Total allowances given (£12,500 + £4,000 + £9,375 + £5,000)		30,875
WDV c/f	31,875		WDV c/f		28,125

It is important to note that a short-life asset election is *not* beneficial if the asset is to be sold for more that its tax written down value. This is because the disposal would result in a balancing charge.

Illustration

Continuing with the above example, assume instead that the asset was sold for £8,000.

Without election			*With election*		
	General pool			General pool	SLA
Year 2	£		*Year 2*	£	£
WDV b/f	43,500		WDV b/f	37,500	6,000
Disposal	(8,000)		Disposal	–	(8,000)
	35,500			37,500	(2,000)
BC	–		BC		2,000
WDA	(8,875)		WDA	(9,375)	
WDV c/f	26,625		WDV c/f	28,125	–

As you can see, by leaving the asset in the general pool, the balancing charge is avoided.

Where the asset qualifies for 100% FYA (eg computer bought by a small business) an SLA election should not be made as a balancing charge would arise on any eventual proceeds.

 An SLA election could also be a disadvantage if a balancing charge is about to arise on the general pool. An addition to the general pool would reduce it £1 for £1. If instead it is kept separate in an SLA column, it cannot achieve this saving.

3.13 Additional considerations

Hire purchase transactions

Allowances for assets bought on hire purchase are calculated on the full cash price (excluding interest). The allowances commence on the date the asset is acquired, irrespective of the dates on which instalments are payable. The capital allowances claimed are thus not affected by the fact that the asset is bought on hire purchase rather than outright.

Interest included in instalments is an allowable Schedule D Case I expense for the period in which the instalments are payable. (This means that there will be no adjustment for hire purchase interest deducted in the profit and loss account).

Part exchange transactions

If an asset is given in part exchange for a new asset, this is treated as a separate acquisition and disposal as follows.

♦ The addition should be recorded in the capital allowances working at *full* price, ie cash paid plus part exchange allowance.

♦ The disposal proceeds deducted in the capital allowances working are taken as the part exchange allowance (restricted to original cost if lower).

VAT on capital purchases

VAT is covered later in the text, but you should note that VAT at 17.5% is normally reclaimed on all purchases, including capital additions, with the exception of cars. The cost of a car for capital allowance purposes is therefore its VAT *in*clusive cost. Other assets are recorded at their VAT *ex*clusive cost.

When capital assets are sold, VAT will be included in the sale price. However, the disposal value for capital allowances will be the VAT *ex*clusive price, with the exception of cars on which no VAT is charged. Most questions involving capital allowances ignore VAT, but not all.

4 Basis periods for capital allowances

4.1 The impact of the accounting period length

As you have seen, capital allowances are computed for accounting periods and deducted in calculating Schedule D Case I profits.

The writing down allowances calculated so far were all for 12 month accounting periods.

Where the accounting period is less than 12 months long, the WDA must be scaled down accordingly. You must perform this calculation to the nearest month.

If the period for which accounts are drawn up exceeds 12 months, the capital allowances are computed in two stages – the first 12 months, then the balance.

Note that first year allowances are given in full even if the length of the accounting period is less than 12 months.

4.2 Example

KNN Ltd started to trade on 1 June 2002 and, on that day, purchased an asset costing £21,900. KNN Ltd does not qualify for FYAs. Calculate the writing down allowances due for the accounting period(s) based on the first period of account on the assumption that accounts are made up to:

(i)   31 May 2003
(ii)   31 March 2003
(iii)   31 December 2003.

4.3 Solution

		(i)	(ii)	(iii)
First period of account		31 May 2003	31 March 2003	31 December 2003
		£	£	£
Cost		21,900	21,900	21,900
WDA	25%	(5,475)		
	$25\% \times \frac{10}{12}$		(4,563)	
	25%			(5,475)
				16,425
	$25\% \times \frac{7}{12}$			(2,395)
WDV c/f		16,425	17,337	14,030

Note that, as already explained in Chapter 1, in (iii) corporation tax is charged separately on an accounting period of 12 months ending on 31 May 2003 and on an accounting period of 7 months ending on 31 December 2003.

4.4 Business cessation

In the accounting period of cessation no WDAs or FYAs will be given.

Any additions and disposals in the final period are allocated to the appropriate columns in the capital allowance working.

At the end of the period there will be no tax WDV carried forward, so there must be a balancing adjustment on *all* categories in the capital allowances working.

♦   If there is a positive balance remaining, a balancing allowance is given.
♦   If there is a negative balance remaining, a balancing charge arises.

4.5 Example

DRN Ltd had been trading for many years, preparing accounts to 31 December, when it decided to cease trading on 30 June 2003.

Expenditure on plant had been as follows.

Date	*Cost*
	£
1 October 2002	4,600

All items of plant were sold on 30 June 2003 for £5,000 (no item was sold for more than cost).

The tax written down value of the pool at 1 January 2002 was £12,600.

Required

Calculate the capital allowances due for the year ended 31 December 2002 and the six months ended 30 June 2003. (Ignore VAT).

4.6 Solution

Capital allowances computation

	£	*General pool* £	*Allowances* £
Year ended 31 December 2002			
Tax WDV brought forward		12,600	
WDA at 25%		(3,150)	3,150
		9,450	
Addition qualifying for FYA 1 October 2002	4,600		
FYA at 40%	(1,840)		1,840
		2,760	
Tax WDV carried forward		12,210	4,990
6 months ended 30 June 2003			
Disposals		(5,000)	
		7,210	
Balancing allowance		(7,210)	7,210

Note: If plant is not sold until after the date of cessation, the proceeds eventually realised are used as the market value on cessation. In effect it is treated as if sold on cessation for market value.

4.7 Timing of expenditure

Capital allowances are given in the period in which capital expenditure is incurred, and in subsequent periods until the expenditure is fully relieved.

If a business intends to incur substantial expenditure qualifying for capital allowances, incurring it just before the end of an accounting period will achieve relief earlier than if the expenditure had been incurred just after the start of the next accounting period.

The rate of tax relief is also relevant. Capital allowances should not be advanced if relief would be obtained at the small companies rate rather than the full rate or the small companies marginal rate. Relief at the starting rate of nil% is, in particular, wasted relief.

Practice question 2 *(The answer is in the final chapter of this book)*

RBT Ltd

RBT Ltd commenced trading on 1 January 2002 and immediately registered for VAT. The first accounts were prepared to 30 June 2002 and thereafter to 30 June annually.

The following purchases and sales of fixed assets occurred.

| | | Invoice details | | |
| | | Net | VAT | Total |
Purchases		£	£	£
1 January 2002	Secondhand loom	10,000	1,750	11,750
1 February 2002	Motor car (used)	–	–	5,750
30 September 2002	Motor car (new)	10,383	1,817	12,200
1 October 2002	Motor car (used)	–	–	6,210
1 October 2002	Computer	8,478	1,484	9,962
1 February 2004	Motor car (new)	15,319	2,681	18,000
1 June 2004	Motor car (new)	13,728	2,402	16,130
Sale				
1 June 2004	Loom originally purchased 1 January 2002, a cheque for £4,700 being received as proceeds			

The car purchased on 1 February 2004 had a carbon dioxide emission rating of 118 grams per kilometre.

Compute the capital allowances for the first three periods of account taking advantage of any beneficial elections available. Assume that RBT Ltd is a medium sized business.

Approach to the question

Note the following points.

♦ You need to decide whether to use VAT inclusive or VAT exclusive figures. Use the fraction $^{40}/_{47}$ if you need to convert a VAT inclusive figure into a VAT exclusive figure.

♦ Watch the length of the first accounting period. Remember that WDAs must be scaled down if the accounting period is less than 12 months long. However, FYAs are never scaled down in such circumstances.

♦ Consider how best to treat the loom as it has been sold at a loss within a couple of years of its purchase.

5 Summary

Capital allowances are granted to give tax relief, over the life of an asset, for the asset's net cost to the business.

A tabular layout is essential for computing capital allowances on plant and machinery. The table should have separate columns for each of the following.

♦ General pool
♦ Each 'expensive' car
♦ Each short–life asset

When an asset is expected to have a short life, and to decrease in value substantially, it may be beneficial to exclude it from the general pool and treat it as a short–life asset.

When an accounting period is less than 12 months long, writing down allowances must be scaled down accordingly. First year allowances are never scaled down.

Multiple choice questions 1 - 5 *(The answers are in the final chapter of this book)*

Each of the questions below has only one correct answer.

1   Lincoln Ltd, an industrial paint manufacturer, incurred the following capital expenditure (including VAT) during a particular VAT quarter.

	Net £	VAT £	Total £
Two cars for salesmen (private use permitted)	12,200	2,135	14,335
Motor van	9,000	1,575	10,575
Second-hand container lorry	22,400	3,920	26,320

How much VAT cannot be reclaimed?

A   £6,055

B   £3,710

C   £2,135

D   £7,630

2   Happy Days Ltd, a holiday camp operator, incurred the following items of capital expenditure in the year ended 31 December 2003.

	£
Children's paddling pool	45,000
False ceiling in the fast food restaurant to hide the services and the wiring	15,000
Murals of tropical beaches for the Hawaiian bar	5,000

How much of this expenditure qualifies for capital allowances?

A   £45,000

B   £50,000

C   £60,000

D   £65,000

3   Julian Ltd commenced trading on 1 July 2003 and purchased a motor car for £7,200 for the use of a manager (20% private use).

What are the company's capital allowances for the accounting period ended 31 March 2004?

A   £1,080

B   £1,350

C   £1,440

D   £1,800

4   Jonah Ltd began trading on 1 July 1998, preparing accounts to 30 June and has been registered for VAT since commencement. In the year ended 30 June 2003 the company's capital transactions were as follows.

    4 May 2003   Purchased used Ford car   £6,580

    10 May 2003   Sold computer   £3,525

The tax written down value of the computer (elected for short life asset treatment) was £4,230. There was no balance on the general pool. The prices include VAT at the standard rate.

Jonah Ltd's capital allowances claim for the year ended 30 June 2003 will be

A   £3,862

B   £2,875

C   £2,630

D   £2,350

5   Jarrot Jibs Ltd commenced a small business as a ships chandler on 1 August 2003 making up accounts to 31 March 2004 and 31 March thereafter. The company bought fixed assets as follows.

(1)	15 August 2003	Shop fittings	£20,000
(2)	1 November 2003	Estate car	£16,000
(3)	10 February 2004	Computer	£2,000

What are the maximum capital allowances that the company can claim for the first trading period? (Ignore VAT.)

A   £8,667

B   £10,800

C   £12,000

D   £13,000

CHAPTER 5

Capital allowances on industrial buildings

EXAM FOCUS

Industrial buildings allowance (IBA) tends to be examined in one of three ways. It may feature as part of a question on capital allowances in general. Alternatively, it may be a full question in its own right. It could also possibly be included as part of a larger question requiring the computation of profits chargeable to corporation tax. Flat conversion allowances are a relatively minor topic, but have been examined.

LEARNING OUTCOMES

This chapter covers the following learning outcome of the CIMA syllabus:

> Calculate the capital allowance entitlement of a company (in respect of industrial buildings and flat conversions).
>
> Demonstrate the importance of timing in tax planning.

In order to cover this learning outcome the following topics are included:

> Eligible expenditure for IBA purposes
> Allowances available for new buildings
> The disposal of an industrial building
> Allowances for secondhand purchasers
> Non-industrial activity
> Flat conversion allowances
> Approach to a typical CT question

1 Eligible expenditure for IBA purposes

1.1 Qualifying expenditure

In examination questions you often need to identify the correct *amount* of expenditure eligible for IBA. You may also need to state the *types* of buildings which qualify for IBA.

Buildings qualify for IBA if they are of an industrial nature and are used in an industrial trade. This includes the following.

- A mill, factory or any building used in a manufacturing trade.
- Warehouses for the storage of stock (ie raw materials, finished goods) provided they are used in or derived from a manufacturing trade.
- Buildings used for the repair or maintenance of goods or materials.
- Sports pavilions used in any trade.
- Canteens and other welfare buildings provided for workers in a manufacturing business.
- Drawing offices in factories (*CIR v Lambhill Ironworks Ltd*).
- Qualifying hotels.
- Any commercial building in a designated enterprise zone.

The qualifying costs of constructing such buildings or acquiring a new building include the following.

- Professional fees (eg architects, legal fees).
- The costs of preparing land (eg levelling, tunnelling, drainage).
- Associated structural undertakings (eg a car park adjoining a factory).

1.2 Non-qualifying expenditure

There are also some frequently examined exclusions which do *not* qualify.

- Land (including any costs pertaining to the land itself, eg legal fees).

- General offices, shops, showrooms and dwelling houses.

- Retailers' warehouses, ie used for storing bought in finished goods.

- Items which qualify alternatively for plant and machinery allowances (eg central heating, fire and safety equipment, ventilation, thermal insulation).

Non-industrial parts

Any 'non-industrial' portion of an industrial building (eg general offices) is only excluded if its cost represents more than 25% of the total building costs.

1.3 Example

The cost of a factory, incurred in September 2003, is shown below.

	£
Purchase price of land (including £1,700 legal costs)	17,000
Buildings (including drawing office £4,900, canteen £10,000, general office £30,000)	144,000
	161,000

Required

(a) What amount is eligible for industrial buildings allowance?

(b) If the general office had accounted for £37,000 of the £144,000 cost of the building, what would the eligible expenditure be?

1.4 Solution

(a) There is no allowance for the purchase price of the land. The drawing office and the canteen both qualify for IBA in their own right. The cost of the general offices will also qualify as it represents 20.8% (£30,000/£144,000) of the total building cost, ie not exceeding 25%. IBA will therefore be based on £144,000.

(b) If the general offices had cost £37,000, this would amount to 25.7% (£37,000/£144,000) of the total cost. As this exceeds 25%, none of the £37,000 would be allowable. IBA would therefore be based on £107,000 (£144,000 - £37,000).

1.5 Additions to a building

Whenever there is an addition (eg an extension) to an industrial building, the 25% test must be recalculated. This may mean that part of the industrial building which previously qualified now becomes disallowable.

1.6   *Example*

Holt Ltd purchased a new factory for the following cost.

		£
Manufacturing area		200,000
Showroom		10,000
General office		30,000
Drawing office		5,000
Land		10,000
		255,000

Two years later the company built an office extension at a cost of £35,000.

Required

What is the eligible expenditure which qualifies for IBA

(a)   on purchase and
(b)   on the subsequent addition?

1.7   *Solution*

(a)   The cost of land never qualifies for IBA. The remaining expenditure (£245,000) could qualify subject to the 25% rule for non-industrial parts. The showroom and the general office are non-industrial parts.

The non-industrial proportion is therefore £40,000/£245,000 = 16.3%. As this is less than 25%, the whole £245,000 qualifies.

(b)   When the extension is added, the building cost becomes £280,000 (£245,000 + £35,000). The non-industrial portion becomes £75,000 (£40,000 + £35,000).

The non-industrial proportion is now £75,000/£280,000 = 26.8%. As this is greater than 25%, the whole of the non-industrial part is no longer eligible for future allowances. Allowances from that point are granted on £205,000 only (ie £280,000 – £75,000).

1.8   *Ownership*

In order to be eligible to claim IBA, the claimant must have the *relevant interest*. This means that the claimant must be either

♦   the freeholder, or
♦   the holder of a long lease (more than 50 years).

In the latter case, a joint election must be made by the tenant and the landlord, to allow the tenant to claim the allowances on the lower of the eligible cost and the premium paid to enter the lease.

A landlord can claim IBAs on a factory (etc) provided the tenant uses the building as an 'industrial building'. The IBAs are set against the Schedule A rental income of the landlord.

A tenant could claim IBAs on any additions he makes during the tenancy of the lease.

1.9 Hotels

A hotel qualifies for industrial buildings allowances if it is a hotel which is open for at least four months between 1 April and 31 October each year ('the season').

When open in the season:

♦ it must have at least 10 bedrooms available to the public for short-term letting (not more than one month at a time);
♦ the sleeping accommodation must comprise wholly or mainly letting bedrooms; and
♦ the services normally provided for guests must include the provision of breakfast and an evening meal, the making of beds and the cleaning of rooms.

It is a hard definition to satisfy. For example, a convalescent home in which guests stay for only two or three weeks would not qualify even though the above conditions are met. It simply is not a 'hotel' in the normal use of the word.

2 Allowances available for new buildings

2.1 Introduction

Three areas of allowance need to be considered.

♦ Initial allowances
♦ Writing down allowances
♦ Balancing adjustments on disposal (see Section 3).

2.2 Initial allowances (IA)

These may be available in the accounting period in which the expenditure is incurred. For example, an initial allowance of 20% was available for qualifying expenditure incurred between 1 November 1992 and 31 October 1993.

Varying percentages of IA have been available over the years. There is no current IA, but you may need to use relevant percentages from earlier years. These will be provided in the examination where applicable.

2.3 Writing down allowances (WDA)

WDA is given on a *straight line* basis of 4% per annum. This means that unless an IA is available it takes 25 years to obtain full relief, and so industrial buildings are often described as having a 25 year tax life. This tax life commences from the date the building is first put into use, industrial or otherwise, and lasts for 25 years regardless of whether an IA was given.

A claimant is entitled to WDA provided the building is in industrial *use* at the *end* of the accounting period. The WDA and any IA can both be given in the initial period of expenditure, provided the building is brought into industrial use before the end of the period.

Periods of temporary disuse during the ownership of the building (eg during contraction of trade) are ignored and allowances still given provided the building had been in industrial use.

For the purpose of calculating allowances, each new building or addition has its own 25 year tax life, and should therefore be kept as a separate item.

No WDA is given in the accounting period in which a building is sold.

2.4 Enterprise zone allowances

Any commercial building (eg shop, office or factory) situated in a designated enterprise zone attracts an initial allowance of up to 100%. If the full IA is *not* claimed, 25% straight line WDA is claimed in subsequent periods.

Before considering the third area of allowances, the balancing adjustment which arises on a disposal, here is a basic IBA question for you to practise the learning points so far.

Practice question 1 *(The answer is in the final chapter of this book)*

Plummer

Required

(a) Briefly explain whether industrial buildings allowance is due on the following buildings.

(i) A warehouse purchased by a clothes manufacturer to store cloth which is to be made into suits.

(ii) The works canteen of a shoe manufacturer.

(iii) An office block used to accommodate the sales office of a heavy engineering manufacturing company.

(iv) A repair workshop used by a lawn mower manufacturer to repair and service lawn mowers.

(b) Bertha Plummer is financial director of Plummer Toys plc, a company which manufactures toys and dolls. Plummer Toys plc makes up accounts to 31 December annually.

The company constructed a factory between January and March 1995 and brought it into use on 1 July 1995. An extension was constructed in November 1998 and brought into use on 1 December 1998. Both the factory and the extension were used for industrial purposes throughout. The costs for each were as follows.

	Factory £	*Extension* £
Land	25,000	–
Construction	175,000	39,000
	200,000	39,000

Required

Prepare for Mrs Plummer a statement showing the maximum allowances available to Plummer Toys plc for all years up to and including the year ended 31 December 2003.

3 The disposal of an industrial building

3.1 Balancing adjustments

When a building is sold, this triggers a *balancing adjustment*. Where insufficient allowances have been claimed, a balancing allowance will be given. Otherwise, a balancing charge will occur. Remember that the total allowances given must equal the net cost of the building.

The easiest way to identify the balancing allowance or charge is to compare the 'net cost' of the building with the allowances claimed, as follows.

		£
Eligible cost		X
Less	Sale proceeds	(X)
Net cost		X

'Sale proceeds' in this calculation cannot exceed the eligible cost.

The net cost is therefore the real capital cost (ignoring inflation) incurred by the business.

◆ Where the net cost is greater than the total allowances claimed, a balancing allowance for the difference arises.

◆ Where the net cost is less than the total allowances claimed, the difference is clawed back as a balancing charge.

◆ The net cost will be nil if the building is sold for more than its original eligible cost. A balancing charge will therefore arise, to claw back all of the allowances given.

No balancing adjustments are required if a building is sold after its tax life has expired. This is an important planning point where a sale is proposed near the end of a building's tax life.

Just as the cost of the building has to exclude the land element and the cost of offices etc if not 'de minimis' (ie under 25%), sale proceeds are also restricted to the qualifying portion. If the exam question just gives 'sale proceeds' you should assume the land etc elements are excluded.

3.2 Example

Gray Ltd makes up accounts to 31 March. On 1 August 2001 it began to use a newly constructed factory which cost £60,000, including £4,000 for the land and £2,500 for offices. On 1 February 2004 the factory was sold to Heath Ltd for £64,200, including £12,000 for the land.

Required

Calculate the allowances for Gray Ltd. Also consider the effect if the sale proceeds were alternatively £53,000 and £71,340 (in each case including £12,000 for the land).

3.3 Solution

	£	£
Cost excluding land (offices allowed, because not over 25%)		56,000
Year ended 31 March 2002 WDA 4%	2,240	
Year ended 31 March 2003 WDA 4%	2,240	
		(4,480)
Residue before sale (RBS)		51,520

There is no WDA in the period of sale (the year to 31 March 2004).

Year ended 31 March 2004

Net cost (cost – proceeds)	(a)	(b)	(c)
(a) (£56,000 – £52,200)	3,800		
(b) (£56,000 – £41,000)		15,000	
(c) (£56,000 – £56,000)			Nil
Allowances given	(4,480)	(4,480)	(4,480)
Balancing charge	(680)		(4,480)
Balancing allowance		10,520	

Practice question 2 *(The answer is in the final chapter of this book)*

Leaden

Leaden Ltd is a manufacturer of plumbing components making up accounts to 31 March annually. In December 2003 the company sold one of its workshops, the details of which are as follows.

Cost	£115,000
Sale proceeds	£190,000
Industrial buildings allowances received to date	£55,200

The above figures exclude the value of the land.

Required

(a)   Calculate the balancing adjustment that arises as a result of the sale.

(b)   Recalculate the balancing adjustment on the assumption that the sale proceeds were alternatively:

(i)   £100,000

(ii)   £50,000.

4   Allowances for secondhand purchasers

4.1   Revised WDAs

So far we have looked at the allowances available to the purchaser of a new industrial building. For the purchaser of a used industrial building, however, the normal 4% writing down allowance is not available.

Instead, the purchaser of a used industrial building receives a special writing down allowance which spreads relief for the unrelieved original expenditure evenly over the remaining tax life of the building. The WDA is therefore calculated as follows.

$$\frac{\text{Residue after sale (or purchase price if lower)}}{\text{Tax life remaining}}$$

The residue after sale (RAS) is computed as follows:

	£
Residue before sale (ie tax written down value)	X
Plus Any balancing charge or	X/(X)
Less Any balancing allowance	
Residue after sale	X

The tax life remaining must be computed to the nearest month.

4.2   Example

Using the details in the earlier example (Gray Ltd) calculate the allowances for Heath Ltd, the secondhand purchaser, under the three sale proceeds options.

4.3   Solution

	(a) £	(b) £	(c) £
Residue before sale	51,520	51,520	51,520
Balancing charge	680		4,480
Balancing allowance		(10,520)	
Residue after sale	52,200	41,000	56,000

All that is happening here is that the Inland Revenue is sharing the eligible cost between the buyer and the seller. Any amount 'clawed' back as a balancing charge from Gray Ltd (the seller) is instead given to Heath Ltd (the buyer). Any allowance already given to the seller (ie £10,520 in option (b)) is not available for the buyer.

Heath Ltd then spreads this residue over the remaining tax life.

Tax life from 1 August 2001 to 1 February 2004 = 2 years 6 months
Therefore remaining life = 25 years – 2 years 6 months = 22 years 6 months

Heath Ltd's allowance per annum is therefore as follows.

	(a) £	(b) £	(c) £
	$\dfrac{52,200}{22.5}$	$\dfrac{41,000}{22.5}$	$\dfrac{56,000}{22.5}$
	2,320	1,822	2,489

Practice question 3 *(The answer is in the final chapter of this book)*

Brown

During the year ended 31 December 2002, Brown Ltd incurred the following capital expenditure on the construction of an industrial building.

		£
12 April 2002	Land	50,000
15 May 2002	Ground levelling	3,125
		53,125

The architect's certificates included the following.

		£
25 June 2002	Construction of building	351,750
5 October 2002	Car park for employees	12,000
20 December 2002	Ventilation equipment	39,400
20 December 2002	Central heating system	41,500
30 December 2002	Road construction	16,250
		460,900

		£
12 October 2002	Quantity surveyor's fees	5,250
21 October 2002	Architect's fees	11,875
		17,125

The surveyor's and architect's fees relate wholly to the construction of the building. The building was brought into use on 25 January 2003.

On 24 February 2004, owing to subsidence, the building was sold to Smith Ltd, a company also with a 31 December year end, for £250,000. The purchase price included £40,000 for the land and £30,000 for fittings.

Required

Compute the industrial buildings allowances due to Brown Ltd and Smith Ltd for the years ended 31 December 2002 to 2004 inclusive. Discuss briefly the tax allowances available to Brown Ltd in respect of the expenditure on the ventilation equipment and central heating system.

Approach to the question

The first step is to identify the qualifying *eligible* expenditure.

In claiming WDA consider when the building goes into *industrial use*.

Go through the *disposal procedure* outlined earlier to ascertain the balancing adjustment. Remember there is no WDA in the year of disposal.

Remember that the secondhand purchaser does not get 4% straight line WDA. Instead, you need to work out the WDA using the residue after sale divided by the remaining tax life.

5 Non-industrial activity

5.1 Impact on the writing down allowance

There may be periods during the ownership of an industrial building when it is used for non-industrial activity. This has an impact on both the writing down allowance and any balancing adjustment on disposal.

Where an industrial building is in non-industrial use at the *end* of an accounting period the impact is as follows.

♦ No WDA is claimed.
♦ A notional WDA reduces the tax balance (ie WDV) to be carried forward.

The reason for this is that the tax life of the building continues to diminish even though the claimant is not entitled to the allowances.

5.2 Disposal of the building

The procedure for identifying the balancing adjustment is essentially the same as before, but with an additional step to take account of the non-industrial activity.

Step 1 (identify the net cost)

	£
Eligible cost	X
Sale proceeds (restricted to eligible cost)	(X)
Net cost	X

Step 2 (this is the new step)

Calculate the adjusted net cost. The adjusted net cost represents the cost of using the building for industrial purposes only and is calculated by simple time apportionment.

$$\text{Adjusted net cost} = \text{Net cost} \times \frac{\text{Period of industrial use}}{\text{Total period of ownership}}$$

This calculation is done to the nearest month.

Step 3 (calculate the balancing adjustment)

If the adjusted net cost is greater than the allowances already given, a *balancing allowance* arises.

If the adjusted net cost is less than the allowances already given, a *balancing charge* arises.

5.3 Example

AST Ltd sold a factory in the year ended 31 December 2003.

Details of the building are as follows.

Allowable cost	£195,000
Total period of ownership	9 years
Period of non-industrial use	2 years
Sale proceeds	£150,000
IBAs given	£54,600

Required

Calculate the balancing adjustment on disposal.

5.4 Solution

	£
Allowable cost	195,000
Sale proceeds	(150,000)
	────────
Net cost	45,000
	────────
Adjusted net cost £45,000 × $\dfrac{\text{(Period of industrial use)} \quad 7 \text{ years}}{\text{Total period of ownership} \quad 9 \text{ years}}$	35,000
IBAs actually given	(54,600)
	────────
Balancing charge (12 months ended 31 December 2003)	(19,600)
	────────

5.5 Example

TSA Ltd prepares accounts annually to 31 December.

A factory costing £375,000 was bought on 30 November 2001 and put into industrial use on 31 December 2001.

Between 1 March 2002 and 31 January 2003 it was used for non-industrial purposes.

The factory is to be sold on 31 March 2004 for alternatively:

(a) £400,000 or
(b) £267,000

Required

Compute the industrial buildings allowances for both first and second users.

5.6   *Solution*

(a)   **IBAs to first user**

	Cost £	Claimed £	Notional £
Year ended 31 December 2001	375,000		
WDA (£375,000 × 4%)	(15,000)	15,000	
Year ended 31 December 2002 notional WDA (in non-industrial use on 31 December 2002)	(15,000)		15,000
Year ended 31 December 2003			
WDA at 4%	(15,000)	15,000	
IBAs given		30,000	15,000
Tax WDV at 31 December 2003	330,000		

Year ended 31 December 2004	£
Disposal of building (No WDA in year of disposal)	
Qualifying cost	375,000
Sale proceeds (£400,000 but limited to cost)	(375,000)
Net cost (see note below)	Nil
IBAs claimed	(30,000)
Balancing charge	(30,000)

Note   Where the net cost is nil, the adjusted net cost is also nil.

IBAs to subsequent user

$$\frac{\text{WDV before sale + balancing charge}}{\text{Tax life remaining}}$$

£330,000 + £30,000 = £360,000

ie $\dfrac{360,000}{25 - 2 \text{ years } 3 \text{ months} = 22 \text{ years } 9 \text{ months}}$ = £15,824 per annum for 22 years

and £11,872 in year 23.

(b)   **IBAs to first user**

For WDA see (a) above.

£

Year ended 31 December 2004
Disposal of building
Qualifying cost   375,000
Sale proceeds   (267,000)
                                                                                    ─────────
Net cost   108,000
                                                                                    ─────────

Adjusted net cost £108,000 $\times \dfrac{16 \text{ months}}{27 \text{ months}}$ 64,000

WDAs given   (30,000)
                                                                                    ─────────
Balancing allowance   34,000
                                                                                    ─────────

IBAs to subsequent user

$$\dfrac{\text{WDV before sale - balancing allowance}}{\text{Tax life remaining}}$$

WDV before sale – BA   = £330,000 – £34,000 = £296,000

Since this exceeds the actual price paid of £267,000, the sale price is substituted ie:

$$\dfrac{267,000}{22 \text{ years } 9 \text{ months}} = £11,736 \text{ per annum for 22 years (£8,808 in year 23)}$$

Practice question 4 *(The answer is in the final chapter of this book)*

Mellor

Mellor Ltd has carried on a cutlery making business since 1 May 1998 making up accounts to 30 April each year.

On 1 September 1998, the company purchased a factory for £335,000 (including £35,000 for the land) and brought it into use immediately.

On 1 September 1999, Mellor Ltd ceased manufacturing cutlery and let out the factory as artists' studios. On 1 May 2001, Mellor Ltd restarted manufacturing in the building and on 1 June 2002 sold it for £395,000 (including £35,000 for the land) to Major Ltd, whose accounting date is 31 August.

Required

(a)   Calculate the IBAs available to Mellor Ltd for all years.

(b)   Calculate the IBAs available to Major Ltd for all years.

(c)   Calculate Mellor Ltd's balancing allowance if the factory had instead been sold for £215,000 (including £35,000 for the land).

(d)   Calculate the figure on which Major Ltd will obtain allowances if the factory is sold for £215,000 (as in (c) above).

Approach to the question

♦ Identify the *eligible* expenditure for IBA purposes.

♦ In claiming the WDA you must check that the building is in *industrial use* at the *end* of the period.

♦ Go through the disposal procedure for Mellor Ltd. Remember there is no net cost if Mellor Ltd sells the building for more than its original cost. In that situation, there will always be a balancing charge. Under the alternative scenario in part (c) you will need to use the extra step to find the adjusted net cost.

♦ When working out the writing down allowance for Major Ltd in part (d) watch the rule about the *lower* of residue after sale and purchase price paid.

6 Flat conversion allowances

6.1 Introduction

100% initial allowances are available on capital expenditure incurred on or after 11 May 2001 in converting premises above shops and other commercial buildings into flats.

6.2 Conditions

When the building was first built, the premises converted must have been intended for use as a dwelling. For the year before the conversion they must have been unused or only used for storage.

The building must have been built before 1 January 1980, and must have had no more than four storeys above ground level.

The flat must have a separate access not through the shop or commercial building. It must be used for short term letting (ie not more than 5 year terms), not be a high value flat, nor have more than four main rooms. A high value flat is one that can be let out for a rent in excess of a prescribed limit (you should assume the limit is not exceeded in an exam question).

6.3 Allowances

100% initial allowances are given on the capital costs of the conversion or renovation against Schedule A income. If less than the full IAs are claimed, a 25% WDA is given on a straight line basis until the cost is fully relieved.

If the flat is sold within seven years a balancing charge or balancing allowance is made on sale, based on the difference between the sale proceeds and the qualifying expenditure. A balancing charge cannot exceed the amount of allowances the landlord has actually received.

7 Approach to a typical CT question

You have now covered most of the basic areas of corporation tax and should be able to see how they fit together in examination style questions.

You are now going to tackle a question with all the basic ingredients to enable you to produce the full CT computation. A methodical approach is essential, so follow the procedure below.

♦ Always present the answer first, supported by workings.

♦ Start by identifying which headings are needed for the proforma and key workings. Then use your workings to construct the computation.

♦ Simple workings can be done on the face of the computation (eg DIII, gains).

Stage 1 Finding PCTCT

The starting point is to set up a Schedule D Case I working. This will reveal that you need to prepare the capital allowance computation as this feeds into the Schedule D Case I profit. The question contains plant and machinery allowances only (ie no industrial buildings allowances).

Here is a procedure for tackling capital allowances, which will form working 2.

♦ Identify the tax written down values (WDV) brought forward at the beginning of the CAP.

	Pool	Expensive car
Tax WDV	X	X

♦ Allocate any additions or disposals in the period to existing or new categories.

♦ Calculate the allowances due.

Watch out for the following points.

♦ You will need to distinguish between those additions which qualify for the first year allowance (FYA) and those which only qualify for writing down allowance (WDA). A 40%FYA is available for assets (excluding cars) purchased after 1 July 1998.

♦ WDA on each expensive car is restricted to £3,000 per annum *maximum*.

Complete working (1) for Schedule D Case I.

Always assume that interest payable is for a trading purpose (unless there is information to the contrary) and therefore is correctly deducted as a trading expense.

Similarly, patent royalties payable are likely to be a trading expense (unless you are told otherwise) and are allowable on an accruals basis so should require no adjustment. Royalties received are trading income unless you are told the rights are held as an investment (therefore DVI).

Next tackle the investment income in the CT computation. Ask yourself four key questions.

♦ Is the income received net or gross?
♦ If *net* what is the correct grossing up rate?
♦ Is it assessed on an accruals or receipts basis?
♦ How should the income be described (DIII) etc?

'Profits' for a company also include gains, so follow the summary procedure for gains outlined earlier.

Capital losses (whether brought forward or current) cannot be used against any other profits.

Finally, to compute PCTCT you need to deduct charges on income. Since 1 April 2002 the only charges you are likely to encounter are Gift Aid payments.

Stage 2 Computation of liability

♦ Find 'P' where any dividends were received. Otherwise PCTCT and P are the same.

♦ Consider the financial years which affect the CAP, to identify the correct tax rates. 'P' then determines which of these rates should be used.

♦ Calculate the tax on PCTCT.

The calculations can be done on the face of the computation but if they are likely to be significant, they are best done in a working.

Stage 3 The ACT set off

You only need to consider ACT if there is an unrelieved surplus brought forward at the start of the accounting period.

Stage 4 The IT set-off

Ascertain whether there is an IT set-off using the procedure described earlier. Again this is best done as a working.

Practice question 5 *(The answer is in the final chapter of this book)*

Straw

Straw Ltd has the following results for the year ended 31 January 2004.

	£
Adjusted trading profit before capital allowances	298,400
Building society interest accrued and received	1,200
Interest accrued and received from £400,000 $8\frac{1}{2}$ % Local Authority Stock	34,000
Chargeable gain	49,400
Gift Aid payment to charity	2,000

The adjusted trading profit is after deducting gross debenture interest, accrued and paid on 1 July 2003, of £10,000. All the debenture holders are individuals. Capital losses brought forward at 1 February 2003 were £2,000.

The Local Authority stock interest is received gross half yearly on 30 June and 31 December.

The company's plant and machinery pool had a tax written down value of £12,000 at 1 February 2003. On 1 August 2003 the company bought a new motor car for the managing director costing £22,000. Prior to this, all motor cars used by the company had been leased. The managing director uses the car 75% for business purposes. The company also acquired a van for £7,500 on the same date.

Required

Compute the MCT payable for Straw Ltd for the year ended 31 January 2004.

Practice question 6 *(The answer is in the final chapter of this book)*

Unimaginable

Unimaginable Utilities Ltd is a United Kingdom resident trading company which manufactures motor vehicle components. It has been trading since 1986 and has no associated companies.

The company's results for the year ended 31 May 2003 are summarised as follows.

	£
Trading profits (as adjusted for taxation but before capital allowances)	311,000
Dividend from UK company	8,437
Local Authority stock interest received (gross)	4,760
Bank interest received	1,250

Included in the adjusted trading profit is a deduction for debenture interest of £4,000 (gross amount). The debentures were for trading purposes and were held by individuals.

In the year ended 31 May 2003 the amounts of interest paid and received are the same as the amounts shown in the accounts on an accruals basis.

Capital acquisitions and disposals during the year were as follows.

Acquisitions	£
'Expensive' motor car	16,000
Two other cars (£7,500 each and to be used by the company's salesmen)	15,000
Plant	48,000

Disposals	
Plant (sold for less than cost)	24,000
'Expensive' motor car (the one owned at 1 June 2002 – see below)	8,000
Two cars (both costing less than £8,000)	4,000

Written down tax values at 1 June 2002 were as follows.

	£
Main pool	32,500
'Expensive' motor car	11,000

The company has operated from two factories, neither of which is in an Enterprise Zone. Factory 1 was acquired in 1991 when new, and cost £250,000 including land £50,000 and integral administration offices £40,000. Factory 2 was purchased second-hand on 1 June 1997 for £120,000, when the residue of expenditure after sale was £100,000 and the building was five years old.

Factory 2 was sold on 1 July 2002 for £170,000 and not replaced. There has not been any non-qualifying use of either factory. The capital gain on the sale of the factory was £29,000.

Notes

(1)   The dates in brackets are those upon which the transactions occurred.
(2)   Income tax has been deducted from the debenture interest paid.
(3)   The company has no losses to bring forward on 1 June 2002.

Required

You are required to calculate the mainstream corporation tax payable for the year ended 31 May 2003.

8   Summary

This concludes the material on capital allowances, a core area for the examination as it can feature in both compulsory and optional questions.

The key points concerning IBA are as follows.

♦   Land never qualifies for IBA.

♦   The non-industrial parts of an industrial building will qualify for IBA if they amount to less than 25% of the total cost.

♦   The initial purchaser of an industrial building receives a 4% WDA, calculated using the straight line method, if the building is in industrial use at the end of the accounting period.

♦   The purchaser of a secondhand industrial building receives a WDA based on the residue after sale (or the purchase price paid, if lower) divided by the remaining tax life.

Multiple choice questions 1 - 5 *(The answers are in the final chapter of this book)*

Each of the questions below has only one correct answer.

1   Cecil Security Ltd, a manufacturer of burglar alarms, incurred the following expenditure on the construction of a new building in its accounting year ended 31 March 2004.

	£	£
Freehold land (including £1,800 legal fees)		30,000
Planning permission		3,000
Site clearance		2,500
Groundwork (including £1,200 for new road)		4,000
Construction of building		
Reception and administration offices	24,000	
Raw materials store	5,500	
Design office	4,000	
Manufacturing workshop	53,000	
Installation of services	4,000	
Finished goods warehouse	5,500	
	———	
		96,000
		———
		135,500
		———

The qualifying expenditure for industrial buildings allowances is

A   £78,000

B   £79,800

C   £81,000

D   £105,500

2   Which of the following structures does not qualify for industrial buildings allowance?

A   Access road to factory

B   Gymnasium on factory site used by employees

C   Drawing office in factory

D   Estate agent's office

3   Bill Ltd sells a building to Ben plc for £75,600 on 31 March 2003. Bill Ltd purchased the
        building new on 31 March 1998 for £84,000 and moved into it on 1 April 1999. There
        was no non-industrial use. Bill Ltd prepares its accounts to 31 March each year and
        Ben plc prepares its accounts to 30 September each year.

        To how much industrial buildings allowances is Ben plc entitled for the year ended
        30 September 2003?

        A   £3,600

        B   £3,780

        C   £4,000

        D   £4,200

4   Fraser Furniture Ltd, which prepares accounts to 31 December each year, had an
        industrial building erected in 1986 which the company brought into use before the end
        of that year. The building cost £90,000; an initial allowance of 25% was claimed.

        The building was sold on 31 August 2003 for £180,000 including £50,000 for the land.
        Fraser Furniture Ltd used the building for industrial purposes throughout, apart from
        the period 1 September 1990 to 30 June 1992 when it was used as offices.

        What is the balancing charge on sale?

        A   £50,400

        B   £72,900

        C   £76,500

        D   £80,100

5   During the year ended 31 May 2003 Foster plc, which manufactures wheels, purchased
        a plot of land for £50,000 and had a factory built. The cost of this development was as
        follows.

	£
Levelling the land	3,000
Building (including drawing office £8,000 and general offices £21,000)	100,000
	103,000

        The expenditure on which industrial buildings allowances can be claimed is

        A   £74,000

        B   £79,000

        C   £100,000

        D   £103,000

CHAPTER 6

Capital gains: principles and computation

EXAM FOCUS

Under the old exam structure there was always a compulsory question on capital gains. This was typically worth between 17 and 20 marks. The new exam structure allows candidates to avoid a *full* question on capital gains. However, this does not mean that you can ignore this area of the syllabus. There will always be some elements of capital gains on the paper and they may represent a major part of a question.

This is the first of three chapters devoted to capital gains. It concentrates on the procedure for identifying gains or losses, key basic computations and key variations.

LEARNING OUTCOMES

This chapter covers the following learning outcome of the CIMA syllabus:

> Identify chargeable assets for taxation as capital gains.

In order to cover this learning outcome the following topics are included:

> The charge to tax
> The three basic computations
> Calculating the tax payable
> Key variations affecting the basic computations.

1   The charge to tax

 A charge to taxation of capital gains tax arises on *the disposal* of a *chargeable asset* by a *chargeable person*.

A *disposal* includes any of the following.

- Sale of an asset
- Sale of part of an asset
- Gift of whole or part of an asset
- Loss or destruction of an asset
- Compensation in connection with an asset

A *chargeable person* may be an individual, a company, or partners in a partnership business. For examination purposes, however, you will only be concerned with disposals by companies.

The term *chargeable asset* includes all assets except exempt assets (most such assets relevant to companies are listed below).

 Exempt assets relevant to companies in the list below need to be learned so that you can identify them in a question.

- Wasting chattels
- Other chattels, where the consideration and cost is £6,000 or less
- Motor cars

- Sterling currency, ie legal tender in the UK, notably gold sovereigns minted after 1837
- Any form of loan stock. Gain and losses on any form of lending are dealt with under the loan relationship rules (ie under Schedule D Case III).

2 The three basic computations

2.1 Introduction

There are three basic methods for computing a capital gain or allowable loss. The type of computation primarily depends upon the date the asset was acquired.

- Assets acquired after 31 March 1982.
- Assets acquired before 31 March 1982, with a rebasing election.
- Assets acquired before 31 March 1982, with no rebasing election.

Each of these will be considered in sequence.

2.2 Assets acquired after 31 March 1982

The following proforma is used.

		Notes	£	£
Disposal value		1		X
Less	Incidental costs of sale	2		(X)
Net sale proceeds				NSP
Less	Allowable expenditure			
	Acquisition cost	3	X	
	Incidental costs of acquisition	2	X	
	Enhancement expenditure (Section 4 of this chapter)	3	X	
				(Cost)
Unindexed gain		4		X
Less	Indexation allowance: Cost × 0.XXX			(IA)
Chargeable gain				Gain

Notes to the proforma

(1) Disposal value is usually the sale proceeds. However, where a transaction is not at arm's length (eg a gift), or is between connected persons, then *market value* will be substituted. A company is connected with

- the person who controls it
- another company under common control.

(*Note* See Chapter 10 for the treatment of disposals between members of a capital gains group).

(2) The incidental costs incurred on the disposal of an asset are an allowable deduction. Examples of such costs include valuation fees, advertising costs, legal fees, auctioneer's fees. Similarly any incidental costs on acquisition are deductible.

(3) The purchase price of an asset acquired since 31 March 1982 is the main allowable deduction. In addition, any further capital expenditure (known as enhancement expenditure) is deductible.

(4) The gain after deducting the costs above is known as an unindexed gain, because an indexation allowance may then be available to reduce that gain. This allowance is based upon the retail prices index (RPI) and is intended to give relief for inflation. It was introduced for periods from 31 March 1982.

2.3 The indexation allowance

The indexation allowance runs from the date of the acquisition expenditure to the date of disposal. It is computed by multiplying the acquisition cost by an indexation factor. The indexation factor will be provided in the examination.

2.4 Example

ELI Ltd sells a chargeable asset on 31 March 2004 for £24,600 after deducting auctioneer's fees of £400. The asset was acquired on 1 May 1989 for £10,000. What is the chargeable gain?

Assume that the indexation factor from May 1989 to March 2004 is 0.605.

2.5 Solution

	£
Sales proceeds (March 2004)	25,000
Less Incidental costs	(400)
Net sale proceeds	24,600
Allowable cost (May 1989)	(10,000)
Unindexed gain	14,600
Indexation allowance = 0.605 × £10,000*	(6,050)
Indexed gain	8,550

*Ensure you index the allowable expenditure and *not* the unindexed gain.

Indexation allowance cannot be used to turn a gain into a loss, nor is it available where there is an unindexed loss.

2.6 Example

JNN Ltd is considering selling a painting at auction in August 2003. It acquired the painting in August 1984 for £10,000 and the sale proceeds are likely to be one of three results.

(a) £25,000
(b) £12,000
(c) £8,000

What is the capital gain or loss under each of these alternatives?

The indexation factor from August 1984 to August 2003 is 1.015.

2.7 Solution

	(a)	*(b)*	*(c)*
Sale proceeds	25,000	12,000	8,000
Cost	(10,000)	(10,000)	(10,000)
Unindexed gain or (loss)	15,000	2,000	(2,000)
Indexation allowance 1.015 × £10,000 = £10,150	(10,150)	(2,000)*	Nil**
Indexed gain or allowable loss	4,850	Nil	(2,000)

*Restricted, because indexation cannot create a loss.

**No indexation because indexation cannot increase a loss.

Practice question 1 *(The answer is in the final chapter of this book)*

JHN

JHN Ltd made the following disposals in the year ended 31 March 2004.

(1)   On 9 June 2003 it sold some plant for £15,000. The plant was bought in October 1988 for £8,000.

(2)   On 5 September 2003 it sold a painting which had been purchased for £7,500 in November 1989. Sale proceeds were £6,500.

(3)   On 1 March 2004 it sold a car, a Trabant, which was bought in February 1983 for £3,000. By the time of the sale, it had become a collector's item and JHN Ltd managed to obtain proceeds of £9,000, out of which it paid £450 in auctioneer's fees.

(4)   On 3 March 2004 it sold a collection of military memorabilia for £19,000. It had cost £7,000 in March 1983.

(5)   Also on 3 March 2004, it sold some land which was purchased in April 1982 for £15,000. It was sold for £25,000.

Required

Calculate the capital gains chargeable on each of the above transactions in the year ended 31 March 2003. You should use the following indexation factors.

April 1982 – March 2004	1.278
February 1983 – March 2004	1.225
March 1983 – March 2004	1.221
October 1988 – June 2003	0.648
November 1989 – September 2003	0.531

Approach to the question

It is important that the gain or loss on each transaction is *separately* computed. Finally, prepare a summary adding gains and losses together to arrive at one overall figure.

2.8   Assets acquired before 31 March 1982

The Finance Act 1988 exempted all gains prior to 31 March 1982. This is known as *rebasing*. If an asset was owned on 31 March 1982, the computation of the gain or loss needs to be varied to take this into account. The precise method differs depending on whether or not the company has made a rebasing election.

♦   With a rebasing election, use the 31 March 1982 market value only.

♦   With no rebasing election, compare the gain or loss using both cost and 31 March 1982 value.

2.9   Rebasing election

If a company wishes to make a rebasing election, it must do so within two years of the end of the accounting period in which the first disposal after 5 April 1988 of an asset held on 31 March 1982 is made.

Use the following proforma for an asset acquired before and held at 31 March 1982 if there is a rebasing election in force.

Proforma

		£
Sale proceeds		X
Less	Market value (MV) at 31 March 1982	(X)
Less	Indexation allowance 0.XXX × MV at 31 March 1982	(X)
Indexed gain		X

The 31 March 1982 value replaces cost in the computation as the main allowable deduction and for indexation purposes.

Indexation runs from March 1982 (it can never run prior to this) until the date of disposal.

In exam questions check whether a rebasing election has been made or you could be wasting time doing calculations based on cost.

2.10   Example

NHJ Ltd sells a painting on 15 February 2004 for £30,000. It had acquired the painting on 1 May 1980 for £11,000. It was valued at £8,000 on 31 March 1982, and there is a rebasing election in force.

You are required to calculate NHJ Ltd's chargeable gain.

The indexation factor from March 1982 to February 2004 is 1.319.

2.11   Solution

	£
Sale proceeds	30,000
Less March 1982 value (see note)	(8,000)
Unindexed gain	22,000
Indexation allowance 1.319 × £8,000	(10,552)
	11,448

Note   This replaces costs incurred before 31 March 1982 when an election is in force.

This may seem unfair because had NHJ Ltd used the cost of £11,000 it would have resulted in a much lower gain. However, where there is a rebasing election, it is irrevocable and applies to *all* assets acquired before 31 March 1982.

So whilst it is disadvantageous in this case, NHJ Ltd presumably made the election on the basis of its overall position on assets held at 31 March 1982.

2.12   No rebasing election

Where there is no rebasing election, the capital gain or loss has to be computed using both cost and 31 March 1982 value as alternative deductions. A decision is then made as to which result should apply.

Proforma

	Cost	31 March 1982
Sale proceeds	X	X
Cost or MV at 31 March 1982	(Cost)	(MV 1982)
Unindexed gain or loss	X	Y
Less Indexation allowance (not with an unindexed loss)	(IA)	(IA)
	A	B

Result

♦ If A and B are both gains, take the smaller gain.
♦ If A and B are both losses, take the smaller loss.
♦ If one is a loss and the other a gain, the gain or loss is taken as nil.

The indexation allowance is calculated on the *higher* of cost and 31 March 1982 value so it is the same in both columns (unless of course it is restricted because it would create a loss).

2.13 Example

Use the details from the example of NHJ Ltd above, but on the assumption that there is *no* rebasing election in force.

2.14 Solution

	Cost £	1982 value £
Sale proceeds	30,000	30,000
Cost	(11,000)	
1982 value		(8,000)
Unindexed gain	19,000	22,000
Indexation allowance 1.319 × £11,000 (higher of cost and 1982 value)	(14,509)	(14,509)
	4,491	7,491
Decision: two gains, so take the smaller gain	£4,491	

Practice question 2 *(The answer is in the final chapter of this book)*

JMY

JMY Ltd sold a holiday cottage for £33,000 on 2 July 2003. The cottage was acquired in June 1974 for £12,000 for occasional use by senior staff. Its value at 31 March 1982 was £10,000.

Required

Calculate the chargeable gain or loss on the assumption that:

(i)   there is a rebasing election in force for assets acquired before 31 March 1982

(ii)   there is no such election in force.

The indexation factor from March 1982 to July 2003 is 1.277.

3   Calculating the tax payable

3.1 Introduction

Gains are calculated for chargeable accounting periods. Once you have calculated all the individual gains and losses for an accounting period, summarise them as follows.

	£
Gain (1)	X
Gain (2)	X
Loss (3)	(X)
Net gains/(losses) for the current year	X
Capital losses brought forward	(X)
Chargeable gains	X

The chargeable gains are then put into the CT computation and the tax liability is calculated in the normal way. If there is an overall loss, it is carried forward and set against future gains. It cannot be relieved against other income.

3.2 Example

Z Ltd has the following results for its year ended 31 March 2004.

Capital losses brought forward	£10,000
Gains	£50,000
Schedule DI profits	£270,000

Required

Calculate the corporation tax payable by Z Ltd on its chargeable gains for the year ended 31 March 2004.

3.3 Solution

The style of this example has featured in several past examination questions. To work out the tax on the chargeable gains, it is necessary to work out the corporation tax liability for Z Ltd both with and without the chargeable gains.

The corporation tax payable by Z Ltd on its total profits for the year ended 31 March 2004 is as follows.

	£
Schedule DI	270,000
Chargeable gains (£50,000 - £10,000)	40,000
PCTCT	310,000

The company's PCTCT falls between the upper and lower limits, therefore small companies' relief applies.

	£
PCTCT £310,000 × 30%	93,000
(£1,500,000 - £310,000) × 11/400 =	(32,725)
	60,275

If the chargeable gains are excluded from the PCTCT, the company is only liable at the small companies' rate. The corporation tax payable by Z Ltd on its profits is then as follows.

PCTCT (£310,000 - £40,000) × 19% = £51,300

The corporation tax payable by Z Ltd on its chargeable gains is therefore £8,975 (£60,275 - £51,300).

The amount of corporation tax payable on the chargeable gains could alternatively be calculated by identifying the relevant rate of corporation tax. In Z Ltd's case, part of the gains are effectively taxed at the small companies' rate, with the balance falling into the marginal rate band.

Lower limit less PCTCT (excluding gains)	
£300,000 - £270,000 = 30,000 × 19% =	£5,700
Gains in excess of the lower limit	
£40,000 - £30,000 = £10,000 × 32.75% =	£3,275
Tax due on chargeable gains	£8,975

4 Key variations affecting the basic computations

4.1 Introduction

This section is concerned with some key variations on the three basic computations. The section deals with:

♦ enhancement expenditure
♦ part disposals
♦ chattels
♦ leases.

4.2 Enhancement expenditure

The main allowable deduction in computing an unindexed gain is the acquisition cost (including incidental costs) or 31 March 1982 value. Any additional capital expenditure on the asset is also an allowable deduction. This normally takes the form of improvement (ie enhancement) expenditure, but can also include expenditure incurred to establish, preserve or defend title to the asset.

As the additional expenditure is incurred later than the original expenditure, there will be an impact on the calculation of indexation allowance. Indexation can only be calculated from the actual date of expenditure; therefore where there is cost plus enhancement expenditure *two* indexation calculations will be required. It is easy to overlook this extra step.

4.3 Example

RMY Ltd bought a shop in November 1986 for £13,200. The company spent £3,800 on improvements in May 1989. The shop was sold for £35,000 in October 2003.

The indexed rise from November 1986 to October 2003 is 0.830 and from May 1989 to October 2003 is 0.580.

You are required to calculate the gain on the sale of the shop.

4.4 Solution

	£
Sale proceeds	35,000
Cost (November 1986)	(13,200)
Enhancement (May 1989)	(3,800)
Unindexed gain	18,000
Indexation allowance	
(a) £13,200 × 0.830	(10,956)
(b) £3,800 × 0.580	(2,204)
Indexed gain	4,840

4.5 Assets acquired before 31 March 1982

You need to be careful when calculating indexation where the enhancement expenditure relates to an asset acquired before March 1982. The precise impact of the enhancement expenditure depends upon whether it is incurred before or after 31 March 1982. All costs (original and enhancement) incurred before 31 March 1982 will have to be compared with 31 March 1982 value (which replaces *all* costs up to that point) for indexation purposes.

4.6 Example

ALX Ltd bought a freehold office building for £200,000 in January 1970. In July 1976 the company installed air conditioning at a cost of £75,000 and in July 1995 an extension which cost £50,000. The building was sold in September 2003 for £800,000; the 31 March 1982 value was £340,000. There is no rebasing election in force.

The indexed rise from March 1982 to September 2003 is 1.283 and from July 1995 to September 2003 is 0.217.

What is the chargeable gain?

4.7 Solution

Set up a two column proforma, as cost and 31 March 1982 value will have to be compared.

	Notes	Cost £	1982 value £
Sale proceeds		800,000	800,000
Cost (original)		(200,000)	
Enhancement (1976)		(75,000)	
31 March 1982 value	1		(340,000)
Enhancement (July 1995)	2	(50,000)	(50,000)
Unindexed gain		475,000	410,000

Indexation allowance

(a)   Higher of cost and 1982 value
         Cost £275,000 or 1982 value £340,000

therefore £340,000 × 1.283		(436,220)	(410,000)

(b)   Post 31 March 1982 enhancement

£50,000 × 0.217		(10,850)	-
		27,930	-

The result is no gain/no loss.

Notes

(1)   This replaces all costs up to 31 March 1982.
(2)   This expenditure occurred *after* 31 March 1982, and needs to be in both columns.

4.8   Part disposals

 The disposal of part of an asset is a chargeable disposal. However, only part of the cost or 1982 value is allocated to the part disposal. The proportion is computed as follows.

$$\text{Cost or 31 March 1982 value} \times \frac{A}{A + B}$$

A = Consideration received for the part disposal
B = Market value of the remainder

Incidental and other costs which relate wholly to the part sold are deductible *in full*.

4.9   Example

	£
JNS Ltd bought a chargeable asset in August 1985 for	18,000 (including expenses)
Part disposal January 1997 for consideration of	21,000
Expenses of disposal (January 1997)	1,200
Market value of remainder in January 1997 is	31,500
Remainder sold February 2004 for net sale proceeds of	38,000

The indexed rise on the part disposal is 0.617 and on the remainder 0.929.

You are required to calculate the gains arising in January 1997 and February 2004, assuming JNS Ltd makes up its accounts to 31 March annually.

4.10   Solution

January 1997

	£
Sale proceeds	21,000
Less Expenses	(1,200)
Net sale proceeds	19,800
Less Part cost £18,000 × $\dfrac{21,000}{21,000 + 31,500}$	(7,200)
Unindexed gain	12,600
Less Indexation allowance (0.617 × £7,200)	(4,442)
Assessed in year ended 31 March 1997	8,158

February 2004

	£
Net sale proceeds	38,000
Less Cost (£18,000 – £7,200)	(10,800)
	27,200
Less Indexation allowance (0.929 × £10,800)	(10,033)
Assessed in year ended 31 March 2004	17,167

Practice question 3 *(The answer is in the final chapter of this book)*

Time

Time Ltd sold two pieces of land in March 2003 for £25,000 each.

The first had been bought in January 1982 for £9,800 and had a value of £8,500 on 31 March 1982. The second was part of a larger piece of land which had been bought for £12,000 in February 1981. Its value on 31 March 1982 was £17,000. The value of the plot remaining was £16,000 in March 2003 and Time Ltd sold the remaining part in December 2003 for £28,000. Time Ltd had other profits in its accounting periods to:

	£
31 March 2003	200,000
31 March 2004	300,000

The company does not receive any dividend income.

The indexed rise from March 1982 to March 2003 is 1.265 and from March 1982 to December 2003 is 1.302.

Required

(a)   Calculate the gains or losses arising in each accounting period.

(b)   Calculate the CT liability on the gains (to do this you need to identify the effective rate of corporation tax on all profits).

No rebasing election has been made.

4.11   Chattels

A chattel is tangible *moveable* property (alive or dead).

There are two types of chattels: wasting chattels and other chattels.

Wasting chattels are those with an expected life of less than 50 years. Examples include:

- racehorse
- greyhound
- boat or caravan
- clocks
- plant and machinery.

The Revenue accept that machinery is 'an apparatus for applying mechanical power' and that, as plant and machinery is held by statute to have a predictable life of less than 50 years (regardless of any expectation to the contrary) antique clocks and guns will count as wasting chattels.

Other chattels have an expected life of more than 50 years. Examples include:

- antiques (unless incorporating machinery)
- jewellery
- paintings.

Wasting chattels are exempt, with the exception of plant and machinery eligible for capital allowances (ie where the owner conducts a trade and does or could claim capital allowances in respect of the asset). Therefore, unless a company holds plant as an investment instead of for its trade, the wasting chattel exemption cannot apply.

Other chattels with a value of less than £6,000 on disposal and which cost less than £6,000 to acquire are exempt. Plant and machinery eligible for capital allowances but worth less than £6,000 could therefore be exempt under this rule.

Other chattels to which the £6,000 rule does not apply are treated as follows.

- With chattels bought for up to £6,000, but sold for more than £6,000, do the normal calculation but then compare any gain (not applicable to a loss) to the following amount:

  $\frac{5}{3}$ (gross sale proceeds – £6,000) = £x. The lower of the gain and this amount is then chargeable. This is known as the $\frac{5}{3}$ rule.

- Chattels bought for more than £6,000 and sold for more than £6,000 are chargeable in full.

- For chattels bought for more than £6,000 but sold for less than £6,000, replace actual sale proceeds with £6,000 and then proceed as normal. There will always be an allowable loss, so no indexation will apply.

These rules are summarised in Figure 6.1.

Figure 6.1   The £6,000 rule for chattels

Buy \ Sell	Proceeds $\leq$ £6,000	Proceeds > £6,000
Cost > £6,000	Allowable loss, but actual proceeds are replaced by deemed proceeds of £6,000	Normal rules apply
Cost $\leq$ £6,000	Exempt	Chargeable but $\frac{5}{3}$ rule applies

4.12 Example

LOS Ltd bought an antique table for £2,500 in May 1990.

In September 2003 the table was sold for:

(a) £5,800 (after deducting selling costs of £100).
(b) £6,400 (after deducting selling costs of £100).

The indexed rise from May 1990 to September 2003 is 0.437.

You are required to calculate the chargeable gain in each case.

4.13 Solution

(a) As cost is less than £6,000 and it is sold for only £5,900 (gross proceeds) this is exempt.
(b) Cost is less than £6,000 but gross proceeds are greater than £6,000.

The normal calculation

	£
Net sale proceeds	6,400
Cost	(2,500)
Unindexed gain	3,900
Indexation allowance 0.437 × £2,500	(1,092)
Indexed gain	2,808

Using the $\frac{5}{3}$ rule

$\frac{5}{3}$ (£6,500 – £6,000) = £833

This is the chargeable gain, because £833 is less than £2,808.

Where sale proceeds are only marginally over £6,000 the $\frac{5}{3}$ should provide a lower result; hence the rule is sometimes described as a marginal relief. The gross proceeds must be used for the $\frac{5}{3}$ rule.

 Note that indexation allowance does not reduce the gain calculated under the $\frac{5}{3}$ rule.

4.14 Example

An antique chair cost £7,000, including expenses, in May 1990. It was sold for £4,000 in September 2003.

Expenses of sale were £240.

You are required to calculate the allowable loss.

4.15 Solution

Bought for more than £6,000

Sold for less than £6,000
Therefore replace proceeds with £6,000.

	£
Sales proceeds (substitute)	6,000
Incidental costs	(240)
Cost	(7,000)
Allowable loss	(1,240)

We now present a consolidation question which covers various capital transactions covered in the chapter.

Practice question 4 *(The answer is in the final chapter of this book)*

Mangle

During December 2003 Mangle Ltd had the following capital transactions.

(a)   It sold for £13,000 a desk which it had acquired in May 1970 for £4,000. The value of the desk on 31 March 1982 was £5,000.

(b)   It sold for £220,000 a property bought in April 1978 for £3,000. It was worth £58,000 on 31 March 1982. Mangle Ltd had incurred the following expenditure on improvements to the property.

		£
October 1979	New extension	1,500
October 1984	New central heating system	4,000

(c)   It sold an antique table bought for £1,000 in July 1984 for £7,200.

(d)   It sold a watercolour for £150, its market value. This was purchased for £7,500 in July 1984 when it was believed it to be a Constable.

Use the following indexation factors.

March 1982 – December 2003	1.302
July 1984 – December 2003	1.053
October 1984 – December 2003	1.017

Required

Calculate the chargeable gains of Mangle Ltd for its year ended 31 December 2003.

4.16   The treatment of leasehold disposals

For capital gains tax, leases are categorised as short leases (50 years or less to run – a depreciating asset) or long leases (more than 50 years to run).

♦   Disposal of a long lease follows normal capital gains rules.
♦   Disposal of a short lease is subject to special rules explained below.

When a short lease is disposed of, the cost/1982 value must reflect the 'wasting' nature of the lease. The calculation is as follows.

$$\text{Cost/1982 value} \times \frac{\%\ \text{lease remaining at disposal}}{\%\ \text{lease when expenditure incurred/MV 1982}}$$

The percentage is provided from the lease depreciation table.

4.17   Example

A Ltd disposed of a leasehold building for £60,000. The lease had 40 years and six months to run at the date of disposal. It was acquired at a cost of £45,000 when it had 47 years to run.

The indexation factor to use is 0.182.

Lease table extract

40	95.457
41	96.041
47	98.902

Required

Calculate the capital gain.

4.18 Solution

	£
Sale proceeds	60,000
Cost	
$£45,000 \times \dfrac{95.749*}{98.902}$	(43,565)
Unindexed gain	16,435
Less: Indexation allowance	(7,929)
$0.182 \times 43,565$	
Gain	8,506

$* \ 95.457 + \dfrac{6}{12} \ (96.041 - 95.457) = 95.749$

Note the depreciated cost is used in the indexation allowance calculation – not the full original cost.

4.19 The grant of a lease

The grant of a lease is a part disposal. There are three main situations:

- grant of a long lease out of a freehold or a long lease. This follows the normal $\dfrac{A}{A+B}$ rule, where A is the premium received, and B is the value of the remainder. This remainder value is the capital value of the rental stream and right to the property at the end of the lease, although you would not be required to calculate it.

- grant of a short lease out of a freehold or a long lease. In this case the $\dfrac{A}{A+B}$ rule also applies but the amount chargeable to income tax is excluded from the proceeds in the CGT computation and is excluded from 'A' in the numerator of the fraction but not from the denominator.

- grant of a sub-lease out of a short lease. In this case the cost of the part disposal is the part of the cost of the original lease that wastes away during the period of the sub-lease, calculated using the percentage depreciation table. The amount chargeable to Schedule A is deducted from the gain.

4.20 Example

In June 2000 X Ltd granted a 40 year lease over a plot of land to Y ltd for a premium of £50,000. The freehold interest in the land had cost X Ltd £36,000 in March 1997. The value of the remainder was £10,000 taking account of the lease terms.

In June 2003 Y Ltd granted Z Ltd a 10 year sub-lease for a premium of £40,000.

The indexation factor from March 1997 to June 2000 is 0.101, and from June 2000 to June 2003 is 0.058.

Lease table extract

40	95.457
37	93.497
27	83.816

Required

Calculate the capital gain on the grant of the lease by X Ltd and the grant of the sub-lease by Y Ltd.

4.21 Solution

X Ltd	£
Lease premium	50,000
Less: Schedule A charge $\frac{51-40}{50}$ x £50,000	(11,000)
Capital element	39,000
Less: cost $\frac{39,000}{50,000+10,000}$ x £36,000	(23,400)
	15,600
Less: Indexation allowance 0.101 x £23,400	(2,363)
Capital gain	13,237

Y Ltd	£	£
Lease premium		40,000
Less: cost depreciating over 10 years of sub-lease		
£50,000 x $\frac{93.497-83.816}{95.457}$		(5,071)
		34,929
Less: indexation allowance		
0.058 × £5,071		(294)
		34,635
Deduct amount charged under Schedule A:		
$\frac{51-10}{50}$ × £40,000	32,800	
Less allowance for premium paid		
$\frac{10}{40}$ × £11,000	(2,750)	
		(30,050)
Capital gain		4,585

5   Summary

A charge to taxation of capital gains arises on the disposal of a chargeable asset by a chargeable person.

Basic computations fall into three categories depending on the date when the chargeable asset was acquired.

- After 31 March 1982
- Before 31 March 1982, with a rebasing election
- Before 31 March 1982, with no rebasing election

Four key variations to the basic computations occur frequently in exam questions.

- Enhancement expenditure
- Part disposals
- Disposals of chattels
- Leases

Multiple choice questions 1 - 3 *(The answers are in the final chapter of this book)*

Each of the questions below has only one correct answer.

1   Danegeld Ltd bought an antique table for £3,000 in July 1990. In August 2003 an auctioneer sold it for £7,000 and charged £100 commission.

Indexation allowance of £1,500 is available.

The indexed gain is

A   £167
B   £1,500
C   £1,667
D   £2,400

2   How many of the following four types of asset are 'exempt assets' for capital gains purposes?

Half share in a race horse worth £120,000
Vintage cars
Antique sideboard costing £600 and valued at £5,800
UK Government securities

A   1
B   2
C   3
D   4

3   Which of the following assets is not chargeable to tax on capital gains?

A   Computerised lathe used as a fixed asset, disposal proceeds of £86,000, originally purchased for £52,000
B   60 year lease on confectioner's shop
C   Racing greyhound owned by a business syndicate
D   2 acres, out of total holding of 10 acres of farmland

CHAPTER 7

Capital gains: shares and securities

EXAM FOCUS

Transactions concerning shares were examined regularly in papers set under the old syllabus. This is expected to continue under the new syllabus.

The calculations are complicated because of the piecemeal way in which shares are acquired and sold. However, it is best to view the process as essentially another variation of the basic computations studied in the previous chapter.

LEARNING OUTCOMES

This chapter covers the following learning outcome of the CIMA syllabus:

> Calculate the gain arising on the disposal of quoted securities using the pooling system.
>
> Apply the substantial shareholdings exemption.
>
> Demonstrate the importance of timing in tax planning.

In order to cover this learning outcome the following topics are included:

> The identification rules
> The operation of a 1985 pool
> The operation of a 1982 pool
> Bonus issues, rights issues and takeovers
> The substantial shareholdings exemption.

---

1 The identification rules

1.1 Introduction

What distinguishes a share disposal from other asset disposals is the need for *identification* rules. These have undergone regular changes. Before considering what these identification (or matching) rules are, it helps to understand why we need them.

1.2 Illustration

Suppose that a company makes the following purchases of shares in A plc.

1 July 1998	500 shares for	£1,000
3 February 1992	300 shares for	£1,000
1 September 1989	800 shares for	£2,000

On 1 November 2003 400 of these shares are sold – but *which* 400?

- ◆ It could be the 300 acquired in 1992 and 100 acquired in 1989.
- ◆ It could be 400 out of the 500 acquired in 1998.
- ◆ It could be based on 400 out of the total 1,600 with costs being averaged.

We need identification rules so that we can establish which shares have been sold, and consequently what acquisition costs and indexation allowances can be deducted from the disposal proceeds. The rules dictate the order in which the shares disposed of are matched with acquisitions.

1.3 Identification rules for companies

If there is more than one disposal, deal with the earlier disposals before the later disposals.

A disposal by a company is matched with acquisitions in the following order.

(1)   Same day acquisitions
(2)   Shares acquired in the nine days before the sale
(3)   1985 pool (shares acquired from 1 April 1982 onwards)
(4)   1982 pool (shares acquired before 1 April 1982)

Categories (1) and (2) are *not* usually examined. You can cope with 'shares' by mastering the two pooling techniques as explained below.

1.4 Example

In September 2003, P Ltd sold 4,000 shares in TUV plc. The shares were acquired as follows.

May 1980	2,000
August 1982	1,000
September 1985	2,000

Required

Match the shares sold with the relevant acquisitions.

1.5 Solution

Shares sold	4,000
Same day acquisitions	Nil
Acquisitions in the previous nine days	Nil
1985 pool (1,000 + 2,000)	(3,000)
1982 pool 1,000/2,000	(1,000)

After the disposal, P Ltd is left with 1,000 in the 1982 pool.

2 The operation of a 1985 pool

2.1 Basic rules

Any acquisitions from 1 April 1982 are 'pooled'. Indexation will apply from acquisition to the date of disposal. To enable the correct indexation to be calculated, a separate working is needed to identify the amount available. The working is also used to find the average cost of a partial disposal.

The working follows a strict proforma which should always be used.

Proforma for 1985 pool

	Number	Cost	Indexed cost (cost plus indexation to date)
Acquisitions 1.4.82 - 31.3.85	X	X	X
Index to April 1985 (This is done separately for each acquisition)			X
Balance at 1 April 1985	X	X	X*
Index to next event			X
Purchase	X	X ⟶	X
	X	X	X
Index to next event			X
	X	X	X
Sale	(X)	(X) W1	(X) W2
Pool carried forward	X	X	X

* This will include indexation on additions up to 1 April 1985 and is most likely to be the start point provided in the exam.

The purpose of the working is to find:

♦ the *cost* of shares disposed of = working 1
♦ the *indexation* of shares disposed of = working 2 – working 1.

Workings 1 and 2 then feed into a normal post 31 March 1982 computation.

	£
Sale proceeds	X
Cost (W1)	(X)
	X
Indexation (W2 – W1)	(X)
Gain	X

 Indexation is always applied to the pool between *events*, and is applied to the *indexed cost* column. Events include both sales and purchases.

A partial disposal from a 1985 pool uses straight line apportionment of cost and indexation.

2.2 Example

FDC Ltd has purchased shares in DCC Ltd. The 1985 pool information of FDC Ltd is given below.

			Cost £
1 June 1985	4,000 shares for		8,000
30 July 1994	1,800 shares for		9,750

FDC Ltd disposed of 2,000 of its shares in DCC Ltd for £20,571 in March 2004.

The indexed rise from June 1985 to July 1994 was 0.509 and from July 1994 to March 2004 was 0.282.

What is the gain on the 1985 pool shares?

2.3 Solution

1985 pool working

	Note	Number	Cost	Indexed cost
Balance at 6 April 1985		Nil	Nil	Nil
Purchase 1 June 1985	1	4,000	8,000 →	8,000
		4,000	8,000	8,000
Indexed rise to July 1994 £8,000 × 0.509	2			4,072
Purchase – July 1994		1,800	9,750	9,750
		5,800	17,750	21,822
Indexed rise to March 2004 £21,822 × 0.282				6,154
		5,800	17,750	27,976
Sale of 2,000 shares	3	(2,000)		
$\dfrac{2,000}{5,800} \times £17,750/£27,976$			(6,121) W1	(9,647) W2
Carried forward		3,800	11,629	18,329

Notes

(1)   Any entry in the cost column must also be made in the indexed cost column.

(2)   Indexation must be added *before* the purchase in July 1994 is added to the pool.

(3)   Use apportionment, *not* part disposal rule, to allocate cost and indexed cost, *unless* the market value of the remainder is supplied (which is rare).

Then complete the computation.

	£
Sale proceeds	20,571
Cost (W1)	(6,121)
Unindexed gain	14,450
Indexation allowance (£9,647 – £6,121)	(3,526)
Chargeable gain	10,924

Now try a basic question to practise how to construct a 1985 pool.

Practice question 1 *(The answer is in the final chapter of this book)*

KNN

KNN Ltd had 1,800 shares in CYZ plc, a quoted company, as at 1 April 1985. Their cost was £3,100; their indexed cost was £3,428. They were all acquired since 1 April 1982. KNN Ltd then carried out the following transactions.

	Number	*£*
Purchase 9 September 1988	3,200	9,600
Sale 10 October 2003	2,000	13,000

The indexed rise from April 1985 to September 1988 is 0.144 and from September 1988 to October 2003 is 0.676.

Required

What is the chargeable gain?

3 The operation of a 1982 pool

3.1 Basic rules

Shares acquired prior to 1 April 1982 are grouped into a 1982 pool. For identification purposes this category is the final one on the list.

The computation is essentially a pre 31 March 1982 computation, so you will need to consider whether a rebasing election is in force or not.

Where there is only a partial disposal, then the cost and 1982 value will need to be apportioned using a simple working. Note that there is no indexation in the working.

3.2 Example

Augustus Ltd has the following transactions in QPR plc.

	Number	*Cost* *£*	*Proceeds* *£*
Purchase 10 March 1971	1,700	2,110	
Sale 15 February 2004	1,200		3,600

The March 1982 value is £1.90 per share. The indexed rise from March 1982 to February 2004 is 1.319. Compute the gain for Augustus Ltd, which has no rebasing election in force.

3.3 Solution

Set up a proforma for pre 31 March 1982 asset.

	Cost *£*	*1982 value* *£*
Sale proceeds	3,600	3,600
Cost or 1982 value (W1)	(1,489)	(2,280)
	2,111	1,320
Indexation on higher of cost or 1982 value £2,280 × 1.319	(2,111)*	(1,320)*
	Nil	Nil

*The indexation is restricted as it cannot create a loss.

Working

This is not the same as the 1985 pool working. No indexation is calculated in the working.

	Number	Cost £	1982 value £
Purchase 1971	1,700	2,110	3,230
Disposal	(1,200)		
$\dfrac{1,200}{1,700} \times £2,110/£3,230$		(1,489)	(2,280)
Carried forward	500	621	950

The following question focuses on the identification rules and the different computations of 1985 pool and 1982 pool acquisitions when dealing with a disposal of shares.

Practice question 2 *(The answer is in the final chapter of this book)*

Spencer

Spencer Ltd had the following transactions in the shares of Tracy plc.

		No	£
6 May 1972	Purchase	300	4,750
10 August 1987	Purchase	100	3,000
6 May 1998	Purchase	150	5,700
14 May 2003	Sold	350	14,000

Each share was valued at £17 on 31 March 1982.

Use the following indexation factors.

March 1982 - May 2003	1.273
August 1987 - May 1998	0.601
May 1998 - May 2003	0.105

Required

Calculate Spencer Ltd's chargeable gain, assuming the company has not made a rebasing election in respect of assets acquired before March 1982.

Approach to the question

♦ Classify the acquisitions between the 1982 pool and the 1985 pool.

♦ Match the disposal to the correct category.

♦ Apportion the sale proceeds between the 1982 pool and the 1985 pool.

♦ Compute the gains in the following order.

- 1985 pool
- 1982 pool

♦ Summarise the gains.

4 Bonus issues, rights issues and takeovers

4.1 Introduction

This section deals with share reorganisations, such as when a company makes a bonus or rights issue of shares to shareholders, or when a company's shares are taken over by another company in exchange for other shares or cash.

In dealing with these situations, it is necessary to understand the fundamental nature of these types of transaction.

4.2 Bonus issues and rights issues

 A bonus issue is the distribution of free shares to shareholders based on existing shareholdings.

A rights issue involves shareholders paying for new shares, usually at a rate below market price and in proportions based on existing shareholdings.

In both cases, therefore, the shareholder is making a new acquisition of shares. However, for *identification* purposes, such acquisitions arise out of the original holdings.

 Bonus and rights issues therefore attach to the original shareholdings for the purposes of the identification rules.

4.3 The effect on indexation

As there is no expenditure involved with a bonus issue, there is no impact on the indexation allowance. However, a rights issue involves a payment and indexation allowance is only due from the time of payment.

4.4 Example

Alma Ltd acquired shares in S plc, a quoted company, as follows.

2,000 shares acquired June 1987 for £11,500.

In October 1988 there was a 1 for 2 bonus issue. In December 1994 there was a 1 for 4 rights issue at £3 per share. Alma Ltd sold 2,600 shares in December 2003 for £30,000.

The indexed rise from June 1987 to December 1994 is 0.433 and from December 1994 to December 2003 is 0.253.

You are required to calculate the gain on disposal.

4.5   Solution

All the share acquisitions belong to the 1985 pool as the original acquisition was after 1 April 1982.

1985 pool	Notes	Number	Unindexed cost £	Indexed cost £
Brought forward at 6 April 1985		–	–	–
Acquisition June 1987		2,000	11,500	11,500
Bonus issue October 1988 (1 for every 2)	1	1,000	–	–
		3,000	11,500	11,500
Indexed rise to December 1994	2			
£11,500 × 0.433				4,980
		3,000	11,500	16,480
Rights issue (1 for every 4) at £3		750	2,250	2,250
		3,750	13,750	18,730
Indexed rise to December 2003				
£18,730 × 0.253				4,739
		3,750	13,750	23,469
Disposal December 2003		(2,600)		
Allocate costs $\frac{2,600}{3,750}$ × £13,750/£23,469			(9,533) W1	(16,272) W2
Carry forward		1,150	4,217	7,197

Computation of gain – 1985 pool

	£
Proceeds	30,000
Cost (W1)	(9,533)
Unindexed gain	20,467
Indexation (£16,272 – £9,533) W2 – W1	(6,739)
Chargeable gain	13,728

Notes

(1)   No indexation of pool because no change in costs.

(2)   Indexation must be updated prior to rights issue, because there is a purchase.

Practice question 3 *(The answer is in the final chapter of this book)*

Scarlet

On 20 September 2003 Scarlet Ltd sold 1,500 ordinary shares in Red plc for £4,725. The company's previous transactions were as follows.

Balance on 1985 pool at 5 May 1986 2,500 shares with a qualifying cost of £3,900 and an indexed cost of £4,385.

Transactions from 5 May 1986 were as follows.

4 April 1987	Took up 1 for 2 bonus issue
19 January 1988	Took up 1 for 3 rights issue at 140p per share

The indexed rise from May 1986 to January 1988 is 0.056 and from January 1988 to September 2003 is 0.756.

Required

Calculate Scarlet Ltd's chargeable gain on the disposal on 20 September 2003.

4.6 The 1982 pool and bonus issues

The impact that a bonus issue has on a 1982 pool is twofold. Firstly, there is an increase in the number of shares. Secondly, the 31 March 1982 value is diluted because of the additional shares.

4.7 Example

Mac Ltd has the following transactions in Arthur plc.

		Cost £	Number
June 1981	Purchase	16,000	12,000
June 1988	Bonus issue	–	3,000

At 31 March 1982 the value of each share held was £1.50.

What is the cost and 1982 value of each share?

4.8 Solution

1982 pool working

	Notes	Number	Cost £	1982 value
At 31 March 1982	1	12,000	16,000	18,000
Bonus issue		3,000		
		15,000	16,000	18,000
Cost/1982 value per share	2		£1.07	£1.20

Notes

(1)   The 31 March 1982 value is based on the actual holding at 31 March 1982: £1.50 × 12,000 = £18,000.

(2)   The addition of bonus shares dilutes both the cost and the 31 March 1982 value.

4.9 The 1982 pool and rights issues

The impact of a rights issue is more complex, because account must be taken of the rights issue cost. This affects both the cost and the 31 March 1982 value of the shares. In addition, indexation allowance must be calculated separately on the rights issue 'enhancement'.

The best way to tackle this is to keep the rights issue cost separate in the 1982 pool working as though it was an 'enhancement'. Upon a disposal, allocate the appropriate part of the rights issue cost to both the cost and 1982 value columns in the gains computation. The indexation allowance can then be separately computed on:

♦   the higher of cost and 31 March 1982 value
♦   the rights issue expenditure (or allocated portion thereof).

4.10   Example

On 6 December 2003, J Ltd sold 1,500 shares in K plc for £18,200. The company's previous transactions in these shares had been as follows.

Acquisitions	Shares	Cost £
Frozen 1982 pool	1,500	6,799

In September 1985 there was a 1:4 rights issue at £6 per share which J Ltd took up. The value of the shares on 31 March 1982 was £5.00.

The indexed rise from March 1982 to December 2003 is 1.302 and from September 1985 to December 2003 is 0.916.

You are required to calculate the chargeable gain.

4.11   Solution

The disposal will be identified with the 1982 pool, as both the original shares and the rights issue shares are allocated there as follows.

1982 pool working

	Number	Cost £	1982 value £	Rights issue £
Frozen pool (see note)	1,500	6,799	7,500	
September 1985	375			2,250
	1,875	6,799	7,500	2,250
Disposal	(1,500)			
Allocate cost and March 1982 value				
$\frac{1,500}{1,875} \times £6,799/£7,500/£2,250$		(5,439)	(6,000)	(1,800)
	375	1,360	1,500	450

Note   There is no indexation updating of a 1982 pool.

The capital gains computation then becomes as follows.

	Cost £	1982 value £
Sales proceeds	18,200	18,200
Cost (W)	(5,439)	
1982 value (W)		(6,000)
Rights (W)*	(1,800)	(1,800)
Unindexed gain	10,961	10,400
Indexation 1.302 × £6,000 (higher of cost and 1982 value)	(7,812)	(7,812)
Indexation September 1985 – December 2003		
0.916 × £1,800 = £1,649	(1,649)	(1,649)
	1,500	939

Take the lower gain of £939.

* This additional cost increases the allowable deduction in both columns.

Practice question 4 *(The answer is in the final chapter of this book)*

Colonel

Peacock Ltd purchased shares in Colonel plc, a quoted company, as follows.

	Number of shares	Cost
		£
December 1975	1,500	4,500
December 1985	1,000	4,000
April 1987 1 for 2 rights issue		£4 per share

In November 2003 Peacock Ltd sold 3,500 shares for £32,000.

The market value of the shares on 31 March 1982 was £3.50 each.

The indexed rises are as follows.

March 1982 –November 2003	1.297
December 1985 – April 1987	0.060
April 1987 –November 2003	0.793

No election has been made, or will be made, to have all pre-31 March 1982 acquisitions re-based to 31 March 1982.

Required

Calculate Peacock Ltd's chargeable gain for its year ended 31 December 2003.

4.12   Takeovers

The final aspect of share reorganisations concerns the situation where a company is taken over by another company. This can either be a straight share for share exchange or can be in the form of shares, cash, loan notes or any combination of these. The precise form of the exchange determines the capital gains position.

4.13   Share for share exchange

The situation here is that Y plc takes over X Ltd, buying up the shares in X Ltd. The shareholders in X Ltd sell their shares in the company, and in return they receive shares in Y plc.

In this situation, the shareholder is simply swapping one form of paper for another.

 There is no immediate CGT liability. However, where the shareholder receives different classes of shares or loan notes, the original cost or 1982 value of the shares must now be allocated between the different classes. This is done on the basis of market values, on the first day of trading following the exchange.

Note that these rules may be overridden by the exemption for substantial shareholdings (see beyond).

4.14   Example

Longterm Ltd acquired 3,000 ordinary shares in Small Ltd (a 5% holding) on 1 December 1985 for £4,000. On 6 May 2003, Small Ltd was taken over by Big plc.

What is the CGT implication for Longterm Ltd if the deal is:

♦   two Big plc ordinary shares for every three Small Ltd shares

♦   one Big plc ordinary share and two Big plc preference shares for every three shares in Small Ltd?

On 7 May 2003 Big plc shares traded at £7.50 per ordinary share and £3.50 per preference share.

4.15 Solution

There is no immediate capital gains implication for Longterm Ltd under either scenario, as both alternatives are 'paper' exchanges.

♦ Where Longterm Ltd receives two Big plc ordinary shares, it will simply take over the original cost of 3,000 Small Ltd shares. On a *subsequent* disposal of Big plc shares, the cost and indexation will be by reference to the original holding.

Before	*After*
3,000 Small Ltd £4,000 cost (1985 pool)	2,000 Big plc £4,000 cost (1985 pool)

♦ Where Longterm Ltd receives a mixture of different types or classes of shares, then the cost needs to be allocated between the *new* types for future disposal purposes. This is done by market values as follows.

Step 1

Find the market value of new shares

New shares – Big plc

1	Ordinary share	}	
2	Preference shares	}	For every 3 Small Ltd shares

		Market value £	Total market value £
Therefore	1,000 ordinary	7.50	7,500
	2,000 preference	3.50	7,000
			14,500

Step 2

Allocate original cost on market value weighting.

		Cost £	Market value £
Ordinary	(7,500/14,500 × £4,000)	2,069	7,500
Preference	(7,000/14,500 × £4,000)	1,931	7,000
		4,000	14,500

Step 3

Longterm Ltd now has two separate 1985 pool shareholdings in Big plc.

	Before	Cost £	*After*	£
3,000	Small Ltd	4,000	1,000 Big plc – ordinary	2,069
			2,000 Big plc – preference	1,931
				4,000

4.16 **Takeovers involving cash**

Often in takeovers, some or all of the consideration received is in the form of cash. In such cases, a chargeable gain arises on the cash element, as there is a deemed part disposal. As cash plus shares is a mixed transaction, the cost of the original shares must be allocated, based on market values, so that the part disposal can be calculated.

4.17 **Example**

Suction Ltd bought 4,000 shares in Little Ltd in April 1987 for £6,000. On 6 June 2003 Little Ltd was acquired by Large plc under the following terms.

£4 cash

1 ordinary share of Large plc $\left.\right\}$ For every Little Ltd share

On the first day of trading following the takeover, a Large plc ordinary share was worth £8.

The indexed rise from April 1987 to June 2003 is 0.773.

Calculate the chargeable gain arising as a result of the takeover.

4.18 **Solution**

Step 1

Find the total market value of the *new* holding.

	£
Cash £4 × 4,000 =	16,000
Shares £8 × 4,000 =	32,000
	48,000

Step 2

Allocate original cost between components based upon market values.

		Cost	*MV*
Cash	(16,000/48,000 × £6,000)	2,000	16,000
Shares	(32,000/48,000 × £6,000)	4,000	32,000
		6,000	48,000

Tutorial note. This step is effectively using the part disposal rule of $\dfrac{A}{A+B}$ ie:

A = Part (deemed) sold = cash = £16,000

B = market value of remainder therefore:

Cost which relates to cash = $\dfrac{16}{16+32}$ = 2,000

There is a capital gains disposal on the holding, in respect of the cash consideration.

£

Sales proceeds (cash)	16,000
Cost (April 1987)	(2,000)
	14,000
Indexation £2,000 × 0.773	(1,546)
Chargeable gain	12,454

5 The substantial shareholdings exemption

5.1 Introduction

If a company disposes of a substantial shareholding then any capital gain arising on the disposal is exempt, provided certain conditions are met. Similarly, if a loss arises it is not an allowable capital loss.

The exemption did not apply to disposals before 1 April 2002.

5.2 The conditions

The conditions that must be satisfied are:

♦ The disposing company must hold at least 10% of the ordinary share capital of the company disposed of, and be entitled to at least 10% of the distributable profits and assets on a winding up.

♦ The substantial holding must have been owned throughout a 12 month period ending not more than two years before the disposal.

♦ The disposing company must have been a trading company or a member of a trading group throughout that period.

♦ The company disposed of must have been a trading company or the holding company of a trading group throughout that period and immediately after the disposal.

The company need not dispose of its entire holding for the exemption to be available, but may make a part disposal. If the part retained was less than a 10% holding, the exemption could only be available on the disposal of the remaining holding if it occurred within one year from the first sale.

5.3 Example

Black Ltd is a trading company. For many years it had held 20,000 ordinary shares of White Ltd, which is also a trading company. White Ltd has an issued share capital of 100,000 ordinary shares.

On 1 May 2003 Black Ltd disposed of 11,000 shares of White Ltd. Black Ltd proposes to sell the remainder of its holding on 1 June 2004.

What are the CGT implications for Black Ltd?

5.4 Solution

The substantial shareholding exemption is available on the sale on 1 May 2003 because:

♦ both Black Ltd and White Ltd are trading companies.

♦ Black Ltd has held a 20% holding throughout the 12 months prior to the disposal.

The exemption is not available on the proposed disposal on 1 June 2004 because Black Ltd only had a substantial shareholding (20%) for the 11 months from 1 June 2002 to 1 May 2003. For the last 13 months, from 1 May 2003 to 1 June 2004, Black Ltd has only had a 9% holding. Had the second sale been made before 1 May 2004 the exemption would have been given.

Note, however, that if the second disposal would generate a loss it would be beneficial not to make it before 1 May 2004 to ensure that the loss was allowable.

5.5   Takeovers

Normally when there is a takeover involving a share for share exchange, there is no capital gain or loss, and the new holding is treated as taking over the cost (and 31 March 1982 value, if appropriate) of the old holding.

If, however, a sale of the old holding would have qualified for the substantial shareholdings exemption, this overrides the takeover rules. Any gain on the disposal is exempt, and the new shares are treated as acquired at market value at the date of exchange.

5.6   Example

Loaders Ltd acquired 20,000 shares in Tiny Ltd in 1997. This was a 25% holding and both companies are trading companies.

Tiny Ltd was taken over by Huge plc on 12 August 2003. Loaders Ltd received 2,000 shares in Huge plc (a 1% holding).

On 12 August 2003 Huge plc shares were worth £5 each, and the indexed cost of Tiny Ltd shares was £4,500.

What are the CGT implications for Loaders Ltd?

5.7   Solution

The substantial shareholdings exemption is available on the disposal of Tiny Ltd shares, and the gain of 2,000 × £5 - £4,500 = £5,500 is exempt.

The shares in Huge plc are treated as acquired on 12 August 2003 at a cost of 2,000 × £5 = £10,000.

6   Summary

When disposing of shares we apply matching rules to identify which shares have been disposed of. These rules are needed so that we can deduct the appropriate acquisition costs from the disposal proceeds.

The identification rules for companies match disposals in the following order.

♦   Same day acquisitions
♦   Acquisitions in the previous nine days
♦   Shares held in the 1985 pool (1 April 1982 onwards)
♦   Shares held in the 1982 pool (shares acquired before 1 April 1982).

Bonus and rights issues attach themselves to the original shareholdings. Takeovers do not give rise to an immediate chargeable gain, unless cash is received.

The substantial shareholding is a very generous relief for disposals of trading companies.

Multiple choice questions 1 - 3 *(The answers are in the final chapter of this book)*

Each of the questions below has only one correct answer.

1   Maribel Ltd realised the following gains on 31 March 2004.

	Gains
	£
£20,000 10% UK Treasury stock 2009	5,000
£10,000 12% Wessex Council stock 2005	6,000

What is the unindexed capital gain arising, if any, on the 31 March 2004 disposals?

A   Nil

B   £5,000

C   £6,000

D   £11,000

2   Roses plc had the following transactions in shares in Stone Ltd.

		£
3 July 1985	10,000 ordinary shares issued fully paid	11,500
24 May 1986	Took up rights issue of 1 for 10 on ordinary shares at 130p per share	1,300
10 October 2003	Sold all 11,000 ordinary shares for	32,000

What is the indexation allowance on this disposal?

Indexation factors to apply:

July 1985 – May 1986	0.028
May 1986 – October 2003	0.857

A   £8,892

B   £9,199

C   £11,568

D   £24,368

3   Swallow plc announced a 1 for 2 rights issue on 1 January 2004, the rights to be taken up by 31 March 2004. Robin plc already held 500 shares which it had acquired in August 1983 and decided to take up the 250 rights shares, paying for them on 24 February 2004.

From what date will indexation allowance run on the 250 rights shares?

A   August 1983

B   January 2004

C   February 2004

D   March 2004

The Financial Training Company

CHAPTER 8

Capital gains: rollover and holdover relief

EXAM FOCUS

Rollover relief is the only significant capital gains relief available to companies. It therefore regularly features in examination questions in both a single company or a group context.

LEARNING OUTCOMES

This chapter covers the following learning outcome of the CIMA syllabus:

Apply rollover and holdover reliefs for tangible and intangible business assets.

Demonstrate the importance of timing in tax planning.

In order to cover this learning outcome the following topics are included:

Rollover relief
Reinvestment in depreciating assets
Relief under the Corporate Venturing Scheme.

1   Rollover relief

1.1 Introduction

 Rollover relief allows a company to defer a chargeable gain, provided certain conditions are met.

In order to qualify for relief, the company must reinvest the proceeds from the sale of a qualifying asset into another qualifying asset. Any gain on the disposal of the first asset is then 'rolled over' against the capital gains cost of the new asset. Capital allowances (if applicable) are still due on the full cost of the new asset.

A typical situation can be depicted as follows.

		£
Asset (1)	Sale proceeds	100,000
	Cost and indexation allowance	(40,000)
	Indexed gain	60,000
Asset (2)	Purchase price	150,000
	'Rolled over gain'	(60,000)
	Revised CGT cost	90,000

Provided at *least* the proceeds are reinvested then *full* deferral

The gain on asset (1) has been deferred against the base cost of asset (2).

On the sale of the second asset a higher gain will result, as this represents both the inherent gain in the second asset and the deferred gain from the first.

	If no rollover relief claimed on asset (1) £		*If rollover relief is claimed on asset (1)* £
Sale of asset (2)			
Sale proceeds	200,000	Sale proceeds	200,000
Original cost	(150,000)	Revised CGT cost	(90,000)
Unindexed gain	50,000	Unindexed gain	110,000

The benefit of rollover relief is that tax, otherwise payable now, is deferred possibly for many years.

1.2 Conditions for relief

Now that we have considered the mechanics, it is necessary to look at the other conditions which apply.

There must be a disposal of and reinvestment in:

♦ a qualifying asset
♦ within a qualifying time period.

 Qualifying assets. The assets must be used in *a trade*. Where they are only partly used in trade then only the gain on the trade portion is eligible. Qualifying assets include the following.

♦ Land and buildings (freehold and leasehold)
♦ Fixed plant and machinery
♦ Ships/hovercraft
♦ Aircraft

Note that *shares* of a company are *never* qualifying assets for rollover relief purposes. There is a separate relief for reinvesting the gains on shares in unquoted companies in further shares in unquoted companies ('corporate venturing relief'), which is discussed later in this chapter.

 Qualifying time period. The qualifying period for reinvestment in the replacement asset is up to 12 months before the sale to within 36 months after the sale. It is important not to miss this window of opportunity.

Prior to 1 April 2002, goodwill was a qualifying asset for reinvestment purposes. Subject to some transitional provisions which can probably be ignored for CIMA purposes, from 1 April 2002 goodwill is dealt with under the FA 2002 intangible asset rules – see Chapter 3.

1.3 Partial reinvestment

Rollover relief may still be available even where only part of the proceeds is reinvested. However, it will be restricted, as there is some cash retained to settle tax liabilities. This is logical as the main purpose of the relief is not to charge tax where cash has been reinvested in the business.

 The amount which *cannot* be rolled over is the lower of:

♦ the proceeds not reinvested
♦ the chargeable gain.

The following example will demonstrate where full relief is available, partial relief is available and no relief is available.

1.4   Example

AB Ltd sold an office block for £500,000 in December 2003. It had been acquired in March 1982 for £200,000 and was used throughout for trade purposes. The indexation on the disposal was £247,200. A replacement office block was acquired in February 2004.

Assuming rollover relief is claimed where possible, calculate the gain assessable on AB Ltd and the base cost of the replacement office block if it cost:

(a)   £610,000
(b)   £468,000
(c)   £345,000

1.5   Solution

Gain on sale of old office block

	£
Proceeds	500,000
Cost	(200,000)
	300,000
Indexation allowance	(247,200)
Indexed gain	52,800

(a)   As all the proceeds have been reinvested, the full gain is rolled over and no gain is immediately chargeable.

Base cost of new asset	£
Cost	610,000
Less gain rolled over	(52,800)
	557,200

(b)   Proceeds not reinvested (£500,000 − £468,000)   £32,000

Hence £32,000 of the gain is immediately chargeable.

Base cost of new asset	£
Cost	468,000
Less gain rolled over (£52,800 − £32,000)	(20,800)
	447,200

(c)   Proceeds not reinvested (£500,000 − £345,000)

£155,000

As this exceeds the gain, the full gain of £52,800 is chargeable and no rollover relief is available.

Base cost of new asset   £345,000

1.6   The 50% rule

In Chapter 6 you learned about rebasing. This allows an asset's value at 31 March 1982 to be used in place of its original cost. Rebasing was not introduced until the Finance Act 1988. Therefore a company could miss out on the benefit of the rebasing provisions if it

♦ purchased an asset prior to 31 March 1982 and sold it prior to 1 April 1988, **and**
♦ reinvested the sale proceeds after 31 March 1982 in an asset which it sold after 1 April 1988.

Figure 8.1 shows the problem in diagrammatical form.

Figure 8.1

Rebasing applies

Asset 1 purchased   Asset 1 sold, Asset 2 purchased

----------------------31/3/82----------------------------------1/4/88---------------------------------

Rebasing does not apply

Asset 1 purchased   Asset 1 sold, Asset 2 purchased

----------------------31/3/82---:1/4/88--------------------------

Assets which were purchased prior to 31 March 1982 and disposed of prior to 1 April 1988 have their gains calculated as follows.

	£
Sale proceeds	X
Less original cost	(X)

Unindexed gain	X
Indexation allowance (See note)	(X)

Indexed gain	X
	—

Note. Indexation is based on the higher of cost and 1982 value if the asset was disposed of on or after 1 April 1985. For disposals prior to 1 April 1985, indexation was always based on cost.

The old rules of calculating a chargeable gain are still relevant in a rollover relief context because, if rebasing does not apply, the rolled over gain is halved if the original asset had been acquired before 31 March 1982.

1.7   Example

GFF Ltd disposed of a business property for £100,000 on 31 December 2003. The property was acquired on 21 June 1986 using the full proceeds from the sale of an office building. The original building was acquired in June 1980 for £20,000 and sold on 1 June 1986 for £60,000. The office building's March 1982 value was £25,000. GFF Ltd claimed rollover relief on the sale of the office building.

Required

Calculate the chargeable gain arising on the December 2003 disposal.

Use the following indexation factors:

March 1982 - June 1986	0.231
June 1986 – December 2003	0.870

1.8 *Solution*

The gain on the first disposal is calculated as follows.

	£
Sale proceeds	60,000
Less Cost	(20,000)
Unindexed gain	40,000
Indexation (based on 1982 value)	
£25,000 × 0.231	(5,775)
	34,225
Rollover relief	(34,225)
Chargeable gain	Nil

The full gain is rolled over as all of the sale proceeds are reinvested.

The gain on the second disposal is calculated as follows.

	£	£
Sale proceeds		100,000
Cost	60,000	
Rolled over gain £34,225/2 =	(17,112)	(42,888)
		57,112
Indexation £42,888 × 0.870		(37,313)
Chargeable gain		19,799

As you can see from the above example, where the 50% rule applies, 50% of the original gain never becomes chargeable. This is to compensate the taxpayer for the loss of rebasing.

Practice question 1 *(The answer is in the final chapter of this book)*

LKK

LKK Ltd purchased a building in January 1980 for £20,000. The building was sold in February 1986 for £35,000. Its value at 31 March 1982 was £25,000. In April 1986 LKK Ltd purchased a building costing £40,000. This building was sold in July 2003 for £95,000.

Required

Calculate the chargeable gain arising in respect of the disposal in July 2003.

Use the following indexation factors.

March 1982 - February 1986	0.216
April 1986 - July 2003	0.852

Approach to the question

Step 1

Calculate the gain on the disposal of the first asset. Note that rebasing does not apply because the asset was disposed of prior to 1 April 1988, however, indexation can be calculated using the March 1982 value as the disposal is after 31 March 1985.

Step 2

Identify how much of the first gain can be rolled over. If the full sale proceeds have been reinvested, the full gain can be rolled over.

Step 3

Deduct the relevant amount of rolled over gain from the cost of the replacement asset and then calculate the gain as normal.

2 Reinvestment in depreciating assets

2.1 Introduction

Certain qualifying assets are depreciating assets. A depreciating asset is one which has a life not exceeding 50 years, or which will become a depreciating asset in the next ten years (ie a 56 year lease at today's date falls within the definition). The two key examples of such assets are:

♦ leasehold buildings
♦ fixed plant and machinery.

Where a claim for rollover relief is desired, and depreciating assets are the replacement assets, then a special form of the relief ensues. This affects:

♦ the duration of the deferral
♦ the method by which the deferral is carried forward.

2.2 The duration of the deferral

The gain on the sale of the 'old' asset is deferred only until the *earliest* of:

♦ the date of sale of the depreciating asset (ie normal rule)
♦ the date the asset ceases to be in trade use
♦ ten years from the date of the acquisition of the depreciating asset.

This effectively means that a depreciating asset can only be used to defer a gain for a maximum of ten years from the date of acquisition.

If the company acquires a non-depreciating asset before the deferred gain 'crystallises' the gain can be rolled over against the non-depreciating asset in the normal way.

2.3 Method of giving relief: depreciating assets

Additionally, where the 'new' asset is a depreciating asset, the gain is *not* deducted from the CGT cost of the 'new' asset. Instead, it is said to be 'held over'. Where this applies, the gain to be deferred must be 'held' separately and 'charged' on the earliest of the three above events.

2.4　Example

FG Ltd, which prepares accounts to 31 October, acquired freehold premises in July 1987 for £50,000. These were sold in December 1995 for £120,000, the company having acquired a 59-year lease on larger premises at a cost of £125,000 in October 1995. The company was unsuccessful, however, and the lease was sold in October 2003 for £168,000.

The indexed rise from July 1987 to December 1995 was 0.480 and from October 1995 to October 2003 was 0.213.

You are required to show the gains chargeable in the year ended 31 October 2003.

2.5　Solution

Gains chargeable in year ended 31 October 2003

	£
Leasehold premises (W1)	16,375
Held over gain crystallising (W2)	46,000
	62,375

Workings

(W1)　Leasehold

	£
Proceeds	168,000
Cost	(125,000)
	43,000
Indexation allowance £125,000 × 0.213	(26,625)
	16,375

(W2)　Freehold

	£
Proceeds	120,000
Cost	(50,000)
	70,000
Indexation allowance £50,000 × 0.480	(24,000)
	46,000

The reinvestment in this example took place within the permitted timescale shown in Figure 8.2.

Figure 8.2　Qualifying period for reinvestment

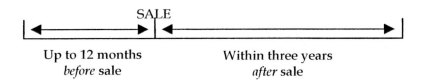

SALE

Up to 12 months
before sale

Within three years
after sale

Practice question 2 *(The answer is in the final chapter of this book)*

DRV

(a)   DRV Ltd makes up accounts to 31 March annually. The company sold the freehold of a factory on 3 March 2004 for £275,000, having previously purchased it as a replacement freehold factory for £190,000 in October 1987. The factory which it replaced was acquired in May 1983 for £65,000 and sold in December 1987 for £130,000.

Required

Calculate the chargeable gains, assuming all available reliefs are claimed.

(b)   Facts as in (a) above, except that the replacement factory purchased in October 1987 cost £115,000.

Required

Calculate the chargeable gains.

The indexed rises are:

May 1983 – December 1987	0.220
October 1987 – March 2004	0.794

3   Relief under the Corporate Venturing Scheme

3.1   Introduction

The corporate venturing scheme was introduced from 1 April 2000 to encourage companies to invest in unquoted trading companies. The following reliefs are available:

(a)   20% of the amount subscribed for the purchase of new shares is given as a credit against corporation tax but cannot lead to a repayment – ie, can only reduce liability to nil.

(b)   Any allowable loss arising when the shares are sold can be deducted from income of the same accounting period or accounting periods ending in the previous 12 months. Note that if the substantial shareholdings exemption applies, any loss will not be allowable.

(c)   Any chargeable gain arising when the shares are sold can be rolled over by further investment in CVS qualifying shares.

3.2   Conditions for the investing company

During the three years following the issue of the shares, or the commencement of the issuing company's trade if later, the investing company

♦   Must not hold more than 30% of the ordinary share capital or voting rights of the issuing company

♦   Must not, with associates, control the issuing company

♦   Must be a trading company or a member of a trading group

♦   Must hold the shares as chargeable assets (ie, not as trading stock)

♦   Must not receive value from the issuing company

3.3 Conditions for the issuing company

During the three years following the issue of the shares, or the commencement of the issuing company's trade if later, the issuing company

♦ Must carry on a qualifying trade. This excludes such trades as property investment and financial services

♦ Must use the funds paid on subscription for purposes of the trade. At least 80% must be used within 12 months of the share issue with the full amount used within 24 months.

♦ Must not have gross assets exceeding £15 million before the issue nor exceeding £16 million immediately after

♦ Must not be quoted on a recognized stock exchange. This condition is relaxed if it obtains a listing within the three years provided this was not planned when the shares were issued.

4 Summary

Rollover relief appears regularly in examination questions. The key points are as follows.

There must be a disposal of and reinvestment in a qualifying asset. The main types of qualifying asset are

♦ land and buildings
♦ fixed plant and machinery.

The reinvestment must take place within the period one year before to three years after the qualifying disposal.

Any proceeds which are not reinvested are immediately chargeable.

The gain can be deferred (not rolled over) for a maximum of 10 years if the replacement asset is a depreciating asset.

Multiple choice questions 1 - 5 *(The answers are in the final chapter of this book)*

Each of the questions below has only one correct answer.

1   Smethwick plc draws up accounts to 31 December each year. On 1 June 2003 the company sold one of its freehold factories upon which it made a substantial chargeable gain.

The company intends to use all the proceeds from the sale of the old factory to assist with the acquisition of a larger factory.

In order to roll over the gain on the old factory, the company must reinvest the proceeds in the new factory not later than

A   1 June 2004

B   31 December 2004

C   1 June 2006

D   31 December 2006

2   Good News Ltd operates a newsagents and a road haulage business. On 5 December 2003 the company sold a freehold shop used in the newsagents business; Good News Ltd had purchased another shop for this business on 11 November 2002. On 10 June 2004 the company purchased an office building for the road haulage business.

Statute provides that Good News Ltd can roll over the gain against the cost of

A   neither asset

B   the shop only

C   the office building only

D   both the shop and the office building

3   Ongar Ltd sold one of its supermarkets in July 2003 for £800,000. The unindexed gain on the disposal was £350,000 and the indexation allowance available was £70,000.

The company used the proceeds from the disposal as follows.

(1)   Purchase of a small supermarket in October 2003 costing £600,000
(2)   Additional working capital - £200,000

How much of the gain on the sold supermarket is eligible for rollover relief?

A   £80,000

B   £150,000

C   £210,000

D   £280,000

4   Penn Ltd purchased a freehold office building in June 1992 for £480,000. Two of the floors have always been occupied by the company for the purposes of its trade. The other floor was let as an office to a political party.

Penn Ltd sold the building in May 2003 for £1,200,000 obtaining an indexation allowance on the disposal of £73,440.

In April 2003 the company had purchased a new building for £720,000 which it occupies for the purposes of its trade.

What is the maximum amount of gain which can be rolled over?

A   £351,040

B   £431,040

C   £566,560

D   £646,560

5   On a disposal resulting in a chargeable gain which of the following assets qualifies for that gain to be rolled over against the cost of a qualifying replacement business asset?

A   A diesel engined road-going oil tanker

B   A diesel engined sea-going oil tanker

C   A warehouse leased to a trading company

D   A company owned house occupied as his residence by the managing director of the company

CHAPTER 9

Relief for company losses

EXAM FOCUS

Under the old syllabus, company losses appeared regularly in both a single company and a group context. This section considers losses in a single company context. It is important for you to gain a good understanding of the topics covered in this chapter as it acts as a foundation for loss relief in a group context, which is covered later in this text.

Throughout this chapter we give the references to statute, eg s393(1). It is not necessary to know the references for exam purposes, but the section numbers do act as a useful tagging device.

LEARNING OUTCOMES

This chapter covers the following learning outcomes of the CIMA syllabus:

> Identify the effect of all forms of loss relief on a company's CT liability
>
> Calculate the form of loss relief which will minimise the CT liability in a single company.
>
> Demonstrate the importance of timing in tax planning.

In order to cover these learning outcomes the following topics are included:

> Relief for trading losses
> Non-trading losses
> Calculating repayments
> Choice of loss relief claim.

1 Relief for trading losses

1.1 Overview

When a company makes an adjusted trading loss, its Schedule D Case I assessment for the period is *nil*. A trading loss is computed in the same way as a trading profit.

There are three forms of relief available to a company which makes a trading loss

♦ current year relief
♦ carry back relief
♦ carry forward relief.

1.2 Current year relief (S393A(1)(a))

A trading loss can be relieved against total profits of the loss making accounting period. The set off is against profits *before* the deduction of any charges.

A claim for current year (or carry back) relief must be made within two years of the end of the loss making accounting period.

The statutory reference for current year relief is S393A(1)(a) ICTA 1988. This is one of the few references that are worth learning and using as a label in your answers.

1.3 Example

Sage Ltd had the following results for the year ended 31 March 2004.

	£
Schedule D Case I	(40,000)
Schedule A	10,000
Chargeable gain	50,000
Gift Aid	10,000

Required

Show how relief would be obtained under S393A(1)(a) in the current period.

Approach to the example

It is *essential* once a loss has been identified to set up a loss memorandum as a working and allocate the loss to it, so that the relief for the loss can be clearly illustrated.

Even where there is a DI loss, this does not alter the basic approach.

- Present the CT computation in the standard proforma.
- Support it with workings (one of which will be the loss memorandum).

1.4 Solution

Sage Ltd

	£
Schedule D Case I	Nil
Schedule A	10,000
Gains	50,000
	———
	60,000
S393A(1)(a) relief	(40,000)
	———
	20,000
Less Charges	(10,000)
	———
PCTCT	10,000
	———

Working

(W1) Loss memorandum

	£
Year ended 31 March 2004	(40,000)
Relieved in current period	40,000
	———
	Nil
	———

Setting off the loss before the deduction of charges may result in the charges becoming excess.

1.5 Example

What if the loss available above had been £60,000?

1.6 Solution

The effect would be as follows.

	£
Total profits (£10,000 + £50,000)	60,000
S393A(1)(a) current relief	(60,000)
	Nil
Less Charges on income	(10,000)

The charges have become excess (ie not used) as there are insufficient profits.

 It is an important principle in the use of most loss reliefs that, where there is an available loss, no restriction in set-off is permitted. This means that it would *not* have been possible here to restrict the loss relief to (£50,000) so as to then relieve charges of (£10,000), and find an alternative use for the remaining (£10,000) loss.

From 1 April 2002 the only type of charge on income still likely to be encountered is a charitable Gift Aid donation.

As Gift Aid is a non-trading charge, excess Gift Aid donations cannot be carried forward or back and are therefore wasted.

 In exam answers you should highlight the fact that non-trading charges are wasted even if not specifically asked to do so.

Patent royalties paid before 1 April 2002 are relieved as trading charges on income. As these were virtually the only type of trading charges you were likely to encounter, we can assume trading charges will not arise after 31 March 2002.

In fact the legislation now defines a charge on income as 'an annuity or other annual payment' subject to a list of exclusions, principal of which are patent royalties and interest. So it is still possible to have trade charges arising in certain rare circumstances but we ignore this remote possibility in this text.

Note that for S393A(1)(a) (current year) loss relief the loss set off takes priority over both trading and non-trading charges.

1.7 Carry back relief – S393A(1)(b)

 A Schedule DI loss may be carried back for relief but only *after* the loss has been relieved against any available current period profits.

The loss carried back is set off against total profits *before* deducting Gift Aid but *after* deducting trading charges. In other words, the order in which the loss is applied is as follows.

♦ First, against total profits of the current year, (*before* Gift Aid and, if relevant, before trade charges).

♦ Second, against total profits of the carry back period (again *before* the deduction of Gift Aid but *after* deducting trading charges).

The permitted carry back period depends upon whether the company's trade is ongoing or is ceasing.

♦ In an ongoing trade, carry back for 12 months.

♦ In a cessation of trade, the loss arising in the last twelve months of trading can be carried back for 36 months (LIFO).

The correct statutory reference is S393A(1)(b) ICTA 1988 and this is a useful label to show in your exam answer.

If trade charges become excess they can be carried forward against future profits of the same trade.

1.8 Example

Marjoram Ltd has the following results for the five accounting periods to 31 March 2004.

	Year ended 30.9.2000 £	6 months to 31.3.2001 £	Year ended 31.3.2002 £	Year ended 31.3.2003 £	Year ended 31.3.2004 £
Trading profits (loss)	1,000	7,500	11,000	9,000	(45,000)
Building society interest	400	–	500	500	500
Chargeable gains	800	–	–	–	4,000
Gift Aid payment (gross)	250	–	250	250	250
Patent royalties paid (gross)	150	–	150	–	–

Required

Show the profits chargeable to corporation tax for all periods affected, assuming that loss relief is taken as soon as possible and that:

(a)   the business continues as a going concern
(b)   the business ceases to trade on 31 March 2004.

Approach to the example

A question utilising company losses often involves several years and a methodical approach is therefore important.

♦   Lay out the years side by side in a table, leaving space to insert any loss reliefs.

♦   Keep a separate working for the trading loss – the memorandum.

♦   Firstly set the loss against the total profits (before Gift Aid and before trade charges) of the year of loss.

♦   Then carry the balance of the loss back against total profits (before Gift Aid but after trade charges) of the previous 12 months (36 months if there is a cessation).

♦   State whether there is any unrelieved loss (and trading charges) remaining.

♦   Keep a running tally in the loss memorandum working.

Here is a suitable proforma for an ongoing trade, the loss being incurred in 2003.

	2002	2003	2004
Schedule DI	X	Nil	X
Loss carry forward			(X)
	X	Nil	X
Other income			
DIII	X	X	X
Schedule A	X	X	X
Gains	X	–	X
	X	X	X
Current period loss relief – S393A(1)(a)		(X)	
	X	Nil	X
Trade charges* - if excess carry forward	(X)		
	X		
Carry back loss relief – S393A(1)(b)	(X)		
	X		
Non trade charges	(X)	(X)	(X)
		If excess then wasted	
PCTCT	X/Nil	Nil	X

*Note that trade charges are unlikely to arise after 31 March 2002 so we are only going to encounter them in a carry back situation.

Loss memorandum

	£
2003 loss	(X)
Current year relief	X
Carry back relief	X
	Nil

1.9 Solution

(a) **Marjoram Ltd – ongoing situation**

	Year ended 31 March 2003 £	Year ended 31 March 2004 £
Schedule DI	9,000	Nil
Schedule DIII	500	500
Gain		4,000
	9,500	4,500
S393A(1)(a) current loss relief (W1)		(4,500)
	9,500	Nil
S393A(1)(b) carry back relief (W1)	(9,500)	
	Nil	Nil
Non trade charge		
Gift aid payment	Wasted	Wasted
PCTCT	Nil	Nil

Working

	£
Loss of year ended 31 March 2004	(45,000)
S393A(1)(a) current relief	4,500
	40,500
S393A(1)(b) carry back 12 months	(9,500)
Loss still available at 1 April 2004	31,000

Note

If the company has no associates it would be within the starting rate Nil band for both years and no loss claims would therefore be made. The example merely shows how the reliefs are applied without considering whether they should be claimed.

(b) **Trade cessation**

This allows a carry back of 36 months on a LIFO basis. If there are sufficient profits in the previous 36 months, then the whole period is treated as one claim. It is important to realise there is just a single carry back claim. You cannot choose to carry back only 24 months, for example, or to skip a period.

Step 1

Set up a corporation tax proforma for all relevant years

Marjoram Ltd

	Year ended 30.9.2000 £	6 months ended 31.3.2001 £	Year ended 31.3.2002 £	Year ended 31.3.2003 £	Year ended 31.3.2004 £
Schedule DI	1,000	7,500	11,000	9,000	Nil
Schedule DIII	400	–	500	500	500
Gain	800	–	–	–	4,000
	2,200	7,500	11,500	9,500	4,500
S393A(1)(a) current year					(4,500)
	2,200	7,500	11,500	9,500	Nil
Trade charges	(150)	-	(150)	-	-
	2,050	7,500	11,350	9,500	Nil
S393A(1)(b) carry back on cessation	(1,100)[4]	(7,500)[3]	(11,350)[2]	(9,500)[1]	
	950	Nil	Nil	Nil	Nil
Non-trade charges	(250)	–	Wasted	Wasted	Wasted
	700	Nil	Nil	Nil	Nil

Step 2

Loss memorandum

	£
Year ended 31 March 2004	(45,000)
S393A(1)(a) current	4,500
S393A(1)(b) carry back	(40,500)
(1) 12m to 31 March 2003	9,500
(2) 12m to 31 March 2002	11,350
(3) 6m to 31 March 2001	7,500
(4) 6m to 30 September 2000 ($\frac{6}{12} \times £2,200$)	1,100
Unused loss	(11,050)

Note

The carry back permitted is 36 months. As the period to 31 March 2001 is only six months a further six months can be relieved in the year ended 30 September 2000. It is arguable that the loss should only relieve $\frac{6}{12}$ ths of the profits as reduced by the trading charge, ie $\frac{6}{12}$ x 2,050 = £1,025. However, by exam convention, either answer is likely to be acceptable. The Revenue interpret the legislation as giving the lower result.

Practice question 1 *(The answer is in the final chapter of this book)*

Alfred Ball

The following are the profits of Alfred Ball Ltd, which commenced trading on 1 January 1990.

	Year ended		
	31.12.01	*31.12.02*	*31.12.03*
	£	£	£
Adjusted trading profit (loss)	42,000	19,000	(67,000)
Bank interest received	3,000	2,000	1,000
Chargeable gains	4,000	4,000	4,000
Gift Aid paid	10,000	10,000	-

Required

Calculate the profits chargeable to corporation tax for all of the accounting periods shown above, clearly indicating how you would deal with the trading loss to obtain relief as soon as possible.

Approach to the question

Ensure that you follow the procedure.

♦   Set up CT proformas in columnar format for each relevant period.
♦   Leave spaces at the appropriate points to slot in the loss reliefs.
♦   Set up a working sheet and open up a loss memorandum.
♦   Determine the reliefs available and update the proforma and memorandum accordingly.

1.10   Carry forward relief S393(1)

Where any loss remains unrelieved after the current year and carry back claims have been made, the carry forward relief is available. This may also be used where no current year and carry back claims are made, as there is no compulsory requirement to use such reliefs.

The carry forward relief automatically allows trading losses (S393(1)) to be set against future trading profits of the same trade as soon as they arise. They cannot be relieved against any other profits.

Similarly, unrelieved trading charges are carried forward as part of the overall trading loss being carried forward.

Such losses have to be used against the first available DI profits.

1.11   Example

Mint Limited has the following results.

	Year ended 31 March		
	2002	*2003*	*2004*
	£	£	£
Schedule D Case I	15,000	(100,000)	40,000
Schedule D Case III	5,000	10,000	10,000
Chargeable gain	–	40,000	–
Patent royalties paid (gross)	3,000	-	-

Required

Show how the loss relief would be claimed as soon as possible.

1.12 **Solution**

Set up CT proformas.

Mint Ltd

Year ended	31 March 2002 £	31 March 2003 £	31 March 2004 £
Schedule D Case I	15,000	–	40,000
S393(1) carry forward relief			(33,000)
Schedule D Case III	5,000	10,000	10,000
Chargeable gain	–	40,000	–
	20,000	50,000	17,000
S393A(1)(a) current year		(50,000)	–
	20,000	–	17,000
Less: trade charges	(3,000)	–	–
	17,000	–	17,000
S393A(1)(b) carry back	(17,000)		
	Nil	Nil	17,000

Working

Loss memorandum

	£
Year ended 31 March 2003	(100,000)
Current year	50,000
	(50,000)
Carry back 12 months year ended 31 March 2002	17,000
Carry forward	(33,000)
Used – 2004	33,000
	Nil

Note: The maximum set off of loss relief under S393(1) in the year to 31 March 2004 is £40,000. If, say, £46,000 of loss was being carried forward, the balance of £6,000 would be carried forward a further year.

2 *Non-trading losses*

2.1 *Introduction*

Both trading and non-trading losses regularly feature in examination questions. Often non-trading losses will occur in questions in isolation, but where a mixture of losses appear it is essential to distinguish the reliefs available.

Non-trading losses may comprise any of the following.

♦ Capital losses
♦ Schedule A losses
♦ Schedule DIII deficits

Each of these will be considered below.

2.2 Capital losses

The treatment of capital losses was covered in Chapter 6. Here is a brief reminder.

♦ A capital loss incurred in the current period is automatically relieved against current gains. Any excess is then carried forward for relief against gains in future accounting periods.

♦ There is no carry back facility and a capital loss cannot be used against any other profit.

Practice question 2 *(The answer is in the final chapter of this book)*

Coriander

Coriander Ltd has the following results.

	Trading profit or (loss) before CAs £	Capital allowances £	Schedule D Case III (gross) £	Patent royalties paid (gross) £	Capital gains or (losses) £
Twelve months ended 30 June 2001	33,000	5,400	1,200	3,000	
Nine months ended 31 March 2002	16,500	4,050	1,300	3,000	(6,000)
Twelve months ended 31 March 2003	(75,000)	6,550	1,400	3,000	
Twelve months ended 31 March 2004	25,000	5,000	1,600	8,000	12,000

The patent royalties are paid at the end of each AP and represent the amount accrued to that date. No deduction for patent royalties has been made against the figures for trading profit or (loss).

Required

Show how the trading loss is relieved, assuming Coriander Ltd has an ongoing trade.

Approach to the question

♦ Set up CT proformas for all years leaving space to enter any loss reliefs.

♦ Set up a loss memorandum for the loss for year ended 31 March 2003.

♦ Ensure when calculating DI profit or loss that you take capital allowances into account. Note that capital allowances in a loss making period will *increase* the loss available.

♦ Similarly, patent royalties must be deducted as a trading expense from 1 April 2002 onwards.

♦ There is also a capital loss to deal with which has more restrictive use than a trading loss.

2.3 Schedule A losses

Losses arising on property income are utilised as follows.

♦ By relief against total profits (including gains) of the current period *before* charges.

♦ By carrying forward against *total* profits of future periods (ie before charges) provided there is still a Schedule A business source.

These reliefs are mandatory – ie they must be taken.

There is no carry back facility for Schedule A losses.

2.4 Schedule DIII deficits

A loss under Schedule DIII is known as a deficit. This could arise where non-trading interest payable (for example, on a loan to acquire rental property) exceeds any non-trading interest receivable.

Such deficits can be relieved as follows.

♦ By relief against total profits of the current period (ie profits before charges)
♦ By carrying back against Schedule DIII profits of the previous 12 months
♦ By carrying forward against *non-trading* profits of future periods

You may find yourself faced with several loss reliefs available against total profits for a current period. Where total profits are not sufficient to utilise all available reliefs then losses must be used in the following order.

♦ Schedule DIII deficit
♦ Schedule A loss
♦ Trading loss

This order refers to losses incurred in the *current* period and should be sufficient for examination questions.

2.5 Example

Comfy Ltd has the following results for the three years ending 31 December 2003.

	2001 £	2002 £	2003 £
Adjusted trading profit or loss before CAs	15,000	(20,000)	4,200
Capital allowances	(2,550)	(14,500)	(200)
Schedule A	2,000	3,000	(500)
Schedule DIII	1,000	(600)	1,000
Gift Aid payments (gross)	(400)	(400)	(400)

Required

Calculate PCTCT, assuming all reliefs are claimed at the earliest opportunity.

2.6 Solution

Set up proforma

	2001 £	2002 £	2003 £
Schedule D Case I (W1)	12,450	Nil	4,000
Carry forward s393(1) trading loss			(4,000)[3]
Schedule A (W2)	2,000	3,000	–
Schedule DIII (W4)	1,000	–	1,000
	15,450	3,000	1,000
Current year reliefs			
Schedule A (W3)			(500)
Schedule DIII (W4)		(600)	
Schedule DI (W2)		(2,400)[1]	
	15,450	Nil	500
Trade charges	Nil	Nil	Nil
	15,450	Nil	500
Carry back relief	(15,450)[2]		
Schedule DI			
Non-trade charges	Wasted	Wasted	(400)
PCTCT	Nil	Nil	100

Workings

(W1) Calculation of DI

	2001 £	2002 £	2003 £
Trading profit	15,000	Nil	4,200
Less Capital allowances	(2,550)		(200)
	12,450	Nil	4,000

(W2) Loss memorandum

Year ended 31 December 2002	£
Trading loss	(20,000)
Capital allowances	(14,500)
	(34,500)
Current year (s393A(1)(a))	2,400[1]
Carry back (s393A(1)(b))	15,450[2]
	(16,650)
Carry forward relief (s393A(1))	4,000[3]
	(12,650)
Carry forward at 31 December 2003	(12,650)

(W3) **Schedule A**

	£
The loss in year ended 31 December 2003 will be relieved against total profits in that period	(500)
Year ended 31 December 2003 relief	500
	Nil

(W4) **Schedule DIII**

	£
The deficit in the year ended 31 December 2001 will be relieved against total profits in that period	(600)
Total profits in that period	600
	Nil

3 Calculating repayments

3.1 Introduction

The effect of the carry back loss relief is to revise the previous figure of PCTCT. However, for the earlier period (or periods as appropriate), corporation tax will already have been paid. This is because the final due date for corporation tax is nine months following the accounting period end or earlier if quarterly instalment payments are required – see Chapter 13. Where the carry back option is examined in a question, you may have to identify any tax repayment due.

The procedure for tackling this aspect is as follows.

(a) Calculate the revised PCTCT, giving relief for any losses, and compute any CT payable.

(b) Calculate the original PCTCT, before relief for the current loss, and compute the CT payable for *earlier* years only.

(c) The repayment due will be (b) – (a).

3.2 Example

The following figures relate to Fennel Ltd, an ongoing trading company.

	Year to 31 March		
	2002 £	2003 £	2004 £
Schedule D Case I profit or (loss)	8,000	31,310	(38,340)
Chargeable gains	–	–	2,430

Required

Show the CT payable or repayable assuming loss relief is claimed at the earliest opportunity. Assume that today's date is 31 March 2004, and that all corporation tax has been paid when due.

3.3 Solution

Step 1

Calculate PCTCT and CT payable – incorporating loss reliefs

	Year ended 31 March		
	2002	*2003*	*2004*
	£	£	£
Schedule DI	8,000	31,310	Nil
Capital gains	–	–	2,430
	8,000	31,310	2,430
Current year relief			(2,430)
Carry back 12 months only		(31,310)	
Revised PCTCT	8,000	Nil	Nil
CT liability @ 10%	800	Nil	Nil

Working

Loss memorandum

	£
Year ended 31 March 2004	(38,340)
Current year relief	2,430
Carry back 12 months only	31,310
Carry forward	4,600

Step 2

Calculate 'original' PCTCT liability – for earlier years only

	2002	*2003*
	£	£
DI and PCTCT	8,000	31,310
CT liability		
10%/19%	800	5,949
Less: $\frac{19}{400} \times$ (£50,000 - £31,310)		(888)
	800	5,061

Step 3

Tax repayment

	2002	*2003*
	£	£
New calculation	800	Nil
Original calculation	800	(5,061)
Difference (= repayment due)	Nil	(5,061)

Note £5,061 is repayable as it would have been paid on 1 January 2004.

Although the claim to relieve profits in the year of the loss saves no tax, as the £2,430 of profits are within the Nil rate band, they have to be relieved before a carry back claim can be made. The effective rate of tax saving is therefore only 15% - £5,061/(£2,430 + £31,310) × 100.

Now you are in a position to tackle an exam standard question including loss reliefs. Consider the question approach before tackling it.

Practice question 3 *(The answer is in the final chapter of this book)*

Unblocked

Unblocked Underground Ltd's recent results have been as follows.

	Profit or (loss) before IBAs (note 1 below) £	Schedule A £	Capital gain or (loss) £	Gift Aid Donation £
Year ended 30.6.2001	47,000		(15,000)	–
Year ended 30.6.2002	156,500	1,500	–	(1,000)
3 months to 30.9.2002	61,250	–	10,800	(1,000)
6 months to 31.3.2003	56,500	–	–	(1,000)
			See below	
9 months to 31.12.2003	(268,750)	–	(note 1) -	(1,000)

Notes

(1) On 1 September 2002 the company had bought a factory, which qualifies for industrial building allowance, from the original owner for £450,000. This factory was first brought into qualifying use by the original owner on 1 September 1987. It had originally cost £250,000. There had been no non-qualifying use before 1 September 2002.

The building was sold on 31 December 2003 for £536,400, realising a capital gain of £71,100.

(2) Unblocked Underground Ltd has unused trading losses of £71,000 at 1 July 2000.

Required

Assuming that relief for trading losses are claimed in the most favourable manner:

(a) calculate Unblocked Underground Ltd's corporation tax payable for all of the accounting periods from 1 July 2000 to 31 December 2003.

(b) calculate the tax refunds that will be due to Unblocked Underground Ltd as a result of the loss relief claims in respect of its trading losses for the period ended 31 December 2003.

Approach to the question

Set up the detailed corporation tax proformas for all relevant years.

Set up the following workings.

Workings

(W1)   Schedule D Case I for each relevant year

		£
Trading profit or loss		X/(X)
Less IBAs (W2)		(X)/X
Or		
Add Balancing charge on industrial building disposal (W2)		X/(X)
		X/(X)

(W2)   Industrial buildings allowances

Industrial buildings allowances including disposal in period ended 31 December 2003.

(W3)   Loss memorandum

Loss memorandum for any losses identified in working 1. Where in a question there is more than one DI loss, losses should be dealt with in chronological date order (ie use earlier year's loss first).

(W4)   Corporation tax liabilities

To calculate the corporation tax liabilities after loss reliefs have revised PCTCT.

For part (b) you need to show PCTCT and CT liabilities on the assumption that there was no carry back relief for the loss in the year ended 31 December 2003 so that you can then compare your findings in (a) with (b) and calculate any tax refunds due.

4   *Choice of loss relief claim*

4.1   *Overview*

In most of the examples so far, you have been told how to relieve the loss. Although this is often the case, there may be occasions when you are required to explain the best choice of relief for a company.

The main consideration in choosing the most appropriate loss relief claim is the rate of tax that will be saved.

Ignoring for a moment the starting rate, there are three different rates of tax a company could be paying.

♦   Large companies pay at the standard rate of 30%.

♦   Small companies pay at the lower rate of 20%.

♦   Companies with profits between the upper and lower limits pay at an effective marginal rate of 32.75%.

The rate of 32.75% is best explained by an example.

4.2   *Example*

Marginal Ltd has PCTCT of £350,000 for the year ended 31 March 2004. It received no franked investment income.

Required

Calculate the corporation tax payable by Marginal Ltd for its year ended 31 March 2004.

4.3   Solution

As Marginal Ltd has profits which fall between the lower limit of £300,000 and the upper limit of £1,500,000 its corporation tax liability will initially be computed using the standard rate of 30%. The tax liability will then be reduced by marginal relief.

	£
PCTCT £350,000 × 30%	105,000
(£1,500,000 – £350,000) × $^{11}/_{400}$	(31,625)
Corporation tax liability	73,375

Suppose instead that Marginal Ltd's profits were only £300,000. In that case it would have paid tax at the small companies rate and its corporation tax liability would have been £57,000 (£300,000 × 19%).

So the £50,000 profits which exceed the lower limit of £300,000 have resulted in extra tax of £16,375 (£73,375 – £57,000). This works out at an effective marginal rate of 32.75% (£16,375/£50,000).

When a company is considering which form of loss relief to claim, it should aim to claim the relief that will result in the highest possible tax savings. That means it should aim to relieve any loss in the following order.

♦   Against profits which fall between the lower and upper limits
♦   Against profits chargeable to tax at the standard rate
♦   Against profits chargeable at the lower rate

 The second consideration is timing. Companies generally aim to relieve their losses as soon as possible. This is because future profits are uncertain and the value of the loss is eroded by inflation if it is carried forward. If tax rates in an earlier year were slightly higher, carrying a loss back may result in a higher rate of tax saving.

The position regarding tax rates is further complicated by the Nil% starting rate. This applies with effect from 1 April 2002.

 Companies with profits falling between £10,000 and £50,000 pay tax at the rate of 19% and then receive a form of marginal relief. This means that profits between £10,000 and £50,000 are taxed at a marginal rate of 23.75%.

4.4   Example

Minute Ltd has PCTCT of £20,000 for the year ended 31 March 2004. It received no franked investment income.

Required

Calculate the corporation tax payable by Minute Ltd for its year ended 31 March 2004.

4.5   Solution

As Minute Ltd has profits which fall between £10,000 and £50,000 its corporation tax liability will initially be computed using the rate of 19%. The tax liability will then be reduced by marginal relief.

	£
PCTCT £20,000 × 19%	3,800
(£50,000 – £20,000) × $^{19}/_{400}$	1,425
Corporation tax liability	2,375

Suppose instead that Minute Ltd's profits were only £10,000. In that case it would have been subject to the starting rate of Nil% and would have paid no corporation tax.

So the £10,000 profits which exceed the lower limit of £10,000 have resulted in extra tax of £2,375. This works out at an effective marginal rate of 23.75% (£2,375/£10,000).

This means that from 1 April 2002 onwards, companies should aim to relieve any loss in the following order.

♦ Against profits which fall between £300,000 and £1,500,000 (32.75%)
♦ Against profits chargeable to tax at the standard rate (30%)
♦ Against profits which fall between £10,000 and £50,000 (23.75%)
♦ Against profits chargeable to tax at the small companies rate (19%)

There is obviously no point in relieving the loss against profits chargeable at the starting rate (Nil%) if that can be avoided.

5 Summary

The use of losses features regularly in corporation tax questions. You need to distinguish between the relief of a trading loss and other losses.

Figure 9.1 summarises the trading loss reliefs for a company.

Figure 9.1   Utilising trading losses

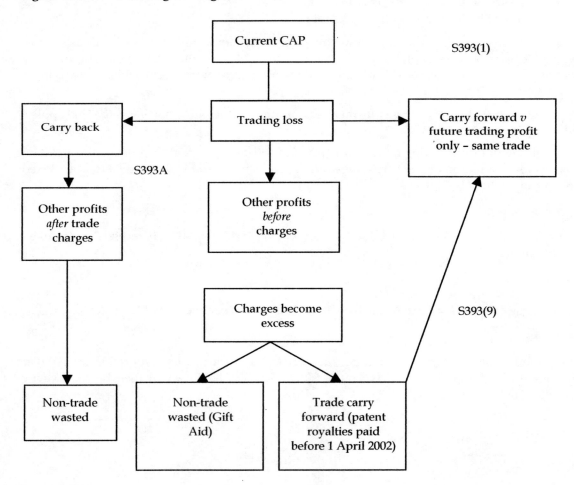

The carry back option can only be considered in conjunction with the current period option.

On cessation of trade *only*, the trading loss and excess trade charges of the last 12 months can be carried back for 36 months on a LIFO basis.

For non-trading losses, such as capital losses, Schedule A losses, or Schedule DIII deficits the relief is more restricted as the following summary indicates.

Relief ⟶	Current period	Carry forward	Carry back
Type of loss			
Capital	Against capital gains only	Against capital gains only	No
Schedule A	Against total profits	Against total profits	No
Schedule DIII	Against total profits	Against 'non-trading' profits	Yes, 12 months against Schedule DIII profits.

Multiple choice questions 1 - 5 *(The answers are in the final chapter of this book)*

Each of the questions below has only one correct answer.

1   Mole Ltd has unrelieved trading losses at 1 January 2003 of £20,000. Its corporation tax computation for the year ended 31 December 2003 shows the following.

	£
Adjusted trading profit	16,000
Less: Capital allowances	(2,000)
Schedule D Case I profits	14,000
Schedule D Case III	1,000
Gift Aid	(2,000)

How much of the loss brought forward will be utilised in the period?

A   £13,000

B   £14,000

C   £15,000

D   £16,000

2   Cloud Ltd was incorporated and started to trade on 1 July 2002. Its results since then have been as follows.

	Six months to 31 December 2002 £	Year ended 31 December 2003 £
Trading profit/(loss)	190,000	(300,000)
Schedule D Case III (gross)	10,000	20,000
Gift Aid paid (gross)	8,000	8,000

The maximum loss which may be relieved against the company's total profits using S393A ICTA88 loss relief is

A   £210,000

B   £212,000

C   £220,000

D   £230,000

3   Stradem Ltd has the following results.

	Year ended 31 October 2002 £	Six months ended 30 April 2003 £
Adjusted loss	-	(£10,000)
Schedule D Case I profit	12,000	-
Capital gains	-	4,000
Trade charges	(1,000)	-

What is the profit chargeable to corporation tax for the year ended 31 October 2002 on the assumption that reliefs are claimed at the earliest opportunity?

A   £1,000

B   £2,000

C   £3,000

D   £5,000

4   Green Ltd had the following results for the year ended 31 March 2004.

	£
Schedule D Case I	175,000
Schedule D Case III	30,000
Capital gains	20,000
Gift Aid paid	10,000

The company had trading losses brought forward of £180,000 and capital losses brought forward of £30,000.

Green Ltd's profits chargeable to corporation tax for the year ended 31 March 2004 are

A   £5,000

B   £10,000

C   £15,000

D   £20,000

5   Wood Ltd had trading losses brought forward at 1 January 2003 of £138,000 in respect of its manufacturing trade. Its corporation tax computation for the year ended 31 December 2003 shows the following before relief for the loss brought forward.

		£
Trading profit	Manufacturing trade	56,000
	Consultancy trade	40,000
Interest from UK government stocks		18,000
Chargeable gains		25,000

The amount of the trading loss which will be relieved against the profits for the year is

A   £56,000

B   £69,000

C   £96,000

D   £138,000

CHAPTER 10

Groups of companies

EXAM FOCUS

Questions on some aspect of the taxation of groups appeared on every paper set under the old syllabus. This is likely to continue under the new syllabus. The topic could be examined as a full optional question in Section C or as part of the compulsory scenario in Section B.

To begin with, you can forget all about consolidated accounts; these have no relevance for taxation purposes. Each individual company within a group is responsible for its own corporation tax; there is no group CT assessment. There are, however, a number of different types of group for taxation purposes. It is important for you to be able to identify them and explain their consequences.

LEARNING OUTCOMES

This chapter covers the following learning outcomes of the CIMA syllabus:

> Identify the effect of all forms of loss relief on a company's, group's or consortium's CT liability

> Calculate the form of loss relief which will minimise the CT liability in either a single company or in a group or consortium

> Identify the CGT reliefs available in a group situation and the anti-avoidance rules relating to pre-entry assets

> Demonstrate the most efficient method of disposing of assets to third parties by a group of companies

> Evaluate the tax efficiency of alternative methods of acquiring other businesses.

> Demonstrate the importance of timing in tax planning.

In order to cover these learning outcomes the following topics are included:

> Associated companies
> 75% groups (group relief)
> 75% groups (capital gains)
> Consortia
> Anti-avoidance
> Alternative methods of acquisition

---

1 Associated companies

1.1 Definition

The starting point for *every* group question is the identification of associated companies.

 A company is *associated* with another where:

♦ one company has *control* of the other (direct or indirect), or
♦ both companies are controlled by the same *person*.

Control means

♦ holding over 50% of the share capital or the voting rights, or
♦ being entitled to over 50% of the distributable profits, or
♦ being entitled to over 50% of the net assets in a winding up.

Person includes a company or individual.

The rules specifically *include:*

♦ overseas resident subsidiaries

♦ any company which is a member of the group at any time during the accounting period (ie joiners and leavers).

A company which does not trade nor carry on any business at any time in the accounting period is excluded from associate status. Earning interest on a deposit account has been held as **not** amounting to the carrying on of a business.

A non-trading holding company is also excluded where it is effectively just linking a sub-group to a main group. It must hold no assets, other than shares in the subsidiaries, must pass on any dividends it receives and have no other income or gains.

1.2 Consequences of being associated

The consequences of being associated are as follows.

♦ The upper and lower limits for small company rate purposes are divided by the total number of associates, and so may increase the effective rate of tax each company pays.

♦ The upper and lower limits for the starting rate of corporation tax are also shared equally. This makes the starting rate of corporation tax very unlikely to apply in a group situation – profits would have to be very low.

♦ Dividends received from associates are excluded from FII in calculating 'profits' (P).

♦ VAT group advantages are available (see Chapter 14).

1.3 Example

Consider the following relationships.

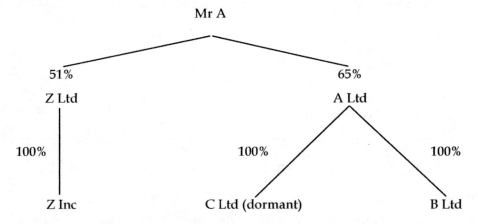

All companies except Z Inc are UK resident and make accounts to 31 March 2004.

Required

How many associates does A Ltd have for corporation tax purposes?

1.4 Solution

A Ltd has three associates: B Ltd, Z Ltd and Z Inc. Although Mr A is the common link between A Ltd and Z Ltd, an individual is not an associated company. C Ltd is excluded as it is dormant.

The impact on A Ltd of having three associates is that the upper and lower limits for small company tax rate purposes are divided as follows

Lower	£300,000/4	=	£75,000
Upper	£1,500,000/4	=	£375,000

Similarly the starting rate band limits are divided as follows

Lower	£10,000/4	=	£2,500
Upper	£50,000/4	=	£12,500

The risk here is that you may forget A Ltd itself when diluting the upper and lower limits.

A Ltd + Three associates = Four companies

2 75% groups (group relief)

2.1 Definition

A 75% group exists where one company

♦ has at least 75% of the ordinary share capital of another company and
♦ is entitled to at least 75% of the distributable profits and
♦ is entitled to at least 75% of the net assets in a winding up.

Note that if a shareholding is held indirectly, the effective interest must be at least 75%.

Note also that although overseas companies are taken into account in determining whether a 75% group exists, only UK companies and UK permanent establishments of overseas companies can claim and surrender group relief.

The following company structures constitute examples of groups for the purposes of group relief.

In the third example, losses can be surrendered between H and S_2 because H indirectly holds 81% (ie the effective interest is at least 75%) of S_2.

2.2 Consequences of being in a 75% group

The consequences of being in a 75% group are the same as for 51% groups, plus losses can be transferred between group members. This is known as group relief. Losses can flow in *any* direction: from H to S, from S to H, and from S_1 to S_N.

Qualifying losses

Qualifying losses are those of the *current* period only and consist of:

♦ Schedule D Case I losses
♦ unrelieved charges on income (both trade and non-trade)
♦ Schedule D Case III deficits
♦ unrelieved Schedule A losses
♦ excess management expenses of an investment company.

Capital losses, and losses under Schedules DV are *not* included.

The surrendering company

The loss making company is known as the surrendering company.

♦ It can surrender all or any part of its loss to any 75% claimant company.

♦ Generally there is no requirement to use the loss against its own profits first. The exception to this is that charges, Schedule A losses and management expenses can only be surrendered if unrelieved in the current period against available profits (ie they must be excess).

The claimant company

The company claiming the loss is known as the claimant company.

♦ It can only set the loss against profits of an identical time period.

♦ The profits available to relieve the loss are calculated after deducting the claimant company's own

    - charges on income
    - trading loss brought forward , and
    - any current year trading loss relief available.

2.3 Example

H Ltd owns 80% of S Ltd. The results of both companies for the year ended 31 March 2004 are as follows.

	H Ltd £	S Ltd £
Adjusted trading profit (loss)	(340,000)	342,000
Capital gain	50,000	
Gift Aid		(2,000)

S Ltd has a trading loss b/fwd of £10,000, and H Ltd has a trading loss b/fwd of £20,000.

Required

What is the maximum group relief H Ltd could surrender to S Ltd?

2.4 Solution

Step 1

Identify whether H and S are in a qualifying 75% relationship. H owns 80% of S, so this condition is satisfied.

Step 2

Identify the 'qualifying loss' to be surrendered.

H can surrender the Schedule DI current loss of £340,000. There is no requirement for H to use the loss against its capital gain (or any other profit) first. It cannot surrender the b/fwd Schedule DI loss of £20,000.

Step 3

Identify the available PCTCT, against which S Ltd could set group relief.

		£
Sch DI		342,000
Less	DI loss b/fwd	(10,000)
		332,000
Less	Gift Aid	(2,000)
PCTCT		330,000

The maximum group relief which can be claimed is £330,000. This is lower than the amount available to be surrendered of £340,000, because S Ltd has to utilise its own DI loss b/fwd and charges on income. Note that there is no restriction on S Ltd's claim because it is only 80% owned. As long as the subsidiary is at least 75% owned the *whole* loss may be surrendered or claimed.

2.5 Overlapping periods

When surrendering or claiming group relief there is a restriction where:

♦ the companies are not members of the same group for the whole period, or
♦ the companies have non-matching year ends.

The following illustrations will demonstrate this 'overlapping' restriction.

 Profits or losses have to be apportioned into common or 'overlapping' periods.

2.6 Example

In the year ended 31 March 2004 H Ltd incurs a Schedule DI loss of £50,000. S Ltd was acquired 100% by H Ltd on 1 October 2003.

Required

What is the maximum group relief which could be surrendered and claimed if S Ltd in the year ended 31 March 2004 has PCTCT of:

(a) £100,000?
(b) £30,000?

2.7 Solution

The maximum H Ltd could surrender is $\frac{6}{12} \times$ (£50,000) loss = (£25,000).

The maximum S Ltd could claim is:

(a) £100,000 $\times \frac{6}{12}$ = £50,000. Therefore group relief is (£25,000)

(b) £30,000 $\times \frac{6}{12}$ = £15,000. Therefore group relief is (£15,000).

In (b) although H Ltd could theoretically surrender £25,000, S Ltd's PCTCT for the overlapping period is only £15,000.

As another example, suppose that H Ltd has a year ending 31 March 2004 and one of its subsidiaries S Ltd makes up accounts to 31 December. If S Ltd had a loss in the year to 31 December 2004 it would be able to surrender only $\frac{3}{12}$ of the loss to H Ltd, in respect of H Ltd's overlapping period 1 January to 31 March 2004.

A loss for an overlapping period can only be used *once*. Suppose that H Ltd incurs a loss of £50,000 in the year ended 31 March 2004. On 1 October 2003 H acquired 80% of S_1 and 80% of S_2. Each subsidiary earned a profit of £40,000 in the year ended 31 March 2004.

H Ltd can surrender £50,000 $\times \frac{6}{12}$ = (£25,000) the 'overlapping period' loss.

In theory S_1 Ltd could claim £40,000 $\times \frac{6}{12}$ = (£20,000) and S_2 could claim (£20,000), bringing the total claim to £40,000, but this is *not* permitted. The loss claimed between S_1 + S_2 is restricted to £25,000 for the six month overlapping period.

2.8   Problems of apportionment

Where a loss making subsidiary leaves the group, losses (for group relief purposes) are normally apportioned between the vendor and purchaser on a time basis. However, either the company or the Revenue could over-rule this if a different basis gave a more 'just and reasonable' result. For example, if M Ltd is bought by N Ltd on 30 September 2003 and makes a loss of £400,000 in its year to 31 December 2003, time apportionment would give a post acquisition loss of £100,000 ($\frac{3}{12} \times$ £400,000). N Ltd, the new holding company, may have instigated a restructuring programme – such as redundancies, refurbishments and new capital investments – resulting in most of the losses for the period. Group relief claims could use losses on an actual rather than time apportioned basis.

2.9   Tax planning issues

The primary consideration where there are qualifying losses for group relief is that they need to be allocated for the maximum benefit of the group (ie to save as much tax as possible).

The approach is as follows.

- Identify the total number of associates, and hence determine the upper or lower limits (eg by drawing the group structure). Remember to divide the starting rate limits of £10,000 and £50,000 as well.

- Rank the eligible companies according to the tax rate currently applying to 'profits' as follows (using FY03 rates).

Class 1	Marginal small company rate (32.75%)
Class 2	Full rate (30%)
Class 3	Marginal starting rate (23.75%)
Class 4	Small rate (19%)
Class 5	Starting rate (Nil%)

- Allocate the losses to Class 1 companies to reduce their 'profits' to the lower limit, then to Class 2 etc.

2.10 Example

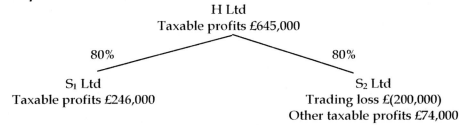

H Ltd
Taxable profits £645,000

80%   80%

S₁ Ltd   S₂ Ltd
Taxable profits £246,000   Trading loss £(200,000)
                                             Other taxable profits £74,000

S₁ Ltd and S₂ Ltd have been owned by H Ltd for several years.

There are no other associated companies. No dividends have been received. All companies make up accounts to 31 March. The above results all relate to the year ended 31 March 2004. S₂ Ltd had no previous profits against which the loss could be set.

Required

Relieve S₂ Ltd's loss within the group so as to save the maximum amount of tax.

2.11 Solution

Adopt a step-by-step approach.

Step 1

From the group diagram, identify associates and the members of the 75% group.

♦ The number of associates is three: H Ltd, S₁ Ltd and S₂ Ltd.
♦ The 75% group also consists of H Ltd, S₁ Ltd and S₂ Ltd. This will not always be the case.

Step 2

The number of associates is used to determine the upper and lower limits which apply.

Small companies' limits

Upper limit $\dfrac{£1,500,000}{3}$ = £500,000

Lower limit $\dfrac{£300,000}{3}$ = £100,000

Starting rate limits

Upper limit $\dfrac{£50,000}{3}$ = £16,667

Lower limit $\dfrac{£10,000}{3}$ = £3,333

Step 3

Find 'profits' (here supplied), separating out any current period 'qualifying' losses into a loss memorandum.

	H Ltd £	S₁ Ltd £	S₂ Ltd £	Loss memorandum
PCTCT	645,000	246,000	74,000	S₂ loss (200,000)
FII	–	–	–	
'P'	645,000	246,000	74,000	

Step 4

Determine the tax rate which currently applies to each company and rank the companies. In this case, priority goes to S₁ Ltd (profits in the marginal band, 32.75%), then to H Ltd (tax at the full rate of 30%).

Step 5

Allocate the losses available to save tax at the highest rates.

	H Ltd £	S₁ Ltd £	S₂ Ltd £	Loss £
PCTCT	645,000	246,000	74,000	(200,000)
Group relief	(54,000)	(146,000)		200,000
Revised PCTCT	591,000	100,000	74,000	
FII	Nil	Nil	Nil	
'P'	591,000	100,000	74,000	

There is no point in allocating any more of the loss to S₁ Ltd. With 'P' down to £100,000 S₁ pays tax at only 19%. The balance of loss should then be allocated to H Ltd.

Although group relief is allocated against PCTCT, sufficient must be allocated to reduce 'P' – ie profits including FII – to the lower limit to maximise relief. Hence if S₁ Ltd had FII of £10,000, £156,000 of loss would have had to be allocated to reduce 'P' to £100,000.

2.12 Other tax planning considerations

Saving tax at the highest rate is the primary factor in using company losses. Consideration should always be given to alternatives such as carrying back a trading loss (after current period relief) as an alternative to group relief, *if* this saves more tax. Another factor which should be taken into account, is whether a group company has *double taxation relief* available for foreign tax credits as the surrender of losses to such a company may reduce the capacity to utilise the credit available. (Double taxation relief is covered in Chapter 12).

Practice question 1 *(The answer is in the final chapter of this book)*

Zeus

Zeus Ltd and its two wholly owned subsidiaries, Thor Ltd and Odin Ltd, are all manufacturing companies. For the year ended 31 March 2004 the taxable trading profits of the three companies were as follows.

	Profit/(Loss) £
Zeus Ltd	640,000
Thor Ltd	165,000
Odin Ltd	(99,000)

These profits and loss are before the following items have been taken into account.

Odin Ltd has unused trading losses as at 31 March 2003 of £18,000. Thor Ltd paid a dividend of £80,000 to Zeus Ltd on 15 January 2004. Thor Ltd received a dividend of £11,160 on 30 June 2003.

Odin Ltd has received rental income of £24,000 for the year.

On 31 March 2004 Thor Ltd paid a royalty of £34,000 to Odin Ltd for the use of a patented manufacturing process. Odin Ltd acquired the patent rights for use in its trade and has written off £10,000 of its value during the year. The payment of £34,000 is the amount accrued for the year.

Required

Calculate the corporation tax liability of each of the group companies for the year ended 31 March 2004. Your answer should include an *explanation* of your treatment of the royalty paid by Thor Ltd, and Odin Ltd's trading losses.

You should assume that reliefs are claimed in the most favourable manner.

Approach to the question

Zeus Ltd concerns group relief

It is essential to have a method when tackling group computational questions. In fact, when planning an answer to a written question, the same considerations have to be made. The following checklist will assist in guiding you through the maze of information.

(1)   Draw a group diagram (if not provided).

(2)   Identify or consider

  ♦   Number of associates
  ♦   75% group(s)

(3)   Calculate upper limit and lower limit for small companies' relief, and for the starting rate of corporation tax.

(4)   Find PCTCT. Consider

  ♦   any current 'qualifying' losses

  ♦   any b/fwd losses – these can normally only be set against same schedule or source (ie a capital loss against a capital gain, trading loss against DI profits of the same trade)

(5)   Find 'P' profits by adding in current FII (exclude group dividends).

(6)   Using information in Steps 3 and 5, identify the current marginal tax rate each company is paying.

(7)   Allocate qualifying losses to optimise the tax relief.

(8)   Consider restrictions such as 'overlapping' period (if companies join or leave a 75% group or have non-coterminous accounting periods)

(9)   Calculate corporation tax payable on revised PCTCT and 'P'.

3 *75% groups (capital gains)*

3.1 *Definition*

A 75% group for capital gains purposes consists of a 'principal' company and all its 75% subsidiaries and their 75% subsidiaries, provided the 'principal' company has overall control (ie more than 50%). It is therefore a sort of hybrid 75% group. This can be demonstrated using the diagrams below.

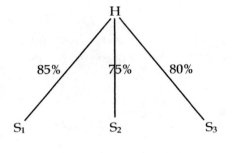

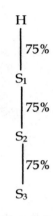

Figure 1   **Figure 2**

♦ In Figure 1, H is the principal company, which together with its three 75% or above subsidiaries forms a capital gains group. The group would also qualify for group relief.

♦ In Figure 2, H is the principal company, which together with S_1 and S_2 qualifies as a 75% group. S_2 qualifies because it is a 75% subsidiary of S_1 with H being able to exercise overall control (ie H's effective interest in S_2 is 75% × 75% = 56.25%). S_3 does *not* qualify as H only controls (75% × 75% × 75%) 42.19%. S_2 and S_3 cannot form a separate capital gains group because S_2 is already in a capital gains group. For group relief (75%) purposes there are three separate groups HS_1, $S_1 S_2$ and $S_2 S_3$.

A capital gains group can exist even if one or more of the companies concerned are resident overseas. So, in Figure 2, S_2 can be in a group with H even if S_1 is resident overseas. However, the only companies that can take advantage of the reliefs available to a capital gains group are:

♦ UK resident companies
♦ Non-resident companies but only in respect of assets used in a trade carried on by a permanent establishment in the UK.

In effect the reliefs apply to assets within the charge to UK taxation.

3.2   Consequences

There are two main consequences of being in a 75% capital gains group. These relate to

♦ the transfer of assets between group members
♦ rollover relief.

3.3   Transfer of assets

The sale or transfer of an asset by a company generally gives rise to an immediate chargeable event. The capital gain or loss is computed using the sale proceeds (or market value if the parties are connected).

Where a transfer of assets is made between 75% group members, it is treated as a 'no gain no loss' disposal. The market value is irrelevant even though the parties are 'connected persons'.

A chargeable event only occurs in the following circumstances.

♦ The asset is eventually sold outside the group – this is treated as a normal disposal.

♦ The transferee company leaves the group, owning the asset, within six years. If that occurs then the deferred gain or loss crystallises in the *transferee* company at the start of the accounting period in which it leaves.

The mechanics of intra-group transfer can be seen in the following example.

3.4 Example

G plc owns 80% of F plc, and both companies prepare accounts to 31 March each year.

On 20 February 1996, G plc bought land costing £121,000.

G plc transferred the land to F plc on 15 July 1998, when its market value was £159,000.

Required

Calculate the chargeable gains arising under the following alternative assumptions.

(a) F plc sold the land to a third party on 8 June 2003 for £300,000.
(b) G plc sold all of its shares in F plc to Y plc on 8 June 2003.

The indexed rise from February 1996 to July 1998 is 0.080 and from July 1998 to June 2003 is 0.107.

3.5 Solution

Step 1

Identify whether the companies are part of a qualifying 75% capital gains group. In this case they clearly are: G owns 80% of F.

Step 2

The transfer of the land from G plc to F plc on 15 July 1998 will be treated as a nil gain or nil loss transfer as follows.

G plc	£
Deemed market value (balancing figure)	130,680
Cost	(121,000)
	———
Unindexed gain	9,680
Indexation	
(February 1996 – July 1998)	
£121,000 × 0.080	9,680
	———
	Nil gain/Nil loss
	———

Step 3

Upon the sale by F plc to a third party on 8 June 2003 the computation on F plc is as follows.

	£
Sale proceeds	300,000
Deemed market value	(130,680)
	———
	169,320
(Indexation July 1998 – June 2003)	
0.107 × £130,680	(13,983)
	———
Indexed gain	155,337
	———

Step 4

If instead G plc sold F plc, which holds the land transferred in 1998, this is within six years of the intragroup transfer, and the gain that should have occurred in 1998 crystallises on F plc.

	£
Actual market value	159,000
Deemed market value	(130,680)
Indexed gain	28,320

This gain is deemed to crystalise on 1 April 2003 (start of AP of leaving) and would therefore be chargeable on F plc in the year ended 31 March 2004.

For computing the gain on a future actual disposal, F plc is deemed to have acquired the land at a cost of £159,000 on 15 July 1998.

3.6 Tax planning issues

The ability to transfer assets for no gain/no loss can be used to 'match' gains and losses. For example, suppose that C Ltd has a building it intends to sell which would realise a gain of £50,000. D Ltd and E Ltd are also members of the same capital gains group. Each has capital losses of £20,000.

C Ltd could transfer the building to either D Ltd or E Ltd under intra-group transfer of assets. The transferee company could then sell the asset realising the gain and offset this against its own capital loss, leaving only £30,000 chargeable.

The transfer of assets rule could also be used to save tax. For example, using the illustration details above, which is the best company to transfer the asset to if D Ltd pays tax at 30%, E Ltd at 19%?

D Ltd has a capital loss of £20,000 (like E Ltd) but pays tax at 30%. Therefore, it would be preferable to transfer the asset to E Ltd as the remaining gain would only be charged at 19%.

 From 1 April 2000, an asset no longer has to be moved between companies in order to match capital gains and losses. Instead, an election can be made specifying which company in the group is treated for tax purposes as making the disposal. The election must be made by both companies concerned within two years of the end of the accounting period in which the asset is disposed of outside the group.

The advantage of the election is that tax planning can now be done retrospectively. It should also mean a saving in legal and administrative costs as assets no longer have to be actually transferred. The election can be made in respect of part of an asset, enabling a group to achieve the optimum result for tax purposes. In the above example 40% of the building could be treated as transferred to D Ltd to cover its capital loss, and the remainder to E Ltd. The resultant net gain of £50,000 × 60% - £20,000 = £10,000 would be taxed at 19%.

For companies leaving a group on or after 1 April 2002 any gain that crystallises in respect of intra group transfers within the previous 6 years (see 3.5 above) can also be transferred by election to another company in the 'old' group.

3.7 Rollover relief

Rollover relief enables the gain on a qualifying business asset to be deferred where another qualifying business asset is acquired.

 Where companies operate within a qualifying capital gains group, there is greater flexibility, as one company can realise the gain, but another company can make the appropriate replacement investment.

The gain made by one company is simply deducted from the base cost of the replacement asset acquired by the other company.

Rollover relief can apply to gains which have crystallised on a company leaving a group on or after 1 April 2002, whether the gain remains in the leaving company or has been transferred to another company in the 'old' group.

 Practice question 2 *(The answer is in the final chapter of this book)*

Pears

Pears Ltd is the holding company of a trading group. The group consists of the following companies.

> Apple Ltd is a 90% subsidiary of Pears Ltd.
> Banana Ltd is a 100% subsidiary of Pears Ltd.
> Orange Ltd is a 51% subsidiary of Pears Ltd.
> Nectarine Ltd is a 100% subsidiary of Orange Ltd.
> Pomegranate Ltd is a 75% subsidiary of Apple Ltd.

For the accounting period ending 31 March 2004, all companies having the same year end, the following is contemplated.

(1)   Banana Ltd has allowable capital losses of £500,000 at 1 April 2003. It is proposed that all members of the group sell investment assets at full market value to Banana Ltd for onward sale outside the group.

(2)   Pomegranate Ltd has an investment in quoted shares currently valued at £400,000, the disposal of which would give rise to a chargeable gain of £175,000. It is intended that Pomegranate Ltd will sell the investments, for current value, to Pears Ltd, the consideration being settled in cash.

Required

Explain the capital gains implications of the actions contemplated.

Approach to the question

 It is essential to draw a group structure to identify the qualifying 75% capital gains group or groups.

Consider each of the suggestions separately with reference to the information in the group diagram.

4 Consortia

4.1 Definition

A consortium exists where two or more companies (UK or overseas) own at least 75% of another company, and each company's holding is at least 5%. Ownership includes ordinary shares and assets and profits as for a 75% group.

The investing companies are *consortium members*.

The target company is a *consortium owned company*.

The difference between a UK tax group and a consortium is illustrated as follows.

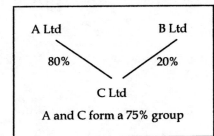

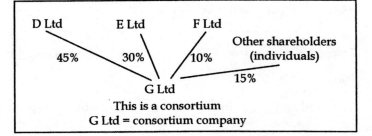

Figure 1 demonstrates that where a company (C Ltd) is controlled at the 75% level by *one* company then it cannot be a consortium company, because at least two companies must have 75% control between them. However, it is possible for a company to be a consortium company and be a member of a 51% group, as the illustration below demonstrates.

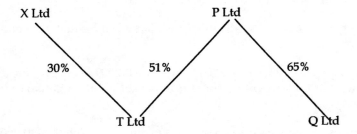

PQT are a 51% group.

PXT is a consortium with T as the consortium company.

Qualification as a consortium company is extended to cover the following specific situation.

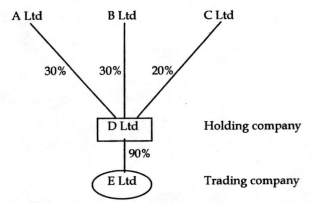

The consortium members own a consortium company which in turn holds at least 90% of a trading company. In effect the trading company is treated as the consortium company.

Practice question 3 *(The answer is in the final chapter of this book)*

Zoo plc

Zoo plc is the holding company for a group of companies. The group structure is as follows.

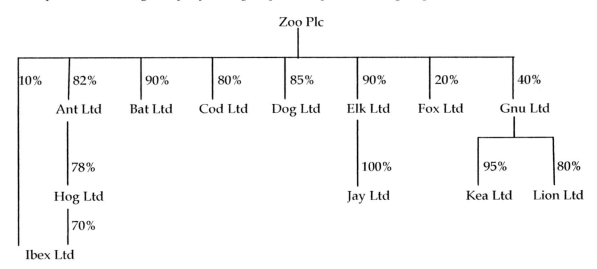

Each percentage shareholding represents a holding of ordinary share capital. The remaining share capital of Fox Ltd is held by Unit plc. The remaining share capital of Gnu Ltd is held equally by Volt plc and Watt plc. Unit plc, Volt plc and Watt plc are not otherwise connected with the Zoo plc group of companies. The remaining share capital of all the other companies is held by individual members of the general public. The shareholdings will all be held throughout the year ended 31 March 2004, with the exception of Zoo plc's 90% shareholding in Bat Ltd, which was acquired on 1 December 2003, and its 80% shareholding in Cod Ltd which was sold on 30 November 2003.

All of the Zoo plc group of companies have an accounting date of 31 March, with the exception of Bat Ltd which has an accounting date of 30 November. Bat Ltd is to produce accounts for the four month period to 31 March 2004 so as to make its accounting period coterminous with the other group companies.

The companies are all resident in the UK except for Elk Ltd, which is resident in the country of Overseabia. The companies are all trading companies except for Zoo plc and Gnu Ltd, which are holding companies, and Dog Ltd which has not yet commenced trading. For the year ended 31 March 2004, the trading companies are all forecast to be profitable, although some of them have made trading losses in the past.

Required

(a)   State the number of associates that Zoo plc has and the upper and lower limits for small companies' rate purposes. State also the starting rate thresholds.

(b)   Define the main 75% group as at 31 March 2004.

(c)   If a 51% group level of control was required, how would this be different to (b)?

(d)   Identify any consortia.

4.2 Consequences

Consortium relief can be claimed. This is a special type of group relief.

4.3 Differences between consortium relief and group relief

There are two major differences between consortium relief and group relief.

♦ Relief is limited to the relevant percentage of the consortium owned company's profit or loss.

♦ The amount of loss a consortium owned company can surrender is reduced by its own current year profits.

These distinctions are best demonstrated by considering the following examples.

4.4 Examples

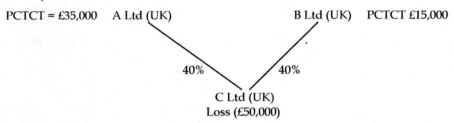

PCTCT = £35,000   A Ltd (UK)   B Ltd (UK)   PCTCT £15,000

40%   40%

C Ltd (UK)
Loss (£50,000)

ABC is a consortium as AB combined own at least 75% of C Ltd.

A consortium member (ie A Ltd or B Ltd) is entitled to a percentage share of C Ltd (consortium company). Where C Ltd has a loss as above, A Ltd is entitled to 40% of (£50,000) ie (£20,000). C Ltd could never surrender a greater amount than £20,000, although it may surrender less. This is in contrast to a 75% group where, if A Ltd owns C Ltd 75%, then C Ltd could surrender the whole loss.

The claimant company (whether under consortium relief or group relief) cannot claim more loss than required to cover the available PCTCT.

A Ltd PCTCT £35,000 –   relief is limited to the £20,000 maximum that can be surrendered by C Ltd

B Ltd PCTCT £15,000 –   relief is limited to £15,000 maximum

Where the consortium company (C Ltd) has a *profit* and a consortium member (eg A Ltd) wants to surrender a loss, the maximum is again restricted to the 'share of the profit' to which A Ltd is entitled. This is illustrated below.

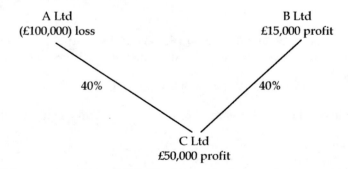

A Ltd
(£100,000) loss

B Ltd
£15,000 profit

40%   40%

C Ltd
£50,000 profit

The maximum consortium relief A Ltd could surrender is *not* 40% of (£100,000) but 40% of £50,000 profit, ie £20,000.

The second distinction concerns a restriction on the amount a consortium company (ie C Ltd) can surrender where it has other profits of its own. Suppose that C Ltd has a trading loss of £100,000 and DIII income of £10,000.

♦ If C Ltd is in a 75% group it could surrender £100,000 (ie total amount).

♦ If C Ltd is a consortium *member* it could surrender the total amount, assuming that its share of the consortium company's profits was sufficient to absorb it.

♦ If C Ltd is a consortium *company* it can only surrender £90,000. This is because a consortium company must use its loss against its own current year profit *before* surrendering to consortium members.

Note also that although consortium members can be resident anywhere in the world, only a UK resident consortium member can claim or surrender losses. This is relaxed, however, for non-resident companies with trading profits or losses of a UK branch or agency just as applies for group relief.

4.5 Flow through arrangements

Where a consortium member is also a member of a group, it is a 'link' company and acts as a route for losses to flow between the group and the consortium company.

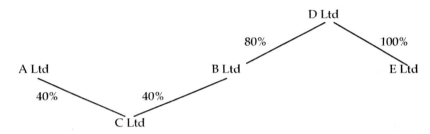

A Ltd and B Ltd are consortium members with C Ltd as the consortium company. B Ltd is also in a 75% group with D Ltd and E Ltd.

40% of C Ltd's losses can be surrendered against the PCTCT of B Ltd, D Ltd or E Ltd (or any mixture thereof).

Similarly, if C Ltd has a profit, 40% of the profit can be relieved by the losses of B Ltd, D Ltd and E Ltd in any combination.

This is just an extension of consortium relief allowing losses to flow (either way) between the consortium company and the consortium member's group.

4.6 Group consortium company

A group consortium company is a company which is owned by a consortium and is also the parent company of a group.

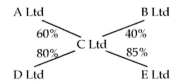

A Ltd and B Ltd are consortium members.

C Ltd is a group consortium company.

D Ltd and E Ltd are members of the C Ltd group.

In this situation both group relief and consortium relief could be available. Priority is given to group relief.

♦ If C Ltd makes a loss, the amount of consortium relief available is calculated on the assumption that the maximum possible group relief has been claimed by D Ltd and E Ltd.

♦ If A Ltd or B Ltd make a loss, the profits of C Ltd available for consortium relief is calculated assuming the maximum possible group relief has been claimed by C Ltd for any losses of D Ltd and E Ltd. Any actual group relief claims made by D Ltd and E Ltd are taken into account in determining the maximum possible group relief available to C Ltd.

4.7 Example

The results of each company for the year to 31 March 2004 are:

	PCTCT/(loss) £
A Ltd	100,000
B Ltd	20,000
C Ltd	(80,000)
D Ltd	5,000
E Ltd	15,000

D Ltd and E Ltd are assumed to have claimed group relief of £5,000 and £15,000 respectively.

The loss of C Ltd available for consortium relief is £(80,000 – 5,000 – 15,000) = £60,000.

A Ltd can claim consortium relief of 60% × £60,000 = £36,000.

B Ltd can claim consortium relief of £20,000, as this is less than 40% × £60,000 = £24,000.

4.8 Example

The results of each company for the year to 31 March 2004 are instead:

	PCTCT/(loss) £
A Ltd	(100,000)
B Ltd	20,000
C Ltd	80,000
D Ltd	5,000
E Ltd	(15,000)

♦ If no group relief is claimed by D Ltd for E Ltd's loss, C Ltd's profits available for consortium relief are £(80,000 – 15,000) = £65,000. The consortium relief that can be claimed in respect of A Ltd's loss is 60% × £65,000 = £39,000.

♦ If group relief is claimed by D Ltd for E Ltd's loss, C Ltd's profits available for consortium relief are £(80,000 – (15,000 – 5,000)) = £70,000. The consortium relief that can be claimed in respect of A Ltd's loss is 60% × £70,000 = £42,000.

Practice question 4 *(The answer is in the final chapter of this book)*

A Ltd group

The group structure below shows the various holdings in ordinary shares in other companies. All of the companies are UK resident except for O Inc which is foreign resident and does not trade through a UK permanent establishment.

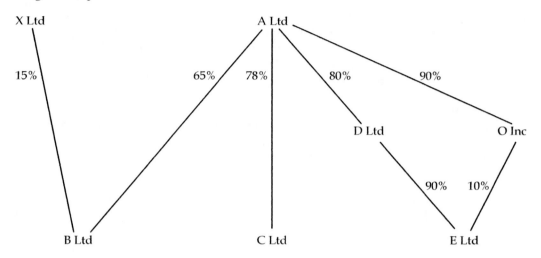

The results for each of the above companies for the accounting year ended 31 March 2004 were as follows.

X Ltd	Loss	(40,000)
B Ltd	Profit	80,000
A Ltd	Profit	103,000
C Ltd	Loss	(60,000)
D Ltd	Profit	35,000
O Inc (foreign resident)	Loss	(30,000)
E Ltd	Loss	(8,000)

Required

(a)   Identify, from the above diagram, the associated companies for small company rate purposes and state the upper and lower thresholds for each of the companies shown. State also the starting rate thresholds.

(b)   Identify any groups and consortia in the above structure qualifying for group relief.

(c)   Compute the MCT payable by each company, assuming loss relief has been claimed in the most efficient manner.

(d)   Advise the directors of A Ltd on the weakness, from a tax point of view, of the existing structure.

Approach to part (c)

Where there are a number of losses in a question, you need to deal with the losses with the most restricted set off first. In a group context, this means you should consider losses in the following order.

♦   Losses which cannot be surrendered to other group members
♦   Losses which can only be surrendered to one other group member
♦   Losses where there are a number of different options.

5 Anti-avoidance

5.1 Introduction

To prevent companies acquiring subsidiaries in order to make use of any losses they may have, there are anti-avoidance rules restricting the use of pre-entry losses and gains.

5.2 Trading losses

Trading losses carried forward can only be set against future profits of the *same* trade. If a trade of a company ceases and a new trade commences, or if the trade changes substantially, then trading losses can no longer be carried forward as the trade is not the same. The restriction on the carry forward of trading losses also applies where a company's activities are negligible prior to a change in ownership and there is a significant revival afterwards.

In addition, the ability to carry trading losses forward is affected where there is *both* a major change in the conduct of the trade *and* a change of ownership within a three year period.

This will be most relevant in group situations where new subsidiaries are acquired or disposed of, as this will constitute a change of ownership.

The new parent company will have to be careful that the trade of a newly acquired subsidiary is not substantially changed for three years or had not been substantially changed in the previous three years. Otherwise the anti-avoidance rules below will apply.

The rules impact as follows.

♦ A trading loss incurred before the change in ownership will not be available for set-off against trading profits arising after the change in ownership.

♦ A trading loss incurred after the change in ownership will not be capable of carry back to a time period before the change in ownership.

This illustrates that the 'block' operates both ways in that a trading loss can neither be carried forward nor carried back where there is a 'change'.

5.3 Pre entry capital losses

At one time companies with large realised capital losses were acquired by groups, so that they could relieve large potential gains using the transfer of assets mechanism.

This loophole was closed with the effect that when a company joins a qualifying capital gains group, it must identify its capital losses (realised and unrealised) at the point of entry. Such capital losses are *not* available for relief except against capital gains on:

♦ own assets held at point of entry

♦ new assets acquired from outside the group for use in a trade existing before it joined the group.

Losses unrealised at the point of entry are normally recognised by time apportionment, but the company can elect for an actual basis, ie by reference to the market value of the asset at the time of entry.

5.4 Example

Techno Ltd was acquired by Forstall Ltd on 30 June 2000. At the date of acquisition, Techno Ltd owned a freehold building with a market value of £180,000 which had cost £220,000 on 30 June 1997. The building was eventually sold on 30 June 2004 for £78,000.

Required

Show the two calculations of the pre-entry loss and comment.

5.5 Solution

		£	£
(i)	Loss by reference to MV at 30 June 2000:		
	220,000 – 180,000		40,000
(ii)	Loss by time apportionment:		
	Total loss 220,000 – 78,000 =	142,000	
	Loss arising up to 30 June 2000:		

$$\frac{30\,June\,1997 - 30\,June\,2000}{30\,June\,1997 - 30\,June\,2004} = \frac{3}{7} \times 142,000 \qquad = \qquad 60,857$$

The lower amount is preferable as this maximises the post-acquisition loss for which the anti-avoidance restrictions do not apply.

5.6 Pre entry capital gains

Similar anti-avoidance rules prevent a group with an unrealised capital loss artificially utilising the loss through the acquisition of a subsidiary with a realised capital gain.

A pre entry capital gain is one which arises in the part of the accounting period immediately prior to a company joining a group.

Pre entry gains can only be matched against:

♦ losses made by the subsidiary before it joined the group
♦ losses arising from assets held by the subsidiary when it joined the group.

6 Alternative methods of acquisition

6.1 Overview

There are two main methods of acquiring the business of another company

♦ The purchase of its shares
♦ The purchase of its assets and trade

In each situation it is necessary to consider the implications for

♦ the vendor
♦ the purchaser
♦ the company itself.

6.2 *Acquisition of shares*

The typical scenario is as follows. Y Ltd group holds 100% of the shares in Z Ltd. All of the shares in Z Ltd are purchased by the X Ltd group.

Before	After
Y Ltd	X Ltd
|100%	|100%
Z Ltd	Z Ltd

Vendor's position (Y Ltd)

♦ On the sale of Z Ltd, there is a disposal of the shares. This will give rise to a capital gain (or loss) which is subject to corporation tax, unless the substantial shareholdings exemption applies.

♦ Group relief (the use of trading losses etc) will be available between the Y Ltd group and Z Ltd up to the date of sale, provided 'arrangements' for the sale were not in existence before that date.

♦ No rollover relief is available on the sale of company shares if the gain is chargeable.

♦ From the beginning of the next accounting period there will be one less associate.

♦ The need to remove the company from VAT group registration (see Chapter 14).

Purchaser's position (X Ltd)

♦ The base cost of the investment, for capital gains purposes, is the price paid for the shares. Stamp duty at the rate of 0.5% is also payable.

♦ Group relief will be available from the date of purchase.

♦ An immediate increase in the number of associated companies.

♦ A consideration of the VAT position of the company and whether a group VAT registration is required (see Chapter 14).

♦ The new subsidiary will qualify for transfer of assets under nil gain nil loss provisions.

♦ The purchaser acquires the company and therefore the losses contained in the company for carry forward (ie trading, capital). Consideration will be needed of the various anti-avoidance provisions. In particular, the group cannot make use of any pre-entry gains and losses.

♦ The target company's tax history is inherited on the acquisition of shares, therefore it is advisable to obtain indemnities from the vendor to cover any outstanding tax and tax related penalties for pre-acquisition events.

The company's position (Z Ltd)

♦ The company's *ownership only* changes. This means that its trade continues and its assets continue to attract capital allowances on tax written down values.

♦ Where the company is leaving one group to join another, then there may be a crystallisation of previous no gain/no loss intra-group transfers, made in the previous six years.

♦ The carry forward of unused trading losses may be prevented if there is a major change in the nature or conduct of the trade in any three year period straddling the date of acquisition.

6.3   *Acquisition of assets and trade*

The alternative route is to acquire the assets and trade of the company. The most important point to note here is that when this occurs the vendor is the *company* itself.

The following figure illustrates the situation.

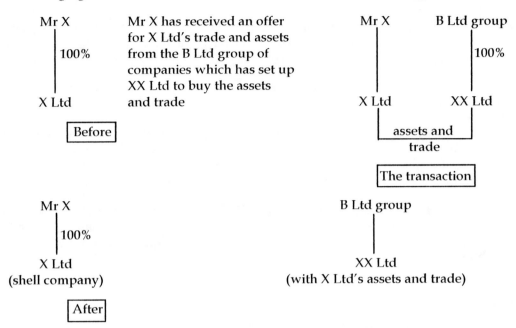

Mr X still owns X Ltd but this is now an 'empty' company; its trade has ceased. Its assets have been sold at market value. XX Ltd commences to trade with X Ltd's assets acquired at market value.

Under this method of acquisition, the purchase price must be allocated between the various assets acquired.

Vendor's position (X Ltd)

♦   There will be balancing adjustments (ie balancing charges or allowances) on the sale of its assets qualifying for capital allowances.

♦   There will be capital gains and/or losses. Gains may be deferred using rollover relief if the relevant reinvestment is made by the company itself (X Ltd) or by a group company, if it is in a group situation.

♦   X Ltd retains its own trading or capital losses. However, if the whole trade is sold, then it is deemed to cease and the losses will also cease.

♦   The transfer of trade will usually qualify as a going concern transfer and be outside the scope of VAT. In this case there will be no output tax to account for but X Ltd will have to notify Customs that its registration should cease (see Chapter 14).

The implications for the buyer company or group

♦   Stamp duty land tax is payable on land, such as freehold property. This can be as high as 4% where total of land transferred exceeds £500,000 in value.

♦   The buyer will be entitled to capital allowances on the market value of the assets acquired for plant and machinery, or under the secondhand building rules for industrial building purposes.

♦   The buyer will not acquire losses or any liabilities. These stay with X Ltd.

♦   The buyer company will normally need to register for VAT, if not already registered, in order for the business transfer to be outside the scope of VAT (see Chapter 14).

7 Summary

This chapter demonstrates that both written and computational elements are likely in a typical examination question. For both types of question, you need to adopt a methodical approach to the key implications. You should initially sort out the key relationships between group members. These are summarised below

Associated companies – one company is under the control of another, or two or more companies are controlled by the same person. The upper and lower limits for both small companies' rate and the new starting rate of corporation tax are shared equally between associated companies.

75% group relief – this requires over 75% effective interest. It enables trading losses to be transferred from one group member to another.

75% capital gains group – this requires a 75% shareholding, but an effective interest of only just over 50%. It ensures intra-group transfers of assets take place on a no gain no loss basis. Group members can elect which company is to be treated for tax purposes as having made a disposal outside the group. All group members are treated as one for the purpose of rollover relief.

Consortium – two or more companies own over 75% of the share capital of another. This enables losses to be transferred between the consortium owned company and the members according to their percentage shareholdings. There are no capital gains reliefs available specifically to a consortium.

Multiple choice questions 1 - 6 *(The answers are in the final chapter of this book)*

Each of the questions below has only one correct answer.

1   The structure of the Rainbow group during the year ended 31 March 2004 was as follows.

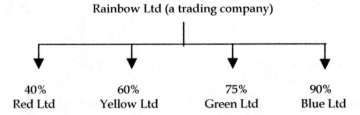

Rainbow Ltd (a trading company)

| 40% | 60% | 75% | 90% |
| Red Ltd | Yellow Ltd | Green Ltd | Blue Ltd |

Green Ltd was disposed of on 30 September 2003. Yellow Ltd was acquired on 1 October 2003.

How many companies are associated for the purposes of determining Rainbow Ltd's corporation tax rate for the year ended 31 March 2004?

A   Two

B   Three

C   Four

D   Five

2   Helton plc and its wholly-owned subsidiary Sithney plc had the following results for the year ended 31 March 2004.

	Helton plc £	Sithney plc £
Schedule D Case I	8,000 loss	12,000 profit
Schedule D Case III	3,000	-
Trading losses brought forward at 1 April 2003	1,000	5,000

What is the maximum amount of group relief that can be claimed by Sithney plc?

A   £5,000

B   £6,000

C   £7,000

D   £8,000

3   Mat Ltd has the following holdings in its subsidiaries.

60% of Neath Ltd
90% of Powys Ltd

Powys Ltd has a subsidiary, Quorn Ltd, of which it owns 80% of the issued share capital.

Between which companies is group relief for losses available?

A   Mat Ltd and Powys Ltd only

B   Mat Ltd, Powys Ltd and Quorn Ltd only

C   Mat Ltd, Neath Ltd and Powys Ltd only

D   Mat Ltd, Neath Ltd, Powys Ltd and Quorn Ltd

4   Holding Ltd owns 100% of the share capital of Sub Ltd and there are no other companies in the group. Both companies have traded since 1 April 2002. In the two years ended 31 March 2003 and 2004, the companies' adjusted Schedule D Case I profits/(losses) were as follows.

	2003 £	2004 £
Holding Ltd	159,000	(124,000)
Sub Ltd	130,000	265,000

What assessable profits will be left in the charge to tax in Sub Ltd for the year ended 31 March 2004 if all available reliefs are utilised to minimise the tax payable?

A   £141,000

B   £150,000

C   £155,000

D   £265,000

5   The following is the structure of the Pets group.

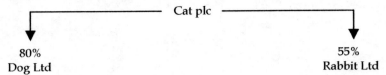

Cat plc acquired an asset for £10,000 and sold it to Dog Ltd for £16,000 when its market value was £18,000.

If Dog Ltd transferred the asset to Rabbit Ltd when its market value was £20,000, what chargeable gains would arise? (Ignore indexation).

A   No chargeable gain arises until the asset is disposed of by Rabbit Ltd to a third party

B   Cat plc would have a gain of £10,000

C   Cat plc would have a gain of £6,000 and Dog Ltd a gain of £4,000

D   Dog Ltd would have a gain of £10,000

6   Wind Ltd and Sail Ltd, its 100% owned subsidiary, prepare accounts to 31 March. In April 1995 Wind Ltd bought an asset for £2,000 and sold it to Sail Ltd in June 1999 for its market value of £6,000. In February 2004 Sail Ltd was sold, at which time the asset was worth £11,000.

Ignoring indexation allowance, Sail Ltd will be assessed to a chargeable gain of

A   £4,000 in the year ended 31 March 2000

B   £5,000 in the year ended 31 March 2000

C   £4,000 on 1 April 2003

D   £5,000 on 1 April 2003

CHAPTER 11

Further aspects of corporation tax

EXAM FOCUS

In Chapters 1 and 2 you learned how to calculate a company's PCTCT and its CT liability. The topics covered in those two chapters are likely to be examined in virtually every paper. This chapter expands on that knowledge and applies it to other areas of corporation tax which are likely to be examined on a less regular basis.

LEARNING OUTCOMES

This chapter covers the following learning outcomes of the CIMA syllabus:

> Calculate the CT liability of a company (including that of small and intermediate companies)

> Contrast the tax implications of financing a company by debt or equity .

In order to cover these learning outcomes the following topics are included:

> Long accounting periods
> Close companies
> Debt and equity finance.

---

1 Long accounting periods

1.1 Introduction

In Chapter 1 you learned that, although a company can draw up financial accounts for a period of more than 12 months, a company's 'chargeable accounting period' (CAP) for corporation tax purposes can never exceed 12 months. Therefore if the financial accounts cover more than 12 months, *two* chargeable accounting periods are required; one for the first 12 months and one for the balance. This section tackles the allocation of income, gains and charges between the two periods, in finding PCTCT.

The table below summarises the rules to be used.

Table 1.1   Allocating income and expenses between CAPs

Item	*Method of allocation*
Trading income before deducting capital allowances	Time apportioned
Capital allowances	Separate computation for each accounting period (see Chapters 4 and 5)
Rents etc under Schedule A	Time apportioned
Schedule DVI (eg, commissions)	Period for which accrued (if the question provides sufficient information)
Schedule DIII	Period for which accrued (if the question provides sufficient information)
Chargeable capital gains	Period of disposal
Charges (eg, Gift Aid)	Period *paid*

Do not miscalculate the number of months in the second period – double check it – as it is crucial for time apportioning calculations and easy to get wrong.

1.2 Example

Printer Ltd has made up accounts for the 17 months to 30 June 2003, with the following information.

	£
Adjusted trading profit before capital allowances	365,000
Building society interest	
Received 30 April 2002 (of which £1,950 related to year ended 31 January 2002)	2,450
Received 30 April 2003	2,675
Accrued on 30 June 2003	200
Rents from property	26,010
Chargeable gains	
Disposal on 31 January 2003	28,700
Disposal on 1 February 2003	49,760
Dividend received from UK company (gross amount) on 1 December 2002	10,000
Gift Aid paid	
Paid 31 July 2002	6,000
Paid 31 January 2003	6,000

Capital allowances for the two CAPs derived from the 17 month period of account are £20,000 and £6,250 respectively.

Show how the company's period of accounts will be divided into CAPs and compute the PCTCT for each CAP. All income is deemed to accrue evenly where relevant.

1.3 Solution

The procedure to be followed is exactly the same as for a 12 month period, but incorporating the allocation rules.

	12 months to 31 January 2003	*5 months to 30 June 2003*
	£	£
Schedule D Case I (W1)	237,647	101,103
Schedule D Case III (W2)	2,382	993
Schedule A (W3)	18,360	7,650
Gains (date of transaction)	28,700	49,760
Less Charges (W4)	(12,000)	Nil
PCTCT	275,089	159,506

Note The dividend received is not relevant for PCTCT.

Workings

(W1)   Schedule D Case I

	Total	*12m*	*5m*
	£	£	£
Adjusted profit (See note)	365,000	257,647	107,353
Capital allowances		(20,000)	(6,250)
		237,647	101,103

Note   Trading profit is time apportioned.

(W2)   Building society interest

The amount which would be included in the profit and loss account for the 17 month period on the accruals basis would be as follows.

		£	12m	5m
Received	30 April 2002	2,450		
	30 April 2003	2,675		
Add	Year end accrual	200		
Less	Opening accrual	(1,950)		
	(See note)	3,375	2,382	993

Note   This is then time-apportioned as the accrual at 31 January 2003 is not supplied.

(W3)   Schedule A

Rental income is assessable under Schedule A, which is assessed on an accrued basis for the 17 months and then time apportioned into the 2 CAPs.

£	12m	5m
26,010	18,360	7,650

(W4)   Charges are relevant when *paid*

	£
31 July 2002	6,000
31 January 2003	6,000
	12,000 in year ended 31 January 2003

Nil in five months to 30 June 2003 as none paid.

The procedure for finding the corporation tax liability now follows the rules outlined earlier, except that you have *two* calculations. The point to watch, however, is that as the second computation is the 'balance' of the accounts it will always be a *short* period. The limits of £300,000 and £1,500,000 therefore need to be reduced proportionately when considering the tax rate to apply.

1.4   Example

Now calculate the CT liability for Printer Ltd for its two accounting periods.

1.5   Solution

Step 1

	12 months to 31 January 2003 £	5 months to 30 June 2003 £
PCTCT (as above)	275,089	159,506
FII (received December 2002)	10,000	–
'Profits'	285,089	159,506

Step 2

Matching the financial years

	FY01 2 months	FY02 10 months	FY02 2 months	FY03 3 months
Lower limit (annual) ($\frac{5}{12}$)	£300,000 small rate		£125,000 marginal	
Upper limit ($\frac{5}{12}$)			£625,000	
Rates to apply	20%	19%	30%	30%

Step 3

	12 months to 31 January 2003 £
PCTCT of £275,089	
£275,089 × $\frac{2}{12}$ × 20%	9,170
£275,089 × $\frac{10}{12}$ × 19%	43,556
CT liability	52,726

	5 months to 30 June 2003 £
PCTCT £159,506 × 30%	47,852
Less marginal relief $\frac{11}{400}$ (£625,000 – £159,506)	(12,801)
CT liability	35,051

As you can see, it is possible to have different tax rates applying even though the information is generated from the same set of accounts.

Practice question 2 (The answer is in the final chapter of this book)

Chinny

Chinny Ltd has for many years prepared accounts to 30 September, but changes its accounting date to 31 December by preparing accounts for the 15 months ended 31 December 2003. The accounts show a profit, as adjusted for tax purposes (but before deducting capital allowances), of £250,000.

Capital allowances for the two CAPs based on the 15 month period of account were £13,450 and £5,818 respectively.

The company also had income in the period as follows.

Building society interest receivable	1 October 2002 – 30 September 2003	£4,420
	1 October 2003 – 31 December 2003	£780
Capital gains	Disposal 15 December 2003	£55,000
Rents received	31 July 2003	£8,000

The rents accrued at 30 September 2002 and 31 December 2003 were £3,000 and £5,000 respectively.

Required

Calculate the amounts of corporation tax payable for this 15 month period of account.

Approach to the question

The approach is exactly the same as developed in Chapter 1, except that you are preparing *two* computations. You first need to check in any question whether the accounts provided exceed 12 months, and determine the CAPs needed.

2 Close companies

2.1 Definition

A close company is essentially a company controlled by either:

♦ five or fewer participators (ie shareholders) or
♦ any number of directors.

Control exists where the participators/directors

♦ hold more than 50% of the issued share capital or the voting rights, or
♦ are entitled to more than 50% of the distributable profits or the net assets in a winding up.

In determining whether control exists, the holdings of associates are taken into account. An associate of a participator is his or her spouse, sibling, (grand) child, (grand) parent or business partner.

The term 'director' includes

♦ any person holding the position of director
♦ any person in accordance with whose instructions the other directors are accustomed to act
♦ any manager who owns 20% or more of the company's ordinary share capital.

2.2 Implications of close company status

The key implications concern the treatment of certain transactions between the close company and its shareholders. The measures are designed to ensure that shareholders and directors cannot use their control over the company to obtain tax advantages. This will be the case in many family companies.

The principal measures cover:

♦ the provision of benefits to shareholders
♦ the provision of loans to shareholders.

In considering the measures, the precise status of the individual must be identified, as this determines both the company's and the individual's tax implications.

♦ The individual may be a shareholder only.
♦ Or he may be both shareholder and director (or employee).

2.3 The provision of benefits

The provision of a benefit to an individual who is a director or employee is covered by the employment income rules. The calculation of amounts assessable under these rules will be covered in Chapter 15.

For the company, expenditure on the provision of benefits to employees and directors is deductible under Schedule DI, as provision of remuneration (in whatever form) is wholly and exclusively for the business.

The provision of a benefit to an individual who is *not* a director or employee *cannot* be assessed on the individual under the employment income rules as there is no office or employment. The provision is instead treated as a distribution of profit. The tax implications for the company are as follows.

♦ The company is deemed to have paid a dividend.

♦ The *amount* (ie value) of the dividend is determined using the benefit rules.

♦ There will, however, be no Schedule DI deduction as the cost of providing the benefit is not 'wholly and exclusively' for business purposes.

2.4 The provision of a loan

The provision of a loan to a shareholder, irrespective of his employment status, has the following implications for the company.

♦ There is a tax charge on the company equal to 25% of the loan advance. This charge is paid at the same time as the mainstream tax (ie nine months following the end of the accounting period) unless the loan has been repaid before that due date. The tax is commonly referred to as 'penalty tax'.

♦ The charge exists to discourage companies from making loans to shareholders.

♦ This tax payment cannot be relieved in any way (ie it cannot be set against profits or the company's CT liability).

♦ The tax is repaid when the loan (or any part thereof) is repaid or the loan is written off. The tax repayment is made nine months after the end of the accounting period in which the loan is repaid or written off.

♦ The reason the tax is repaid if the loan is written off, is that the individual is assessed to tax instead.

The above implications will not apply where the loan fulfils three requirements.

♦ The amount loaned does not exceed £15,000.
♦ The individual is a full-time working employee.
♦ The individual (including associates' interests) owns less than 5% of the shares.

2.5 Example

Nichole and Michele are both shareholders and full time employees in Munch Ltd, a close company. Nichole owns 25% of the company, whilst Michele owns 4%. They are not connected with each other. The company loans each of them £10,000, on 6 April 2003 in the year to 31 March 2004. No interest is charged on the loans.

Required

What are the taxation implications for Munch Ltd?

2.6 Solution

Only the loan to Nichole is caught by the provisions as she owns more than 5% of the share capital. Therefore £10,000 × 25% = £2,500 tax charge to be paid on 1 January 2005. If any part of the loan is repaid by 1 January 2005 then this tax charge is reduced accordingly.

The £2,500 cannot be off set against the company's corporation tax liability and will not be recoverable until the loan is repaid, or written off.

The loan to Michele is not caught by the close company provisions as she owns less than 5% of the share capital, the loan is less than £15,000, and she is a full-time working employee.

Both employees will be assessable under the employment income rules on the benefit of the use of money interest free (see Chapter 15).

2.7 Other close company implications

Where a company is close, but is not a trading company, then it will be classed as a close investment holding company (CIHC). As such, it will be required to pay corporation tax at the ordinary rate (currently 30%), irrespective of the level of profits.

3 Debt and equity finance

3.1 Introduction

Companies have two main ways of financing their operations

♦ debt finance, such as loans and overdrafts
♦ equity finance, such as a new issue of ordinary shares.

These two methods of finance have very different impacts on the corporation tax computation.

3.2 Debt Finance

Debt finance is serviced by the payment of interest. The treatment of interest was covered earlier when we looked at the loan relationship rules. To summarise, payments of interest for trading purposes are deductible in computing Schedule DI profits. Interest paid on a non-trading loan is set against Schedule D III income and any deficit allowed against other profits. This means that interest payments (trading or non-trading) reduce the company's chargeable profits and hence its corporation tax liability.

Repayments of loan capital have no direct impact on either the chargeable profits or the CT liability.

3.3 Example

Borrower Ltd makes trading profits of £200,000 annually. The company needs to purchase some replacement plant and is therefore going to issue £50,000 of debentures paying interest at the rate of 10%.

Required

What impact will the new debentures have on the company's CT liability?

3.4 Solution

Prior to issuing the debentures, the company's CT liability was as follows:

> PCTCT £200,000 × 19% = £38,000

The payment of debenture interest of £5,000 (£50,000 × 10%) is deductible in computing the Schedule DI profits. The company's PCTCT will therefore be reduced to £195,000 (£200,000 - £5,000). Its CT liability will now be £37,050 (£195,000 × 19%).

The payment of debenture interest has therefore reduced the CT liability by £950 (£5,000 × 19%).

Note that although the debentures are paying interest at the rate of 10%, the CT relief reduces this to a real rate of only 8.1%.

	£
Interest payable	5,000
Less CT saving	(950)
Real cost of interest	4,050

£4,050/£50,000 = 8.1%

3.5 Commercial impact

Although debt finance has the benefit of being deductible in computing taxable profits, there is an administrative cost which needs to be taken into account. Companies must pay loan and debenture interest net of 20% income tax when the recipients are individuals. The tax deducted needs to be accounted for under the quarterly CT61 system outlined in Chapter 2.

Interest is a burden which must be met when it falls due. A bank or debenture holder may be able to appoint a receiver to realise sufficient of the company's assets to repay the loan if the company defaults on interest payments. This could prejudice the company's ability to continue trading.

3.6 Equity Finance

 Equity finance is serviced by the payment of dividends. Dividends are not deductible in computing taxable profits. They therefore have no impact on a company's CT liability. Now that ACT has been abolished, the payment of dividends carries no administrative requirements for tax purposes.

Except in the case of preference dividends, the company can choose whether or not to pay a dividend and can set the rate. This can be commercially safer for the company (if not for the 'lenders') than using debt finance. Equity finance is sometimes called 'risk' capital – the risk being for the shareholder.

3.7 Enterprise Investment Scheme (EIS)

Unquoted trading companies may encourage investment through the Enterprise Investment Scheme. This offers certain tax advantages to individuals who subscribe for ordinary shares, including

- 20% income tax relief on the amount subscribed

- tax free capital gains provided the shares are held for at least three years

- CGT reinvestment relief, enabling the investor to defer gains realised on the disposal of other assets. The amount deferred cannot exceed the amount invested, and will crystallise on the disposal of the EIS shares.

In order to obtain these reliefs, the investor must not be connected with the company before the share issue. Connected means

- being an employee or director, or
- owning over 30% of the share capital.

The individual can, however, become a paid director or employee after the share issue.

The company must also satisfy certain conditions

- at the date of the share issue there must be no arrangements in existence for it to become quoted (though there is no requirement that it remains unquoted for a minimum period).

- its assets must not exceed £15 million immediately before, or £16 million immediately after, the share issue

- it must carry on a qualifying trade. This term excludes financial activities, legal and accountancy services and property development.

3.8 Venture capital trusts (VCTs)

Unquoted trading companies can also generate equity capital through the medium of venture capital trusts.

VCTs are quoted on the stock exchange, take subscription money from investors and subscribe for shares in unquoted trading companies. The investors are thereby spreading their risk and able, in theory, to readily realise their investment.

A VCT must invest at least 70% of its funds in unquoted companies (maximum 15% in any one), of which 30% must be in new ordinary shares. The maximum assets of each company is £16 million.

The investor in a VCT receives 20% income tax relief for subscribing up to £100,000 in new shares in any one tax year. There is an added income tax advantage (not available to EIS investments) that VCT dividends are tax free. However, income from the underlying investments is probably spent on VCT manager's fees leaving little income for dividends!

The VCT investor is entitled to CGT reinvestment relief.

The main difference between direct EIS investment and investing through a VCT are the commercial factors of the lesser risk of VCTs and their realisability.

3.9 Other methods of finance

Companies may choose to finance the purchase of assets by leasing or hire purchase.

♦ Leasing costs are deductible in computing chargeable profits.

♦ If an asset is bought on hire purchase, the cash price may qualify for capital allowances. The interest charges are deductible in computing chargeable profits.

4 Summary

A company's chargeable accounting period (CAP) can never exceed 12 months. Where the financial accounts exceed 12 months, they should be divided into a CAP covering the first 12 months and a CAP covering the balance.

Close companies are companies controlled by five or fewer participators, or by any number of participators who are also directors. There are extra rules for close companies to prevent them obtaining tax advantages.

A company may finance its operations using debt or equity. The cost of debt finance is deductible in computing chargeable profits, but the cost of equity finance is not. Capital repayments, whether debt or equity, are never deductible.

Multiple choice questions 1 - 5 *(The answers are in the final chapter of this book)*

Each of the questions below has only one correct answer.

1   Gensing Ltd has a 15 month period of account to 30 September 2003. The company purchased a car on 4 August 2003 for £9,000. The capital allowances pool, brought forward at 1 July 2002 was £18,000.

What are the maximum capital allowances which may be claimed for the period of account?

A   £5,906

B   £6,244

C   £7,594

D   £8,437

2   Freeman Ltd, a small company with 25 employees, has always prepared accounts to 31 March until it changed its accounting date to 30 June and prepared accounts for 15 months to 30 June 2004.

The tax written down value of the general plant pool at 1 April 2003 was £3,500.

During the period of account the following transactions in motor cars took place.

| 10 January 2004 | Sold car | £4,500 |
| 3 March 2004 | Purchased second-hand car | £7,500 |

What are the capital allowances for the accounting period ended 30 June 2004?

A   £305

B   £ 352

C   £1,570

D   £1,930

3   Histon plc drew up accounts for the 15 month period to 30 June 2004. The Schedule D Case I profits for the 15 month period was £30,000. Royalties of £2,000 (gross) were paid to Histon plc on 1 January each year in respect of patent rights held as investments. The company also had a chargeable gain of £1,000 in respect of a disposal on 1 February 2004.

What is the profit chargeable to corporation tax for the accounting period ended 30 June 2004?

A   £6,500

B   £6,200

C   £6,000

D   £6,600

4   Willis Ltd had always prepared accounts to 31 December until it changed its accounting date to 30 April and prepared accounts for 16 months to 30 April 2004.

The tax written down value of the general plant pool at 1 January 2003 was £11,000.

During the period of account the following transactions took place.

10 May 2003	Sold car for	£4,500	(cost originally £7,900)
3 March 2004	Purchased car for	£7,485	

What are the capital allowances for the accounting period ended 30 April 2004?

A   £4,661

B   £3,090

C   £2,655

D   £1,030

5   Millicam Ltd, a close company with a 31 March year end, made a loan of £30,000 on 10 August 2003 to Tex, one of its shareholders. Tex is not a director or employee of the company. Tex repaid £5,000 on 1 December 2004 and six monthly thereafter.

How much penalty tax will Millicam pay on 1 January 2005 and how much tax will be refunded on 1 January 2006 assuming Tex keeps up the repayments?

A   £6,250; £1,250

B   £7,500; £1,250

C   £6,250; Nil

D   £7,500; Nil

CHAPTER 12

Overseas aspects

EXAM FOCUS

Under the old syllabus, this topic formed a minor part of the corporation tax section of the syllabus. Questions on this topic tended to appear in Section C; the optional part of the paper. The new syllabus has increased the emphasis on this topic; it now forms a separate part of the syllabus worth 20% of the total. Questions are still likely to be optional, but worth 20 marks rather than the previous 15 marks. A greater depth of knowledge is therefore required.

LEARNING OUTCOMES

This chapter covers the following learning outcomes of the CIMA syllabus:

Identify the significance of company residences for tax purposes

Evaluate the taxation implications of alternative methods of running an overseas operation

Calculate the CT liability of a UK company which has overseas income, using the rules of double tax relief (but excluding knowledge of Treaties)

Identify transfer pricing problems, calculating any adjustment required and state how this will be reported in its CTSA return

Identify a controlled foreign company (CFC)

Calculate the CT liability arising as a result of the presence of a CFC.

Demonstrate how to maximise DTR.

In order to cover these learning outcomes the following topics are included:

Company residence
Overseas branches and overseas subsidiaries
Double tax relief
Anti-avoidance for overseas activities.

---

1   Company residence

1.1   What determines residence?

 The residence of a company determines its chargeability to UK corporation tax. A company is resident in the UK if

♦   it is incorporated in the UK, or
♦   its central management and control are exercised in the UK.

These rules are illustrated in Figure 12.1.

Figure 12.1 Determining company residence

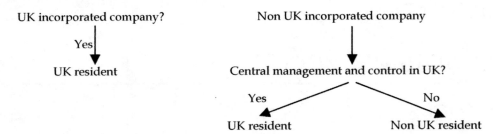

The location of the central management and control of a company is normally where the directors meet for board meetings, as this is where major policy decisions are made.

1.2 UK resident companies

A UK resident company is chargeable to UK tax on its worldwide profits.

Worldwide profits comprise:

♦ all UK profits

♦ overseas branch profits *arising*

♦ profits of overseas (ie non UK resident) companies *remitted* to the UK

♦ other income and gains arising overseas (eg interest on overseas government stocks and gains on sale of foreign property).

Profits from overseas companies are usually remitted in the form of dividends and are assessable as Schedule D Case V income. This applies even if the overseas company is an associated company. Only dividends from UK companies can be exempt as FII.

The above definition of *profits* includes both income and gains. It also introduces an important distinction between the treatment of profits of an overseas branch and those of an overseas company in which the UK company has an investment.

1.3 Non-UK resident companies

A non-UK resident company is chargeable to UK CT if it carries on a trade in the UK through a permanent establishment (eg branch or agency). Only its UK profits are chargeable.

A non-UK resident company is chargeable to *income tax* at the basic rate (currently 22%) on UK non-trading income – eg rents from commercial letting of UK property.

However, the CIMA Guidance Notes state that foreign companies trading in the UK is not an examinable topic.

2 Overseas branches and overseas subsidiaries

2.1 Introduction

 A UK resident company wishing to expand overseas will consider one of two principal methods in setting up a permanent place of business:

♦ An overseas branch
♦ An overseas subsidiary company.

2.2 Overseas branch

An overseas branch is merely an extension of the UK company. All of the profits earned overseas (including capital gains) are included within the computation of the UK company's PCTCT, irrespective of whether they are actually remitted to the UK.

The overseas branch trading profits will be assessed to UK corporation tax as follows.

♦ Overseas branch with UK control: Schedule DI
♦ Overseas branch with overseas control: Schedule DV

The distinction is not particularly important where a branch is profitable.

There is no impact on the upper and lower limits for starting rate or small companies' rate purposes as the branch is not a separate company.

2.3 Overseas subsidiary

A subsidiary is a separate legal entity irrespective of whether it is situated in the UK or overseas. It will therefore be taxed separately on its own profits. Its profits are not accumulated with those of the parent.

An overseas subsidiary does, however, impact on the computation of the parent's CT liability:

♦ if the parent controls the subsidiary, it will be an associated company. It therefore affects the parent's upper and lower limits for starting rate and small companies' rate purposes

♦ a non-UK resident company cannot benefit from the transfer of trading losses, etc (ie group relief) against its overseas profits

♦ the parent will be charged UK CT on any profits remitted to it, for example, dividends or interest. Note that dividends are **not** classed as FII and are therefore included in the computation of PCTCT. Dividends are taxed under Schedule DV; interest is taxed under Schedule DIII under the loan relationship rules.

Note that the level of control does not affect the basic principle of assessing on a remittance basis. However, it may be relevant in determining the amount of overseas profits to be included in the PCTCT if the controlled foreign company rules apply (see beyond).

2.4 Tax differences between the two alternatives

The other differences between operating through an overseas branch or subsidiary are outlined in Figure 12.2.

Figure 12.2   The effects of alternative overseas investment structures

Tax factor	Overseas branch	Overseas subsidiary
Trading losses	Can relieve DI trading losses against UK profits, unless the loss can be relieved in the country in which it arose	The overseas company cannot claim loss relief from the UK company nor surrender losses to the UK company
Capital allowances	Capital allowances on plant and machinery and industrial buildings available on overseas located assets, provided purchased by and used by overseas branch	Not available under UK tax rules
Chargeable gains	Capital gains computed using UK rules, which means that rollover relief is available on reinvestment and capital losses can be utilised	UK rules not applicable

Tax rates	The branch is not a separate entity. The UK company and its overseas branches count as one company for upper and lower limits	If the overseas company is a subsidiary (>50%) then there are two companies (or more) for upper and lower limits purposes
Illustration	UK company has two overseas branches	UK company has two overseas subsidiaries
	UK chargeable	UK chargeable
	'Profits' £250,000	'Profits' £250,000
	Lower limit £300,000	Lower limit $$\frac{300,000}{3} = £100,000$$
	19% tax rate	30% tax rate with marginal relief

2.5 *Planning with overseas structures*

The above comparison between operating through an overseas branch or subsidiary appears to favour the medium of a branch as regards:

♦ trading losses
♦ capital allowances
♦ capital gains reliefs
♦ no dilution of profit limits.

However, it is in the underlying distinction between a branch and a subsidiary that the subsidiary scores. This is shown in Figure 12.3.

Figure 12.3 Profits chargeable to UK tax

	Overseas branch *50% remitted*	*Overseas subsidiary* *100% owned, 50% profits* *distributed each year*
	£	£
Profits	200,000	200,000
	All assessable, remittance irrelevant	Only £100,000 chargeable in UK

The advantage of operating through an overseas subsidiary is the control over the *amount* and the *timing* of the remittances, so that UK corporation tax liability can be minimised if required. There is no such control in respect of a branch.

Because of the above, many overseas operations initially start as a branch and are later incorporated, once early trading losses and start-up capital expenditure have been relieved.

The conversion of an overseas branch into a subsidiary usually requires Treasury consent, as the profits and assets are being removed from the UK charge to tax. Assets are normally deemed to be sold to the new subsidiary at market value. However, the gains may be deferred where:

♦ all branch assets are transferred to an overseas resident company (the subsidiary)
♦ in exchange for shares of at least 75% of the overseas resident company.

3 Double tax relief

3.1 Overview

All overseas profits (whether arising or remitted) must be reflected as *gross* amounts in the corporation tax computation, but the profits may have suffered overseas tax, which must be taken into account as discussed below.

There are *two* types of overseas tax to consider.

♦ *Withholding tax* is physical tax which may be withheld from *any* remittance before it reaches the UK company. This is illustrated below.

♦ *Underlying tax* can be considered in relation to certain dividends or branch profits only.

3.2 Withholding tax (WHT)

Thomas Ltd, a UK company which makes up accounts to 31 March 2004, receives a dividend of £10,500 from an investment in Elisia, an overseas country. Elisia withholds 30% tax on any remittances.

The gross amount to be included as Schedule DV income is as follows.

	£
Dividend received	10,500
WHT	4,500
DV (ie £10,500 × $\frac{100}{70}$)	15,000

If we were to now compute the tax liability of Thomas Ltd, assuming other profits of £200,000, the result would be as follows.

	£	*Overseas tax suffered*
Other profits	200,000	
DV	15,000	4,500
PCTCT	215,000	
FII	Nil	
'P'	215,000	
CT liability @ 19%	40,850	

This means that the overseas income of £15,000 has suffered both overseas tax (£4,500) and UK tax (£15,000 × 19% = £2,850), a total of £7,350.

3.3 Relief for double taxation

The above illustration demonstrates that there is a double charge to tax, where both UK tax and overseas tax have arisen on the same source. There are three mechanisms to relieve the overseas tax suffered, as shown in Figure 12.4.

Figure 12.4 Relief for double taxation

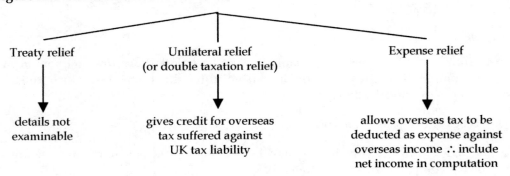

Double taxation relief is the most common form of relief, and the most important for the exam. The alternative, expense relief, is only to be claimed if it is more beneficial. This will only be the case if losses are involved. (Note that unilateral relief will not be given where it is specifically excluded under the terms of a double taxation agreement.)

3.4 Double taxation relief

Double taxation relief (DTR) involves giving credit for the *lower* of

♦ the overseas tax suffered

♦ the UK corporation tax (using the effective rate) attributable to the overseas income.

The rules for relieving overseas tax were revised by the FA 2000 to allow the carry forward and carry back of unrelieved foreign tax, and 'onshore pooling' of foreign dividends.

The CIMA examiner acknowledges that the 'onshore pooling' rules are too complex to be included in the syllabus and are therefore not examinable. We therefore explain DTR but avoid situations which involve 'onshore pooling'.

3.5 Example

Z plc has the following results for the year ended 31 March 2004.

	£
Schedule D Case I	2,000,000
Schedule D Case V_1 (gross)	80,000
Schedule D Case V_2 (gross)	60,000
PCTCT	2,140,000

Schedule DV_1 - foreign dividend on which overseas tax of £23,200 has been suffered.
Schedule DV_2 - foreign rents on which overseas tax of £22,800 has been suffered.

In each case the overseas tax consists entirely of withholding tax.

Note that 'onshore pooling' cannot arise as there is only one source of foreign dividends. In any case, the onshore pooling provisions do not apply to foreign income other than dividends (eg foreign rents are not pooled).

Required

Compute Z plc's corporation tax payable.

Approach to the example

It is essential to use workings to calculate:

♦ the gross overseas income (if not given in the question) and foreign tax
♦ the UK CT on each foreign source separately
♦ the DTR on each foreign source.

Use the suggested approach below.

Z plc corporation tax computation

	£	
DI	X	
DV	X	(From W1)
PCTCT	X	
CT	X	
Less DTR	(X)	(From W2)
CT payable	X	

Working 1

	DV_1 £	DV_2 £	Total £
Income received*	X	X	
Overseas tax (B)	X	X	
Gross DV income	X	X	X

*This will be your starting point if gross income is not supplied in the question.

Working 2

	DV_1	DV_2	Total
UK CT on overseas source (A)*	X	X	
Overseas tax (from W1) (B)	X	X	
DTR (lower of (A) or (B))	X	X	X

*If marginal relief is available, calculate UK CT on each source as $\dfrac{\text{DV income}}{\text{PCTCT}}$ x Total UK CT.

3.6 Solution

£

Z plc corporation tax computation
Year ended 31 March 2004

	£
Schedule D Case I	2,000,000
Schedule D Case V (W1)	140,000
PCTCT	2,140,000
CT @ 30%	642,000
Less DTR (W2)	(41,200)
CT payable	600,800

Workings

			DV_1 £	DV_2 £	Total £
(1)	Overseas tax (supplied)		23,200	22,800	
	Gross (supplied)		80,000	60,000	140,000 DV
(2)	CT (allocated) @ 30%	(A)	24,000	18,000	
	Overseas tax	(B)	23,200	22,800	
	DTR (lower of (A) and (B))		23,200	18,000	41,200

The relief for overseas tax can never exceed the UK liability.

The excess foreign tax on the foreign rents £4,800 (22,800 – 18,000) is wasted. Had there been excess tax on the foreign dividends there would be a facility to carry it back or forward (see para 3.18 below).

There was no need to state net income received as the gross figure was already supplied.

3.7 Maximising double taxation relief

Charges on income and loss reliefs reduce chargeable profits and can therefore cause relief for overseas tax to be wasted or, in the case of dividends, to become excess.

3.8 Example

(Overseas tax £19,000)

	UK profit £000	DV £000	Total £000
Profits before charges	100	100	200
S393A loss relief – allocated to DV		(100)	(100)
PCTCT	100	Nil	100
CT @ 19%			19

As nil overseas profits no UK CT ∴ no DTR possible

If the loss is allocated instead against UK profits:

		UK profit £000	DV £000	Total £000
			(Overseas tax £19,000)	
Profits before charges		100	100	200
S393A loss relief – allocated to UK profits		(100)	–	(100)
PCTCT		Nil	100	100
CT @ 19%			19	19
Less	DTR: Lower of:			
	(a) £19,000 – overseas tax			
	(b) £19,000 – UK tax		(19)	(19)
		Nil	Nil	Nil

The impact of *not* allocating the loss relief to DV is clear. To maximise DTR, you need to avoid setting losses or charges against overseas profits where UK profits could be used instead. Where there are insufficient UK profits available, then allocate in priority to overseas sources which suffer the *lowest* rate of overseas tax.

Note that loss relief under S393(1) – ie being carried against future profits of the same trade – must be used against DI. Only S393A loss relief – ie used in year of loss or carried back – is used against total profits and therefore allows a choice, as do current year Schedule A losses and Schedule D Case III deficits.

3.9 Expense relief

When a company with overseas income does not have a corporation tax liability because it has trading losses, then there is no benefit to be obtained from DTR as a tax credit. An alternative relief, 'expense relief', permits the overseas income to be included *net* of overseas tax in the computation, thus reducing total profits. This in turn means that a lower amount of loss is needed to relieve the profits chargeable, and so a greater loss is available for other reliefs (ie carry forward or carry back). Thus, instead of wasting the tax credit, some use is made of it by setting it off as an expense. It is easy to overlook expense relief.

3.10 Example

Helpless Ltd, a UK resident company which has no associated companies, has the following details for the year ended 31 March 2004.

	£
Schedule D Case I trading loss	(213,000)
Rents from Utopian Company (net of 18% withholding tax)	45,920
Rental income from UK property	90,000

You are required to calculate the profits chargeable to corporation tax for the year ended 31 March 2004. State how much of the trading loss will be available for carrying back or forward at that date, assuming that double tax relief is taken in the most beneficial manner.

3.11 Solution

	With DTR as a credit £		Expense relief £
Schedule DV (gross) $(45,920 \times \frac{100}{82})$	56,000	Schedule DV (net)	45,920
Schedule A	90,000		90,000
	146,000		135,920
Less S393A(1)(a) relief	(146,000)		(135,920)
	Nil		Nil

No DTR as nil liability

Loss available for carrying forward is
(£213,000 – £146,000)   = £67,000

Loss available for carrying forward is
(£213,000 – £135,920)   = £77,080

The expense relief results in the use of a lower amount of loss, thus leaving a greater amount for other loss relief purposes.

Note that expense relief involves surrendering £1 of tax credit for every £1 of loss preserved. If, in the case of foreign dividends, the tax credit could instead be carried back or forward for set-off £1 for £1 against CT in a past or future year expense relief may not be beneficial. The £1 of loss preserved may only save tax at 30% but the £1 of foreign tax credit, if it can be used, is worth £1.

3.12 Underlying tax

We shall now consider the basic concept of underlying tax (ULT). As indicated earlier this is another type of overseas tax which is suffered. It can *only* be considered in the following circumstances:

♦ in respect of *dividend* income from overseas shares, where the UK resident company owns 10% or more of voting power.

♦ on overseas branch profits.

The concept of underlying tax will be illustrated using the figures below (which have been translated into sterling).

Overseas company	£
Profit before tax	100,000
Overseas corporation tax (say 25%)	(25,000)
	75,000
Dividends paid	(20,000)
Retained profit	55,000
A withholding tax of 20% is deducted from dividends.	

If a UK company owned 10% of the above overseas company, it would be entitled to a dividend of £2,000 (£20,000 × 10%), but it would receive cash of only £1,600 as £400 withholding tax would be retained.

In addition, the UK company has effectively suffered its share of 'overseas corporation tax'. This was at a rate of 25% and is known as *underlying* tax.

Both types of tax (WHT and ULT) can give rise to double taxation relief, but the gross amount to be included in the computation of profits must reflect the 'true' income as well.

The following procedure is required to find DV.

	£	Overseas tax
Net income	1,600	
Withholding tax	400	400
	———	
Gross (for WHT)	2,000	
Add Underlying tax 2,000 × $^{25}/_{75}$	667	667
	———	
Gross DV income	2,667*	
	———	———
Available for DTR		1,067
		———

*As you are given the rate of overseas corporation tax, you could calculate the gross DV income by grossing up as: £2,000 × $^{100}/_{75}$ = £2,667.

Take care when applying the above in examination questions, because the income details provided might be net (£1,600) or gross of WHT (£2,000) or gross DV income (£2,667). Read the question carefully.

3.13   Example

The following details relate to R plc.

	Year ended 31.3.04
	£
Dividend received	90,440
Schedule D Case I	2,000,000
Loss relief	(100,000)

The dividend received was from an overseas company, Space Inc, in which R plc had a 30% interest. Withholding tax of 15% had been applied, and the underlying tax rate was 24%.

The loss relief results from a separate trade and arises in the same year (ie S393A available).

Required

Show the CT payable assuming all reliefs available are claimed.

3.14   Solution

First, calculate *gross* DV income as follows.

	£	Overseas tax £	
Net dividend received	90,440		
Add Withholding tax $\frac{15}{85}$	15,960	15,960	
	———		
	106,400*		
Add Underlying tax 106,400 × $\frac{24}{76}$	33,600	33,600	
	———	———	
Gross DV income	140,000	49,560	for DTR
	———	———	

* Where ULT is to be considered this is treated as *net* of underlying tax.

Before applying ULT, check:

♦ 10% voting power
♦ dividend income.

Next, find PCTCT analysed between UK income and DV income.

R plc

Year ended 31.3.04		Total £	UK £	DV £
Schedule	DI	2,000,000	2,000,000	
	DV	140,000		140,000
Less	Loss relief	(100,000)	(100,000)	
PCTCT		2,040,000	1,900,000	140,000

S393A losses are allocated against UK profits, so that DV remains at £140,000, to maximise DTR.

Then calculate the corporation tax liability.

	£	
PCTCT	2,040,000	
FII	Nil	Overseas dividends are *not* FII but *DV*
'P'	2,040,000	

'P' is greater than £1,500,000 so the 30% rate applies.

UK CT

2,040,000 @ 30%	612,000

The DTR limit is found as follows:

		Total £	UK £	DV £
PCTCT		2,040,000	1,900,000	140,000
CT @ 30%		612,000	570,000	42,000
Less DTR				
Lower of	(B) overseas tax: 49,560			
	(A) UK CT on DV: 42,000	(42,000)		(42,000)
CT payable		570,000	570,000	Nil

The unrelieved overseas tax £7,560 (49,560 – 42,000) is excess. It is usually good exam technique to highlight this result even if the question does not specifically ask for it.

Practice question 1 *(The answer is in the final chapter of this book)*

Oxo

Oxo Ltd, a UK resident company with one UK resident subsidiary, has the following holding in voting shares in an overseas company

> M (Inc) resident in Mercia   15,000 shares (a 15% holding)

Oxo Ltd produced the following information in relation to its accounting year to 31 March 2004.

Income

UK trading profit	£8,000
Dividend from M (Inc) (net of withholding tax of 15%)	£7,990

The rate of underlying tax in Mercia is 12%

Rents from property situated in Polia (net of withholding tax of 10%)	£16,200

Charges paid

Gift Aid paid	£5,000

Required

Compute the CT payable for the above period by Oxo Ltd, ensuring that the maximum possible relief is obtained for foreign tax suffered.

Approach to the solution

Ensure that you set up your computation supported by workings to calculate the overseas income and the DTR. Use the example approach above.

3.15   *Calculating the underlying tax*

In the above practice question, the underlying tax rate was provided. This is not always the case in exam questions. Instead, information may be supplied so that the underlying tax can be calculated.

The underlying tax is calculated as follows.

$$\text{Overseas corporate tax paid for period} \times \frac{\text{Dividend received} + \text{withholding tax}}{\text{Distributable profits of overseas company}}$$

The information to calculate the underlying tax may be supplied in the following format.

Overseas company profit and loss account

		£	£
Profit before tax			100,000
Less	Provision for taxation	20,000	
	Deferred taxation	5,000	
	Under-provision in prior year	3,000	
			(28,000)
Profit after tax			72,000
Dividend paid			(30,000)
Retained profit			42,000

Overseas tax eventually paid for the year was £18,000.

Here are some points to watch out for.

♦ The dividend shown in the accounts is *before* the deduction of withholding tax.

♦ Distributable profits will be as for UK accounting purposes. Profit after tax = £72,000

♦ The taxation figure in the accounts is only relevant if it is the actual overseas tax paid. In the format above

Tax per accounts	=	£28,000
Overseas tax paid	=	£18,000

The underlying tax attaching to the total dividends paid is therefore:

$$£18,000 \times \frac{£30,000}{£72,000} = £7,500$$

The amount that would be attributable to a UK investing company depends upon its percentage entitlement to dividend.

3.16 Example

S plc has a 20% shareholding in the above overseas company. The overseas company withholds 10% tax from any dividends remitted. S plc has DI profits of £200,000 for the year ended 31 March 2004.

Using the information above, what is the CT payable?

3.17 Solution

S plc

	£
DI	200,000
DV (W1)	7,500
PCTCT	207,500
CT @ 19%	39,425
Less DTR (W2)	(1,425)
CT payable	38,000
Excess foreign tax 2,100 – 1,425	675

Workings

(W1)   Schedule DV

	£	Overseas tax £
Net dividend (£30,000 per accounts × 20% share × 90%)	5,400	
WHT $^{10}/_{90}$	600	600
Gross (for WHT)	6,000	
ULT (£7,500 × 20%)	1,500	1,500
DV	7,500	2,100

(W2)   Double taxation relief

	UK £	DV £	Total £
DI	200,000		
DV		7,500	
	200,000	7,500	
CT @ 19%	38,000	1,425	39,425
Less DTR: lower of			
(B) Overseas tax £2,100			
(A) UK tax £1,425		(1,425)	(1,425)
CT payable			38,000

3.18   Relief for excess foreign tax on dividends

Where there is a single source of overseas dividends

Any excess WHT or ULT on overseas dividends can be carried back for up to three years or carried forward indefinitely. It is added to the foreign tax credit in a past or future year and is subject to the same overriding set off limit. If a source of dividends carries a tax credit of over 30%, this carry back/carry forward mechanism is unlikely to be beneficial.

If there is more than one source of overseas dividends

There is a complicated tax credit relief system known as 'onshore pooling' but as it is not examinable it is not covered in this text.

4   Anti-avoidance for overseas activities

4.1   Introduction

We have now considered the computational framework for a UK resident company investing overseas. We have identified that if a branch is established, the whole profit is taxable in the UK. However, if the investment is done through an overseas subsidiary, then only remittances are assessable. This can be used to significant advantage in tax planning, as it gives the parent company control over the *amount* and the *timing* of the tax liability.

There are anti-avoidance measures known as the controlled foreign company rules to combat this possible source of abuse and these are discussed in this section.

It is also possible for companies in the same international group to 'export' profits to a low tax country by judicious pricing of inter-company sales. If a UK company sells its products below an 'arm's length' price to another group company overseas, an adjustment may be required to impose a higher price and thereby increase UK profits. This is known as the transfer pricing rules and is discussed below.

4.2   Controlled foreign companies (CFCs)

A controlled foreign company (CFC) is a company which is

♦   resident in a country with a lower level of tax, and
♦   controlled by UK resident persons.

A 'lower level' of tax means less than 75% of the amount which would have been payable if the company had been UK resident. (The Revenue has a list of 'excluded' countries which it does not regard as being low tax countries.)

These rules are illustrated in figure 12.5.

Figure 12.5 Controlled foreign companies

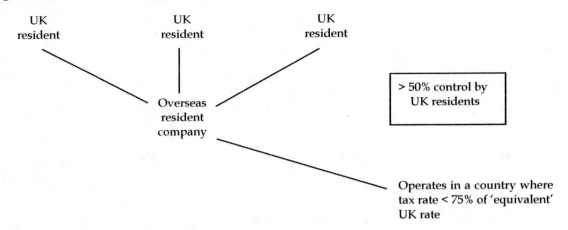

Even if UK residents do not hold more than 50% of the shares the company is a CFC if:

♦ Two persons (one UK and one non-UK) jointly control the company

♦ The UK resident person holds at least 40% of the joint holding

♦ The non-UK resident person holds at least 40% but not more than 55% of their joint holding.

There is no requirement that the two persons are connected but in fact this FA2000 anti-avoidance rule was introduced to combat joint ventures designed to circumvent the CFC rules.

4.3 Example

Pedro SA, a non-UK resident company, holds 30% of the shares in Exprime SA, a non-UK resident company.

Petromime Ltd, a UK resident company, holds a further 30%.

The other 40% is held by non-UK resident individuals, none of which own more than 2%.

Required

Decide whether Exprime SA is a CFC.

4.4 Solution

Exprime SA is not controlled by UK residents but the FA2000 anti-avoidance rule applies as:

1   Pedro SA (non-res) and Petromime Ltd (UK res) control the company having 60% between them (ie > 50%).

2   The UK party (Petromime Ltd) holds more than 40% of 60% ie 24%.

3   The non-UK party (Pedro SA) holds more than 40% (ie more than 24%) but not more than 55% (55% × 60% = 33%).

Therefore Exprime SA is a CFC.

4.5 Exclusions from CFC treatment

Even if a company falls within the above definition of a CFC, it will *not* be treated as such if it satisfies one of the five exclusion tests.

♦ It has an *acceptable distribution policy*. This means it pays at least 90% of its distributable profits as a dividend within 18 months of the end of its accounting period. Profits for this purpose means taxable profits, less gains and foreign tax.

- It is engaged in *exempt activities*. This involves conducting at least 50% of its business with unconnected persons.

- The *public quotation* test. Its shares are listed on a recognised stock exchange and at least 35% of its ordinary share capital is held by the public.

- The *de minimis* test. Its profits are less than £50,000 per annum.

- Avoidance of UK tax was not the main purpose of setting up the CFC. This is known as the *motive* test.

4.6   Consequences of being a CFC

If the overseas company cannot satisfy any of the above tests, its profits may be apportioned to its UK resident corporate shareholders. This means that where a UK resident company (and its associates) has 25% or more entitlement to the profits of a CFC, then the UK company is charged on its share of 'taxable profits less gains', *not* just on amounts remitted to the UK.

Thus the profits of a wholly owned subsidiary which is classed as a CFC will be fully chargeable to UK CT, irrespective of the amount actually remitted to the parent.

The apportioned profits of the CFC must be included in the UK company's corporation tax self assessment return and taxed at the full CT rate (30%). Tax paid by the CFC will also be apportioned appropriately to the UK company.

Under self assessment the onus is on the UK company to decide whether the CFC rules apply and to include the necessary profits when calculating their tax liability. Failure to recognise and act on a CFC situation can result in penalties.

4.7   Example

The following are shareholders in Alfredo SA, a Spanish registered company, resident in the Cayman Islands.

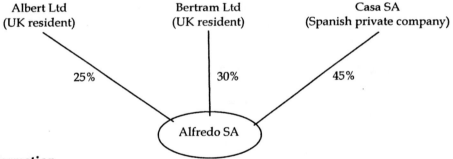

Other information

- Cayman Island tax rate is 20%

- The tax rate applicable to Albert Ltd is 30% and to Bertram Ltd is 19%.

- Albert Ltd and Bertram Ltd are *not* associated with each other.

- Alfredo SA has profits of £80,000 which are not derived from exempt activities, and it is currently not distributing profits.

What is the likely impact for Albert Ltd and Bertram Ltd?

4.8   Solution

(1)   Is Alfredo SA controlled by UK residents? Yes, because Albert Ltd and Bertram Ltd together hold more than 50% of Alfredo SA.

(2)   Is Alfredo SA in a 'tax haven'? From the perspective of Albert Ltd the answer is yes, because Alfredo's 20% tax rate is less than 75% of the UK equivalent (75% × 30% = 22.5%). Therefore CFC rules may apply. From Bertram Ltd's perspective the answer is also yes, because corporation tax is charged on apportioned profits at the full rate (30%).

(3)   Do Albert Ltd and Bertram Ltd own 25% or more of Alfredo SA? The answer is yes in both cases.

(4)   Does Alfredo SA satisfy any of the exclusion tests?

♦ Exempt activities?	No
♦ 35% in public hands?	No (Casa SA is a *private* company)
♦ PCTCT < £50,000?	No = £80,000
♦ Motive?	Difficult to prove
♦ Distribution policy	No not currently

Conclusion: CFC rules apply to Alfredo SA and therefore Albert Ltd will be assessed on 25% × £80,000 = £20,000 with tax payable of £6,000 (30%). Bertram Ltd will be assessed on 30% × £80,000 = £24,000 with tax payable of £7,200 (30%).

4.9   Transfer pricing

Anti-avoidance rules exist to prevent 'price fixing' between a UK resident company and an overseas company in the same group. The anti-avoidance rules replace the transfer price with the true market price based on an 'arm's length' value, so that profits cannot be moved overseas to avoid tax. The rules apply to transactions between a UK company and an overseas company with either one controlling the other or both under common control. 'Price fixing' between a UK resident company and its overseas branch is self-defeating as attempts to increase or reduce branch profits cannot avoid UK corporation tax.

Under self-assessment, the adjustment to market price must be made by the company. A system of advance pricing arrangements (APAs) exists to enable companies to agree in advance with the Inland Revenue that their transfer pricing agreements are acceptable. However, the examiner confirms that no questions will be set on APAs.

Practice question 2 *(The answer is in the final chapter of this book)*

Columbus

Columbus Ltd, a UK resident company, is the manufacturer of the Columbus tractor. The company has for several years been exporting its tractors to the small country of Rowinda. Columbus Ltd is now planning to set up a permanent business establishment in Rowinda on 1 April 2003 to assist with these sales, and to handle the subsequent repair and servicing work. The directors of Columbus Ltd have not yet decided whether to set up the new business establishment as a branch or as a 100% subsidiary company. A permanent director is to be sent out from the UK to run the Rowinda establishment who will be fully responsible for all decision making.

For the year ended 31 March 2004 the Rowindan establishment is expected to make a trading profit of £200,000, irrespective of the business structure chosen. Rowinda has a tax system which taxes profits at the rate of 6%, with any dividends paid out of the country additionally subject to a 3% withholding tax. Columbus Ltd will require the Rowindan establishment to remit 25% of its distributable profits (ie after tax) back to the UK either by way of straightforward payments (if a branch) or dividends (if a company). The remittances will be made during the year to which they relate, there being no problem in sending money out of Rowinda. There is no double taxation treaty between the UK and Rowinda.

Columbus Ltd expects to make a trading profit of £1,200,000 for the year ended 31 March 2004, and a trading loss of £430,000, from a separate UK trade in the same year. Loss relief is to be claimed under S393A – ie against profits of the same year.

Columbus Ltd has no other subsidiaries or overseas establishments.

Required

(a)   Calculate Columbus Ltd's expected mainstream corporation tax liability for the year ended 31 March 2004, if the Rowindan establishment is set up as (i) a branch, and (ii) a 100% subsidiary.

        You should ignore the possibility of the subsidiary being classified as a controlled foreign company.

(b)   Assuming that Columbus Ltd decides to set up its Rowindan establishment as a 100% subsidiary, advise the directors as to whether this subsidiary might be classified as a controlled foreign company. Briefly describe the implications of it being so classified.

        You should note that Rowinda is not on the Inland Revenue's list of those countries ('excluded countries') which it does not regard as low tax countries.

(c)   The profits of the Rowindan establishment have been calculated on the assumption that it is invoiced by Columbus Ltd for exported tractors at their normal trade selling price. What would the implications be for (i) a branch, and (ii) a 100% subsidiary if exported tractors were instead invoiced at cost?

Practice question 3 *(The answer is in the final chapter of this book)*

Mitch

The following details are given in respect of Mitch Ltd, which has no associated companies, for the year ended 31 March 2004.

	£
Trading profits	180,000
Dividends received from a Danish corporation (net of 5% withholding tax)	91,200
Capital gain	68,000
Gift Aid paid	5,000

Mitch Ltd controls 20% of the voting rights in the Danish corporation. The profit and loss account of the Danish corporation is as follows.

		£	£
Profit before tax			1,440,000
Tax charge	current	172,000	
	deferred	468,000	
			(640,000)
Profit after tax			800,000

Following the submission of the Danish corporation's tax return, the tax actually payable was £200,000.

Required

You are required to calculate the corporation tax payable for the year ended 31 March 2004.

Watch out for the level of 'profits' when determining the tax rate.

5 Summary

Questions on this area of the syllabus are likely to focus on the basic distinction between an overseas branch and an overseas subsidiary.

An overseas branch is simply part of a company. All of its profits are included in the computation of PCTCT, irrespective of the amount remitted to the UK.

An overseas subsidiary is a separate legal entity. Only profits remitted to the UK are chargeable to UK corporation tax.

Relief is usually given unilaterally for withholding tax and, subject to a 10% holding, underlying tax.

The computational techniques for ensuring DTR does not exceed the UK tax on the overseas source should become 'second nature'.

Where an overseas subsidiary is resident in a country with a tax rate that is less than three-quarters of the corresponding UK corporation tax rate, the controlled foreign company rules may be applicable.

CHAPTER 13

Corporation tax administration

EXAM FOCUS

This area of the syllabus has great practical relevance for companies, especially as there are numerous financial penalties for non-compliance. The subject is ideally suited to examination in the multiple choice section of the paper; particularly the payment dates and the time limits for submission of returns. The compulsory question in the pilot paper required the preparation of a schedule of payment dates.

LEARNING OUTCOMES

This chapter covers the following learning outcomes of the CIMA syllabus:

Describe the system of Corporation Tax Self-Assessment (CTSA)

Identify key dates for submission of returns

Describe the Inland Revenue's powers of enquiry

Identify the various penalties and interest charges in CTSA

Identify the minimum record-keeping requirements

Prepare a schedule of CT payments of a large company covering a two year period under the new quarterly payment system.

In order to cover these learning outcomes the following topics are included:

Corporation Tax Self-Assessment (CTSA)
The Inland Revenue's powers of enquiry
Record keeping requirements
Quarterly payments dates.

---

1   Corporation Tax Self-Assessment (CTSA)

1.1   Scope

Corporation Tax Self-Assessment (CTSA) applies to accounting periods ending after 30 June 1999. CTSA requires companies to submit a tax return and a self-assessment of any tax payable.

1.2   Filing the return

 A company is required to file a return (form CT600) when it receives a notice requiring it to do so. A company which is chargeable to tax, but which does not receive a notice requesting a return, must notify the Inland Revenue within 12 months of the end of the accounting period. If it fails to do so, it is liable to a penalty of up to the amount of tax unpaid 12 months after the end of the accounting period.

A notice to file a return may also require other information, such as the annual accounts.

The return must include a calculation (self-assessment) of the corporation tax payable for the accounting period covered by the return.

The return must be made within 12 months of the end of the accounting period or, if later, three months from the date of the notice requiring the return.

♦ There is a £100 penalty for failure to submit a return on time. This rises to £200 if the delay exceeds three months.

♦ There is an additional tax geared penalty if the return is more than six months late. This is 10% of the tax unpaid six months after the return was due. This rises to 20% if the return is over 12 months late.

♦ A penalty of up to the amount of tax that would have been lost can be imposed for a fraudulent or negligent return.

1.3 Example

CTT Ltd has produced accounts for the year ended 30 June 2003. The company has calculated that its corporation tax liability for the year is £220,000.

Required

Advise the company of the consequences of each of the following scenarios.

(a) The company received notice from the Inland Revenue requiring a return for the period ended 30 June 2003. The notice is dated 1 October 2003.

(b) The company received notice from the Inland Revenue requiring a return for the period ended 30 June 2003. The notice is dated 1 June 2004.

(c) The company has not received a notice requiring a return.

(d) The company's return was due on 30 June 2004, but was not submitted until 1 February 2005. The company had paid its corporation tax liability by the due date.

(e) The company's return was due on 30 June 2004, but was not submitted until 1 February 2005. The company's corporation tax liability was paid on the same date.

1.4 Solution

(a) The company must file its return by 30 June 2004 (ie within 12 months of the end of its accounting period).

(b) The company must file its return by 1 September 2004 (ie within 3 months of the date the notice was issued).

(c) The company must notify the Inland Revenue of its chargeability to tax by 30 June 2004 (ie within 12 months of the end of its accounting period). Failure to do so could result in a penalty of up to £220,000, assuming this amount was still unpaid.

(d) The company is liable to a fixed penalty of £200 as the return was more than three months late.

(e) The company is liable to a fixed penalty of £200 as the return was more than three months late. It is also subject to a penalty of £22,000 (£220,000 × 10%) as the tax was unpaid six months after the return was due.

1.5 Amending the return

A company can amend a return within 12 months of the filing date.

The Revenue can amend a return to correct errors within nine months of the date it was filed or within nine months of the filing of an amendment. If the company disagrees with the Revenue's amendment it may reject it. This rejection should be made within the normal time limit for amendments or, if this time limit has expired, within three months of the date of correction.

1.6 Errors

A company may make an error or mistake claim within six years of the end of an accounting period. An appeal against the Revenue's decision on such a claim must be made within 30 days. A company is not allowed to make an error claim if its return was made in accordance with a generally accepted accounting practice which prevailed at the time.

1.7 Paying the tax

The tax is payable within nine months of the end of the accounting period. Large companies – ie those paying CT at 30% - have to pay their tax by quarterly instalments (see Section 4 below).

1.8 Interest on late payments of corporation tax

Interest is charged automatically on late paid corporation tax from the due date to the date of payment (the rate of 6.5% pa currently applies).

Where there is an amendment to the self-assessment or a 'discovery assessment' (see below) interest runs from the date the tax would have been payable had it been correctly self-assessed in the first place.

Interest paid is allowable as a Schedule D Case III expense.

1.9 Interest on overpaid corporation tax

If corporation tax is overpaid the Revenue will pay interest from the date of overpayment to the date it is refunded (the rate of 2.5% pa currently applies).

Interest received is assessable under Schedule D Case III.

2 The Inland Revenue's powers of enquiry

2.1 Basic rules

The Revenue may enquire into a return, provided they first give written notice. Notice must normally be given

♦ within a year of the filing date or, if later

♦ within a year of the 31 January, 30 April, 31 July or 31 October following the actual date of delivery of the return.

If notice of an enquiry has been given, the Revenue may demand that the company produce documents for inspection. If the company fails to do so, a penalty of £50, plus £30 a day, may be imposed.

An enquiry ends when the Revenue give notice that it has been completed and notify what amendments they believe to be necessary. The company has 30 days from the end of an enquiry to amend its return. If the Revenue are not satisfied with the company's amendments, they have a further 30 days to amend the return. The company then has a further 30 days in which to appeal against this latest Revenue amendment.

2.2 Example

CTS Ltd has produced accounts for the year ended 30 June 2003. The company filed its return on 1 April 2004. What is the latest date by which the Revenue must give notice of an enquiry?

How would your answer differ if CTS Ltd had filed its return on 1 September 2004?

2.3 Solution

The Revenue must give notice within a year of the filing date. The filing date is 30 June 2004, therefore notice must be given by 30 June 2005.

If the company had filed its return on 1 September 2004, the Revenue would need to give notice by 31 October 2005 (ie 12 months after 31 October following the actual date of delivery of the return).

2.4 Determinations

If a company fails to deliver a return by the filing date, the Revenue may issue a determination of the tax payable within five years from the filing date. There is no appeal against a determination. However, it is replaced if the company makes a self-assessment within

- five years of the filing date or, if later
- 12 months from the determination.

2.5 Discovery assessments

A discovery assessment may be issued if the Revenue believe that insufficient tax has been collected. The time limit for a discovery assessment is six years from the end of the accounting period. This is extended to 21 years if there has been negligent or fraudulent conduct by the company.

3 Record keeping requirements

Companies must keep records until the latest of

- six years from the end of the accounting period
- the date any enquiries are completed
- the date after which enquiries may not be commenced.

Failure to keep records can lead to a penalty of up to £3,000 for each accounting period affected.

The company must keep original records of

- distributions (ie dividends) and tax credits
- payments and any tax deducted
- certificates of payments to sub-contractors
- details of foreign tax paid.

It is acceptable to keep copies of other records. The record keeping requirements will normally be satisfied by the same records that satisfy Companies Act requirements.

4   Quarterly payment dates

4.1   Introduction

Under CTSA a company's tax return must include a self-assessment of any tax payable.

 Large companies, that is companies with profits in excess of the upper limit for small companies' rate purposes, are required to make quarterly payments on account of their CT liability. Note that the upper limit is divided between associated companies. This means that a company with two associates will be required to pay its CT in instalments if its profits exceed £500,000 (£1,500,000/3).

A company is not required to make quarterly instalment payments in the year in which it becomes large, unless its profits exceed £10 million. (This limit is also shared between associated companies.) In addition, a company does not have to make quarterly instalment payments if its liability does not exceed £10,000.

The quarterly payments are based on the **estimated** CT liability for the current year. The first payment is made on the 14th day of the seventh month of the accounting period. The other quarterly payments are due on the 14th day of months 10, 13 and 16.

 Note that the payments begin *during* the accounting period itself, not afterwards. So you must begin counting months from the *start* of the accounting period.

4.2   Example

What are the payment dates for a company with an accounting period ending on 29 February 2004?

4.3   Solution

The payments on account are due on

♦   14 September 2003
♦   14 December 2003
♦   14 March 2004
♦   14 June 2004

Each payment due is a quarter of the CT liability for the year which, for at least the first three and for probably all four instalments, would have to be estimated. The first instalment payment would be a quarter of the best estimate at that date. The second payment would require a revised estimate and add or deduct any difference in respect of the first instalment and so on. The Revenue may expect to see some proof that the estimates were made with care.

Groups of companies can pay their CT on a group-wide basis if they wish, instead of company by company.

4.4   Transitional rules

There are transitional rules which apply for accounting periods ending on or before 30 June 2002 and the examiner still shows an interest in them as they are mentioned in the Guidance Notes.

For the first three years ending on or after 1 July 1999, a company subject to the quarterly payment rules only pays part of its CT liability by instalments. The balance is due nine months after the end of the AP as applies to non-large companies:

Year	Payments on account	Balance
1	60%	40%
2	72%	28%
3	88%	12%
4 onwards	100%	

Year 1 is the first year subject to CTSA, ie the first AP ending after 30 June 1999.

4.5   *Example*

A company makes up accounts to 31 December annually. In the year ended 31 December 2000, it had chargeable profits of £3,000,000 and a CT liability of £900,000. In the year ended 31 December 2001, it had chargeable profits of £3,500,000 and a CT liability of £1,050,000.

Required

Explain how much tax is payable in instalments and how much is payable on the normal due date.

4.6   *Solution*

CTSA applies to accounting periods ending on or after 1 July 1999. The second such accounting period for this company is the year ended 31 December 2000. The CT for this year is payable as follows:

	£	
Total liability	900,000	
Payable by instalments (72%)	648,000	/ 4 = £162,000 per instalment
Payable on normal due date	252,000	

The year ended 31 December 2001 is the third year of CTSA. The CT for this year is payable as follows:

	£	
Total liability	1,050,000	
Payable by instalments (88%)	924,000	/ 4 = £231,000 per instalment
Payable on normal due date	126,000	

4.7   *Non-12 months accounting periods*

If the accounting period is less than 12 months long, each instalment is calculated as $\frac{3}{n}$ of the CT liability where n is the length of the AP in months (to two decimal places where appropriate).

The first instalment is then due 6 months and 13 days after the start of the AP and the last instalment is due 3 months and 14 days after the end of the AP. For a very short AP (eg, one of 2 months) the last instalment date falls before the first instalment date. In which case all the CT liability is due 3 months and 14 days after the AP end.

If the last instalment date falls more than three months after the first instalment date, additional instalments are payable every three months after the previous instalment date. The tax payable on the final instalment cannot exceed the balance that remains payable.

Example

Brevity Ltd is a large company and prepares its accounts for a 10 month AP ending on 31 December 2003. Its CT liability for that period is £800,000.

Each instalment is therefore	$\frac{3}{10}$ x £800,000	£240,000
First instalment	14 September 2003 – pays	£240,000
Next instalment	14 December 2003 – pays	£240,000
Next instalment	14 March 2004 – pays	£240,000
Final instalment	14 April 2004 – pay	£80,000 (balance)
		£800,000

4.8 Interest

Companies should revise the estimate of their CT liability every quarter. It is a good idea to keep records showing how the estimate has been calculated. This will help to justify the size of a payment if the Revenue should dispute the amount paid.

Interest runs from the due date on any underpayments or overpayments. Interest paid by the company is a deductible expense. Interest received by the company is taxable income. Both are dealt with under Schedule D Case III.

Penalties may be charged if a company deliberately fails to pay instalments of a sufficient size.

Practice question 1 *(The answer is in the final chapter of this book)*

Space plc

Space plc, which has profits of £2 million annually, is preparing its budget for the year ending 31 March 2004.

Required

(a)   prepare a plan of projected corporation tax payments based on its results for the year, stating the amounts due and the due dates and

(b)   advise of any other administrative requirements for corporation tax purposes.

Approach to the question

Step 1

Calculate the corporation tax liability.

Step 2

Consider the impact of the instalment system on this *large* company.

Step 3

Consider the *returns* required, and the impact of late payments.

5   Summary

There are numerous deadlines and penalties under CTSA. The key points are summarised as follows.

♦   A company must file a return within 12 months of the end of its accounting period or, if later, three months from the date of the notice from the Revenue.

♦   Failure to submit a return on time results in a penalty of £100.

♦   The company can amend a return within 12 months of the filing date.

♦   The Revenue can enquire into a return provided they give written notice within a year of the filing date.

♦   Companies must keep records for six years from the end of the accounting period. Failure to do so can result in a penalty of up to £3,000.

♦   The due date for corporation tax is nine months after the end of the accounting period.

♦   Companies liable at the standard rate of CT must pay their liability in quarterly instalments, commencing on the 14th day of the seventh month of the accounting period.

♦   The quarterly instalment system is being phased in. Although the phasing in period is practically spent, the examiner may still regard it as an examinable topic.

Multiple choice questions 1 - 5 *(The answers are in the final chapter of this book)*

Each of the questions below has only one correct answer.

1   Jofar Ltd prepares accounts to 30 September and the directors realise that they made an error on the 30 September 2002 Tax Return which they had already submitted to the Revenue on 6 July 2003.

By what date will a correction be permitted, if at all?

A   No correction permitted

B   30 September 2004

C   6 July 2005

D   30 September 2008

2   The Revenue will be able to correct a tax return for obvious errors in a period from the date of filing of

A   3 months

B   6 months

C   9 months

D   1 year

3   In a case of fraud or negligent conduct the latest date for assessment will be

A   9 months from the filing date

B   2 years following the accounting date

C   6 years following the accounting date

D   21 years following the accounting date

4   Rosschips Ltd submitted its CT return for the year to 31 December 2002 on 12 February 2004.

Until what date must the company retain all records used to complete that return?

A   12 February 2005

B   30 April 2005

C   31 December 2005

D   31 December 2008

5   Jancombe Ltd submitted its 31 December 2002 CT return on 13 February 2004.

By what date must the Revenue give notice if they wish to enquire into the return?

A   30 April 2004

B   1 January 2005

C   13 February 2005

D   30 April 2005

CHAPTER 14

Value added tax

EXAM FOCUS

VAT featured regularly as an optional question in the papers set under the old syllabus. The pilot paper for the new syllabus only features one question on VAT; this is included in the compulsory multiple-choice part of the paper. However, the examiner has advised that a significant element of VAT could be included in the compulsory scenario-based question.

LEARNING OUTCOMES

This chapter covers the following learning outcomes of the CIMA syllabus:

Identify the significance of Standard rate, Zero rate and exempt supplies and those supplies outwith the scope of VAT

Identify the correct tax point of a supply and understand its significance

Identify the significance of EU and non-EU countries when dealing with VAT

Identify the VAT registration/de-registration requirements and the rules and penalties in relation to VAT returns.

Discuss the problems and opportunities inherent in a VAT group registration.

Discuss the most efficient method of arranging VAT registrations for groups of companies.

In order to cover these learning outcomes the following topics are included:

Types of supply
Registration and deregistration
Accounts and records
Accounting for VAT
Special accounting schemes
VAT penalties and interest
Appeals and assessments
Property
Partial exemption
VAT group registration
Overseas aspects of VAT

---

1 Types of supply

1.1 How the VAT system works

 VAT is charged on the taxable supply of goods and services in the UK and on the importation of goods from outside the European Union by a taxable person in the course or furtherance of a business. It is a multi–stage tax, charged at each stage of the business cycle on the value added at that stage. The government department responsible for VAT is HM Customs & Excise ('Customs') (*not* the Inland Revenue).

A taxable person (ie a company or partnership or individual) is required to charge and collect VAT from his customers (the *output VAT*). Against this he is allowed to reclaim the tax he has paid to suppliers (the *input VAT*). The end consumer (ie the general public) bears the VAT cost as he is unable to reclaim the VAT.

Illustration

Transaction	Net price	VAT	Trader's VAT account	Paid to Customs & Excise
	£	£	£	£
Importer buys raw materials from outside EU	200	35	35	35
Wholesaler sells to a manufacturer	400	70	70 – 35	35
Manufacturer sells to retailer	800	140	140 – 70	70
Retailer sells to consumer	1,200	210	210 – 140	70
				———
				210
				———

Total VAT payable of £210 is ultimately borne by the end consumer, who pays a total of £1,410 for the finished product (net price £1,200 plus VAT £210).

We refer throughout this chapter to a taxable person as 'he' (rather than 'it') although, of course, the CIMA syllabus is only concerned with VAT registered companies – not individuals.

1.2 Standard rated, zero rated and exempt supplies

For VAT to apply there must be a taxable supply of goods or services.

A *supply* can be any of the following.

- A sale of goods or services by ordinary commercial transactions
- The hire or rental or lease of goods
- Hire purchase or similar transaction (eg credit sale agreement)
- A gift of goods (but *not* services)
- A supply of goods for personal use
- Goods supplied for further processing

The provision of labour by an employee cannot be a taxable supply, so wages are outside the scope of VAT.

Supplies fall into three categories.

Standard rated. These supplies, as in the illustration, are charged at 17.5%. There is a special 5% rate for the supply of domestic power and certain other types of supply   All supplies are standard rated unless they are classified as zero rated or exempt.

Zero rated supplies are taxable supplies, on which VAT is charged at 0%. Where a trader makes zero rated supplies he may still register for VAT, so that any input VAT suffered on purchases can be reclaimed, resulting in a repayment from Customs.

Supplies are zero rated if they fall into one of the following categories.

Food*	Caravans and houseboats
Sewerage and water services	Gold
Books, etc*	Bank notes
Learning aids for blind and handicapped	Drugs, medicines
Construction of residential buildings	Exports outside the EU*
Approved alterations of protected buildings	Sale of donated goods by charities
International services	Children's clothing and footwear*
Public transport	

Most zero rated supplies are necessities or there is a perceived social or commercial argument in favour of zero rating.

You should familiarise yourself with some of the key categories marked *.

Exempt supplies

Certain supplies are *exempt* from VAT (ie are not taxable). This means that the trader is not required to register for VAT if he only makes exempt supplies, and therefore no claim can be made to recover input VAT. Exemption is a misnomer. It is a way of blocking off VAT recovery.

Supplies are exempt if they fall into one of the following categories.

Land	Health and welfare
Insurance	Burial and cremation
Postal services	Subscriptions to and services from trade unions and professional bodies
Betting/gaming/lotteries	Sport
Finance*	Works of art
Education*	Fundraising events
*Key categories	

Both the exempt and the zero rated groups of supplies have specific conditions or criteria which must be met to qualify.

Certain traders make both taxable supplies (standard rated and/or zero rated) and exempt supplies and are classed as *partially exempt*. The treatment of partially exempt traders is discussed in section 9 below.

2 Registration and deregistration

2.1 Introduction

A person who makes or intends to make taxable supplies becomes a taxable person when he is required to become or is registered.

There are two types of registration.

♦ Compulsory
♦ Voluntary

2.2 Compulsory registration

There are two separate tests for compulsory registration.

Test 1

When taxable supplies made by a person exceed £56,000 in the previous 12 months, the person is required to notify Customs within 30 days. Registration is effective from the end of the month following the relevant 12 month period.

Test 2

The alternative test is considered where at any time there are reasonable grounds for believing that taxable supplies in the next 30 days (in isolation) will exceed the £56,000 threshold. Customs need to be notified within the 30 days, and registration applies from the start of the 30 day period.

2.3 Example

Pickle Ltd opened a shop on 1 January 2003 selling books and stationery.

In the first year of trading, sales of stationery were £3,000 a month and sales of books were £1,000 a month.

During the first few months of the year ended 31 December 2004 the business expanded and sales were as follows.

	Books £	Stationery £	Total £
January 2004	1,000	5,000	6,000
February 2004	1,000	6,000	7,000
March 2004	1,300	8,300	9,600
April 2004	1,300	8,500	9,800
May 2004	1,300	8,800	10,100

For the rest of the year sales remained at their May 2004 levels.

Required

Determine the date when Pickle Ltd is required to register for VAT, and give the date from which the registration will be effective.

2.4 Solution

Pickle Ltd's supplies are of books (which are zero rated) and stationery (which is standard rated). Both types of supply are therefore taxable.

Taxable supplies in the previous 12 months are as follows.

End of

December 2003	£48,000 (12 × £4,000)
January 2004	£50,000 (11 × £4,000 + £6,000)
February 2004	£53,000 (10 × £4,000 + £6,000 + £7,000)
March 2004	£58,600 (9 × £4,000 + £6,000 + £7,000 + £9,600)

Therefore Pickle Ltd must notify Customs of its liability to register within 30 days of the end of March 2004, ie by 30 April 2004. The registration will be effective from 1 May 2004, the *end* of the month following the end of the relevant 12 month period.

2.5 Example

Onion Ltd, which is not yet VAT registered, has been trading for two years, with taxable turnover for the past 12 months of £40,000. Owing to the growth of the business, the company anticipates exceeding the £56,000 threshold in three months time. It has now received the offer of a contract of £60,000 which needs to be completed within a month. Assuming the date is 1 April 2004, advise Onion Ltd of its VAT registration position, if it accepts and if it rejects the contract.

2.6 Solution

Without the contract

If the additional contract is not accepted, the taxable annual turnover will exceed the threshold at the end of June 2004. Onion Ltd would then be required to notify Customs of its liability to register by 30 July 2004 and registration would be effective from 1 August 2004.

With the contract

If the additional contract is accepted, then taxable supplies in the next 30 days (£60,000) will exceed the threshold. There is no need to consider past turnover. Onion Ltd will accordingly need to notify liability to register by 30 April 2004, but the registration becomes effective from 1 April 2004. This means the company must immediately commence charging VAT on sales made, using 'proforma' invoices until its VAT registration is confirmed. Once the registration certificate is issued it can issue VAT invoices for the sales made since 1 April 2004.

2.7 Voluntary registration

Voluntary registration may be applied for. The main advantage is the ability to recover input VAT paid. The main disadvantage is the administration of the system. Voluntary registration is particularly advantageous to zero rated traders as they do not charge output VAT but can recover input VAT.

The following is a summary of the advantages and disadvantages of voluntary registration.

Advantages	*Disadvantages*
Hides the size of business, thus giving the impression of being well established.	
Allows trader to recover input VAT.	If customers are not VAT registered, the VAT charged will be a real cost to them. In a competitive market the trader may have to absorb the VAT in his profit margins.
If the business is likely to recover more VAT than it pays, then this will assist cashflow.	
Avoids any further problems when compulsory limits exceeded.	
Imposes discipline on a business to keep accurate records.	Extra administration.
Allows intending trader to reclaim input tax in advance of making taxable supplies.	Risk of penalties for accounting mistakes and late submission of returns etc.

2.8 Relief for pre-registration input tax

Input tax can normally only be recovered if it was incurred on supplies received when the claimant was a taxable person.

However, pre-registration input tax can be recovered (in the first return period) on:

♦ services invoiced in the six months prior to registration.

♦ goods received in the three years prior to registration if still held at the date of registration.

2.9 Deregistration

This is required when a taxable person ceases to make taxable supplies, or may be applied for if expected future turnover is below £54,000. Notification of compulsory deregistration is required within 30 days. The act of deregistration (eg on trade ceasing) is a *deemed supply*. This means that VAT must be accounted for on the value of the business assets at the date of deregistration (ie a final return) unless no input VAT was recovered in the first place on their purchase. Output VAT in this situation is ignored if it is less than £1,000.

3 Accounts and records

3.1 VAT returns and VAT invoices

One of the perceived disadvantages of having to be VAT registered is the administrative burden it places on traders, who are made responsible for collecting VAT for Customs. The following records must be compiled and retained.

The *VAT return*. This is a quarterly return which must be completed and returned within 30 days of the quarter end. The quarter periods are allocated to a trader on registration (eg 30 April, 31 July, 31 October, 31 January). Customs allocate quarter ends (eg 31 January etc, 28 February or 31 March etc) according to industry type so as to spread their own workload evenly through the year. Traders making zero rated supplies can expect to be receiving VAT *repayments* from Customs and can opt to make their returns monthly instead of quarterly.

The *VAT invoice*. This important document is the principal record for a customer to support a claim to recover input VAT. It must contain all of the following details.

♦ An identifying number

♦ The date of the supply and date of issue of the document

♦ The name, address and registration number of the supplier

♦ The name and address of the person to whom the goods or services are supplied

♦ The type of supply by reference to certain specified categories: a supply by sale, on hire purchase or similar transaction, by loan, by way of exchange, on hire, lease or rental, of goods made from customer's materials, by sale on commission, on sale or return or similar terms

♦ A description sufficient to identify the goods or services supplied

♦ For each description, the quantity of the goods or the extent of the services, the rate of tax and the amount payable, excluding tax, expressed in sterling

♦ The gross total amount payable, excluding tax, expressed in sterling

♦ The rate of any cash discount offered

♦ The amount of tax chargeable expressed in sterling at each rate, with the rate to which it relates

♦ The total amount of tax chargeable expressed in sterling

A less detailed invoice can be issued by a retailer, where the value of the supply is less than £100. The tax invoice in this case need only contain the following.

- Name, address and registration number of the retailer
- The date of supply
- Description of the goods or services
- The total amount payable including VAT
- The rate of VAT

Zero rated and exempt supplies cannot be included on this type of invoice.

No tax invoices are needed to recover input VAT in the following cases.

- Telephone calls from public or private telephones
- Purchase through coin operated machines
- Car park charges, excluding on–street parking

3.2 VAT records

Adequate records and accounts of all transactions must be maintained to support both the amount of output VAT chargeable and the claim for input VAT. These records must be kept for six years and include the following.

- VAT account linking the figures in the VAT return with the underlying records.
- Purchase invoices and copy sales invoices
- Orders and delivery notes
- Purchase and sales day books
- Cash book
- Records of daily takings (eg till rolls)
- Annual accounts (balance sheets and profit and loss accounts)
- Bank statements and paying–in slips
- Any credit/debit notes issued

4 Accounting for VAT

4.1 Output VAT

When a trader becomes VAT registered, then the appropriate VAT rate (ie 17.5%, 5% or 0%) will need to be charged on supplies in the correct period. As detailed above, the VAT period is either monthly or quarterly. The correct period is determined by the tax point.

The *basic tax point* of different types of supply is as follows.

- Supplies of goods: date of despatch (ie when goods are removed from stock or made available).

- Supplies of services: date when service is performed (ie when completed).

- Goods on sale or return: date the purchase of the goods is accepted, but with a maximum time limit of 12 months from despatch.

- Continuous supplies: this is the earlier of the issue of the tax invoice or the receipt of payment, and covers situations where there is no tax point.

The *actual tax point* is as follows.

- Normally the basic tax point

- If payment is received or an invoice is issued *before* the basic tax point the earliest date is taken

- If the invoice is issued within 14 days *after* the basic tax point, the invoice date is used unless payment is received earlier, or the trader elects *not* to use the 14 day rule.

Customs can agree to extend the 14 day period at the trader's request. For example, issuing invoices at the month end for sales in the month may be convenient. By agreement the tax point can be the month end where invoices are so issued.

The rules on 'tax point' are highly examinable.

4.2 Example

During the quarter to 31 March 2004, Peanut Ltd, a VAT registered company, sold a bulk order of toys (a standard rated product) amounting to £1,000 (excluding VAT). The customer paid a deposit of £100 (plus VAT) on 12 January 2004 when he placed the order. The toys were collected on 1 March 2004 and Peanut Ltd issued an invoice on 1 April 2004. The remaining £900 (plus VAT) was paid on 8 April 2004. There is no agreement with Customs to extend the normal 14 day invoicing period.

Required

What is the tax point in respect of this sale and how much VAT should be accounted for in Peanut Ltd's return for the three months to 31 March 2004?

4.3 Solution

The basic tax point for a supply of goods is the time the goods are made available to the customer. In Peanut Ltd's case this is 1 March 2004.

The date the supply is deemed to take place is the 'basic tax point' unless:

♦ payment is received before the basic tax point, or
♦ an invoice is issued before the basic tax point, or
♦ an invoice is issued within 14 days after the basic tax point.

The date of supply for the £100 deposit is 12 January 2004, as this is before the basic tax point.

The date of supply for the remaining £900 is 1 March 2004 (ie the basic tax point), since the invoice was issued more than 14 days later and there was no agreement to extend the period.

Output tax to be accounted for in the quarter ended 31 March 2004 is therefore £1,000 × 17.5%, or £175.

4.4 Valuation of supplies

If the consideration for a supply is payable in money, the value of the supply (on which VAT is calculated) is the VAT exclusive selling price.

If the consideration is in kind (eg a barter transaction), VAT is charged on the open market value of the supply.

Similarly, if the consideration is partly in cash and partly in kind (eg a part exchange deal for a car) the open market value is used.

Open market value is defined as the VAT-exclusive amount that would be payable if the vendor and the purchaser were dealing at arm's length.

Certain supplies have special rules in connection with output VAT. These are discussed below.

4.5 Fuel for private use

This applies to private fuel provided to an employee. The business is permitted to recover the full input VAT on fuel purchased. Output VAT is then based on a scale charge, to account for the private use element. There is no scale charge if the employee reimburses the business in full. The scale charge is deemed to be the VAT inclusive amount. It will be given to you in the exam. If the employer does not claim input tax on his car fuel purchases, the scale charge is waived. This might be beneficial if there are only small amounts of fuel purchased.

4.6 Example

An employer provides an employee with a 1600 cc (petrol) car, and fuel is provided for both business and private use. The quarterly fuel bill on this car is £250 inclusive of VAT.

Required

What entries will appear on the employer's quarterly VAT return to 31 January 2004?

4.7 Solution

Output VAT is accounted for based on a scale charge for 2003/04.

This is £300 quarterly (see below). The VAT element is £300 × $\frac{7}{47}$ = £44.68 output tax.

Input VAT can be reclaimed in full so £250 × $\frac{7}{47}$ = £37.23 input tax (but see note below).

		Scale benefit (VAT inclusive)	
VAT fuel scale charge	Engine size	Petrol	Diesel
		£	£
Quarterly	To 1,400 cc	237	225
	1,401 to 2,000 cc	300	225
	Over 2,000 cc	442	283

Note. The fraction of $\frac{7}{47}$ is used because the scale charge figure is VAT inclusive ($\frac{7}{47}$ is the same as $\frac{17.5}{117.5}$).

The scale charge can be avoided (by extra statutory concession) if the employer chooses not to recover input tax on road fuel. Thus neither entry should be made as the output tax exceeds the input tax.

4.8 Bad debt relief

As stated earlier, VAT must be charged in accordance with the tax point of the supply. This means that traders must account for the output VAT to Customs, often before the debt is paid by the customer. Where a debt remains outstanding more than six months from the due date of payment, then bad debt relief may be claimed from Customs provided the following conditions are satisfied.

♦ The debt is written off in the accounts.
♦ VAT on the supply has been accounted for and paid.

The purchaser must repay any input VAT claimed on supplies that have not been paid for within six months of the date of the supply (or the date on which payment is due, if later).

The bad debt relief claim is made by adding the amount recoverable to the input tax figure inserted on the VAT return.

VAT cannot be recovered by issuing a credit note to reverse the original sale where there is otherwise no commercial reason (eg faulty goods).

4.9 Business gifts

The output VAT position is depicted as follows in relation to business gifts.

Supply of goods	Output VAT on value of supply, unless cost is less than £50
Supply of services	No VAT
Trade samples	No VAT, but only *one* item per person

If there is more than one gift, the £50 limit applies to the total cost of gifts made to the same person in any 12 month period.

4.10 Discounts

There are two types of discount on sales invoices which affect output VAT.

♦ *Trade discounts.* VAT is charged on the price *after* trade discount

♦ *Prompt payment discounts.* VAT is charged on the price *after* discount even if the prompt payment option is not taken up.

The rules are demonstrated as follows.

Illustration

An invoice is issued for £1,000 + VAT. A 2% discount is offered for payment within 30 days. The VAT on the invoice is £171.50 (£1,000 × 98 % × 17.5%) even if the customer does not take up the discount option.

4.11 Input VAT

Input VAT is not recoverable on certain purchases and expenses as follows.

♦ **Motor cars**

This disallowance does not extend to vans, lorries etc. The VAT inclusive amount on cars is, however, available for capital allowances. Where a motor car is leased, even though there may be private use, 50% of the VAT charged by the leasing company is reclaimable.

♦ **Entertainment**

Input VAT is not recoverable, except where the expenditure is solely for employees.

♦ **Non–business expenditure**

Input tax on professional fees for company reconstructions and issue of share capital are disallowed as non-business expenditure.

4.12 Preparing the VAT account

Registered traders need to prepare a quarterly VAT account which details the total output and input VAT and the resulting VAT liability or repayment.

For exam purposes, where required, this should be done in a 'T account' format.

VAT account

Input VAT on purchases	X	Output VAT on sales	X
Input VAT on expenses	X	Understatement on previous return (£2,000 maximum)	X
Input VAT on returns to suppliers	(X)	Car fuel charge	X
Bad debt relief	X	Output VAT on returns from customers	(X)
VAT payable carried forward	X		
	X		X

Practice question 1 *(The answer is in the final chapter of this book)*

NCH

NCH Ltd's management accounts for the quarter ended 31 May 2003 are shown below. All figures *exclude* VAT. The following additional information is provided.

♦ NCH Ltd's sales, purchases and other expenses are all standard rated for VAT.

♦ The expenses include the cost of both private and business petrol for the managing director's car which had an engine capacity of 1,800 cc. The quarterly fuel charge (VAT inclusive) of a car with cubic capacity 1,401–2,000 is £300.

♦ The bad debts were written off in May 2003. Payment for the original sales was due 28 February 2003.

♦ The sales and purchases returns are all evidenced by credit notes issued and received.

♦ A sales invoice for £3,000 excluding VAT had been omitted in error from the VAT return for the quarter to 28 February 2003.

♦ The VAT *exclusive* management accounts are as follows.

	£	£
Sales		16,500
Sales returns		(900)
		15,600
Purchases	9,600	
Purchases returns	(300)	
	9,300	
Bad debts written off	1,500	
Other expenses	2,400	
		13,200
Profit		2,400

Required

(a) You are required to complete the VAT account for the three month period ended 31 May 2003, showing how much VAT is payable to Customs.

(b) When is the tax shown above payable?

All workings should be done to the nearest pound.

5 Special accounting schemes

5.1 Introduction

Certain schemes have been introduced to relieve the VAT burden on smaller businesses.

♦ The cash accounting scheme
♦ The annual accounting scheme
♦ The flat rate scheme

There is also a special scheme for large traders to accelerate payments of VAT to Customs.

5.2 The cash accounting scheme

This scheme is primarily designed to ease the cashflow burden on smaller businesses. It provides automatic bad debt relief as VAT is accounted for on the basis of cash received and paid, rather than on invoices issued and received.

The date of payment or receipt (rather than the tax point) determines the VAT return in which the transaction is included.

The scheme can be applied for if expected taxable turnover (excluding VAT) does not exceed £600,000.

To be accepted on the scheme the trader must be up to date with all VAT returns and payments. (There is an exception to this where no more than £5,000 VAT is outstanding and arrangements are in force to pay it.)

The trader must not have been convicted of a VAT offence within the past 12 months.

There is a minimum participation period in the scheme of two years. However, this is overridden where taxable turnover in the previous 12 months (measured by VAT accounting periods) exceeds £750,000, and where it is expected to exceed £600,000 in the next 12 months. In this situation the trader must leave the scheme.

Returns are still prepared quarterly.

5.3 Annual accounting scheme

The aim of this scheme is to reduce the administrative burden of preparing quarterly returns and to even out the VAT payments required for the smaller business, thus aiding cashflow planning.

Businesses with a taxable turnover (excluding VAT) of less than £600,000 may join, provided the business has been registered for at least one year. If taxable turnover is expected to be less than £150,000 the trader may join the scheme from registration without having to wait a year.

Only one VAT return is required on an annual basis. The return and the balancing final payments (see below) must be made within two months of the end of each annual VAT period.

For businesses that have been registered for at least a year, the total VAT liability (for the previous year) is divided by ten, and nine monthly instalments are made commencing at the end of month four. If the trader has not been registered for a year, Customs will agree an estimate of the current year's VAT liability.

Customs can permit an alternative schedule of quarterly payments in which case the procedure is as follows:

♦ Customs estimate the VAT payment for the year (based, where possible, on the previous year's liability).

♦ The trader then makes three quarterly payments at the end of months four, seven and ten of 25% of the total year's estimated liability, with the final payment being made within two months of the end of the period.

Traders must leave the scheme when taxable turnover exceeds £750,000.

5.4 Flat rate scheme

Traders can apply to join a special flat rate scheme if their expected VAT exclusive annual taxable turnover for the next 12 months does not exceed £150,000 and their total turnover (including zero rated and exempt supplies) is not expected to exceed £187,500.

The net tax due to Customs for a return period is then calculated as a flat rate percentage of the total turnover. This includes standard rated and reduced rate standard rated supplies at their tax inclusive amount and zero rated and exempt supplies. Actual amounts of output tax and input tax are irrelevant.

The flat rate percentage depends on the trade sector of the business (and will be provided in the exam room if required). Flat rate traders are still required to issue normal VAT invoices to their VAT registered customers but there are less records for the trader to maintain so there are administrative advantages.

Example

Rivendale Ltd's trade has a flat rate percentage rating of 12% and makes annual VAT inclusive standard rated sales of £130,000 pa. The company makes VAT inclusive purchases of £5,170 for the year.

Without applying the flat rate regime:

Net output tax due for the year:

		£
Output tax	$130,000 \times \frac{7}{47}$	19,362
Input tax	$5,170 \times \frac{7}{47}$	770
VAT due to Customs		18,592

With the flat rate regime:

Net output tax:	$130,000 \times 12\%$	15,600

In this particular situation the company benefits from applying the flat rules for calculating output tax due as it results in almost £3,000 of extra trading profit.

5.5   Large traders

Taxable persons whose annual VAT liability exceeds £2 million must make monthly payments on account of their liability. The amount of each payment is one twelfth of the VAT due based upon the previous year's liability.

6   VAT penalties and interest

6.1   Penalties

The VAT system has a range of penalties and interest. These are designed to enforce the timely and accurate completion of VAT returns. The main penalties are considered below.

Type	*Cause*	*Penalty effect*
1. Late registration	Failure to register when compulsorily required under Tests 1 and 2	Minimum of £50 Graduated effect: 0 – 9 months late – 5% (note 1) 9 – 18 months late – 10% 18 + months late – 15%

2. Default surcharge	Late submission of a VAT return or late payment of tax	A surcharge notice is issued when a return or payment is late. This is known as a *default* notice period. It lasts for 12 months

If a further default occurs (ie during the 12 month period) then:

1st default –	2% (note 2)
2nd default –	5%
3rd default –	10%
4th default –	15%

3. Serious misdeclaration	Where net VAT for a period is under declared by lower of: (a) 30% of the gross attributable tax (output + input VAT added together) = GAT (b) £1 million	15% of the VAT which would have been lost (by Customs) if the inaccuracy had not been discovered.
4. Repeated misdeclarations	Where repeated errors are made. These errors must exceed the lower of: (a) 10% of GAT or (b) £500,000 over a defined period (details not examinable)	15% of the VAT for the return period which would have been lost through the error.

Note 1:   The percentage (5/10/or 15) applies to the net VAT due for the period from the date the registration should have started to the date Customs received notice of liability to register.

Note 2:   Customs will not collect penalties of less than £200 if the charge is at 2% or 5%.

The effect of a further default is also to extend the surcharge period by a further 12 months.

Customs have announced that they will relax their approach to automatic late payment penalties for businesses with a turnover not exceeding £150,000.

6.2   *Example*

A company is registered for VAT and usually makes its returns on time. The following returns, however, are made late.

Return	Tax outstanding
	£
31 December 1999	6,000
30 June 2000	8,000
30 June 2001	9,000
31 March 2002	9,300
31 December 2003	8,100

What are the consequences of these defaults?

6.3 Solution

Period ended	Tax outstanding £	Consequence
31 December 1999	6,000	First default: surcharge liability notice served
30 June 2000	8,000	Penalty 2% (£160) which will not be collected as less than £200
30 June 2001 [1]	9,000	Penalty 5% (£450)
31 March 2002 [2]	9,300	Penalty 10% (£930)
31 December 2003 [3]	8,100	First default: surcharge liability notice served

Notes

1   The effect of 30 June 2000 return being late is that the surcharge period is extended until 30 June 2001 (ie for a further 12 months).

2   The effect of 30 June 2001 return being late is to extend the surcharge period for a further 12 months until 30 June 2002.

3   There is no surcharge penalty when the 31 December 2003 return is late as it is not in a surcharge period, but it starts a new 12 month period.

6.4 Mitigating circumstances

In the four situations above, penalties may be cancelled if the trader has a reasonable excuse. A reasonable excuse may include the following.

♦ Computer breakdown
♦ Illness
♦ Loss of key personnel
♦ Loss of records

However, these have to be unforeseeable events. For example, a bookkeeper's sudden illness just before the VAT return was due might qualify but his continuing illness would not. The business had time to make other arrangements.

Statute specifically states that a reasonable excuse is not:

(a)   insufficient funds to pay any VAT due or

(b)   the reliance on any other person (eg a tax agent) to perform a task and that person was dilatory or inaccurate in carrying it out.

The following do *not* rank as reasonable excuses.

♦ Absence on business or holiday
♦ Misunderstanding or ignorance of VAT law
♦ Pressure of work
♦ Shortage of staff

In the case of late registration and serious and repeated misdeclarations (but not default surcharge), Customs (or a VAT tribunal) have powers to reduce the penalty to whatever amount 'they think proper'. However they are not entitled to take into account pleas for mitigation based on:

(a)   insufficiency of funds to pay the VAT or the penalty
(b)   the fact that no VAT or very little VAT has been lost or
(c)   the fact that the person charged with the penalty (or his agent) had acted in good faith.

In any case, penalties are unlikely to be exacted if certain errors are disclosed voluntarily except where the trader was aware that enquiries by Customs were pending.

6.5   Default interest

Interest for late payment may also be charged from the due date, at an annual rate prescribed. Interest will not be charged on errors of less than £2,000 which are corrected on a return, but will be charged on errors of more than £2,000. Notification of such errors should be done separately and in writing. VAT – default interest

Any interest (or penalties) so levied is not tax deductible for Schedule D purposes.

Practice question 2 *(The answer is in the final chapter of this book)*

Tee Total

(a)   Tee Ltd has been trading for about a year and is VAT registered. The managing director has recently heard that the government has certain schemes available to make VAT easier for small businesses.

Prepare brief notes outlining the schemes available.

(b)   Total Ltd submitted its VAT return for the quarter to 31 May 2003 on 31 July 2003 as the company's accountant has got into arrears with his bookkeeping. After its submission the accountant discovers that he has incorrectly reclaimed input VAT of £8,500. The correct VAT liability for the period was £20,000 being output tax of £24,000 less and input tax of £4,000. No action has yet been taken in respect of this under–declaration.

Outline the possible VAT penalties which Total Ltd has triggered by these actions and advise the company of any action it should take to avoid or mitigate those penalties.

---

7   Appeals and assessments

7.1   Assessments

Where a taxpayer fails to make returns, or Customs consider the returns to be incomplete or incorrect, they may issue *assessments* of the amount due. This is normally done within two years of the period when the fault occurs but can be extended to three years. Where there is fraudulent or negligent conduct the period is increased to 20 years.

7.2   Appeal procedure

Where an assessment is made or other dispute arises with Customs (such as the requirement to register, or the calculation of output VAT) the trader can appeal.

The right of appeal does not apply to every possible grounds for disputes. Instead statute provides a lengthy but not exhaustive list of appealable matters.

The trader has 30 days to appeal in writing against a decision of the local VAT office. The local office can then either confirm the decision or reverse the decision. In either case, the trader can appeal in writing to a VAT tribunal. In the former case, 21 days is allowed, in the latter 30 days.

The role of the VAT tribunal is to hear the appeal. It is normally conducted in public. A further appeal on a point of law can be made to the courts, including the European Court of Justice.

For a VAT tribunal to proceed, all VAT returns and payments (including the tax in dispute unless the trader can show 'hardship') must have been made.

Costs may be awarded by a VAT tribunal to either party.

8 Property

8.1 Introduction

The VAT treatment of land and buildings is complicated and depends on the age and type of property concerned. For example

♦ Sales of new commercial buildings, and those less than three years old, are standard rated.

♦ Sales (or leases for over 21 years) of new residential properties are zero-rated.

♦ Sales of buildings more than three years old, and rental income, are exempt from VAT unless the option to tax has been exercised.

8.2 The option to tax

A landlord who acquires a building for commercial letting can elect to treat the rental as a taxable supply. The election is irrevocable for 20 years and applies to all future supplies of the property (including its sale).

Making the election allows the landlord to recover his input tax, including that paid on the purchase of the property.

Before deciding whether to make the election, the landlord should consider the VAT status of the tenants. If they are registered, they can recover the VAT they are charged. However, if they are exempt or not registered, any VAT charged is an additional expense to them.

If the landlord does not make the election, the VAT incurred on any revenue expenses is deductible in calculating the Schedule A income. The VAT on any capital expenses forms part of the cost of the property in calculating the capital gain on its eventual disposal.

9 Partial exemption

9.1 Input tax recovery

Certain traders make both taxable and exempt supplies. Such traders are known as *partially exempt.*

Input VAT can only be recovered on purchases and expenses which relate to taxable supplies. Therefore, when dealing with a partially exempt trader it will be necessary to adopt the following procedure to determine the amount of input VAT which is recoverable.

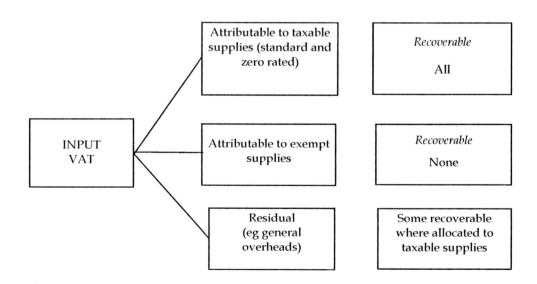

The 'residual' input VAT is split between taxable and exempt supplies using an acceptable allocation method. The standard method adopted uses the value of supplies to determine the split as follows.

$$\text{Residual VAT} \times \frac{\text{Total taxable supplies}}{\text{Total supplies}} \quad \text{(rounded up to nearest whole number \%)}$$

Sales of capital goods are excluded from the fraction. Taxable supplies include both standard rated and zero rated supplies.

Where the total exempt input VAT is below £625 per month on average, and does not exceed 50% of the total input VAT, then all of the VAT is recoverable. (This kind of rule – where the authorities do not pursue trifling sums – is often referred to as a *de minimis* exception).

The partial exemption calculation is done quarter by quarter. At the year end the calculations are done for the 12 months and any over or under recovery of input tax is adjusted for in the first return of the following year.

'Partial exemption' is a common exam topic as it is one of the few VAT areas which can be tested computationally.

9.2 Example

A VAT registered trader pays total input tax in a year of £30,000, made up as follows.

	£
Input tax wholly relating to taxable supplies	18,000
Input tax wholly relating to exempt supplies	2,000
Other input tax	10,000
	30,000

The supplies for the year are analysed as follows.

	£
Taxable supplies	150,000
Exempt supplies	50,000
	200,000

Required

Calculate how much input tax is recoverable.

9.3 Solution

		£
Step 1	Input VAT always recoverable – relating to taxable supplies	18,000
Step 2	Residual input VAT is £10,000. The recoverable amount is	7,500

$$\frac{\text{Taxable supplies}}{\text{Total supplies}} \quad \frac{150,000}{200,000} \times £10,000 =$$

Step 3 Consider the amount of exempt input VAT not currently recoverable £2,000 + (£10,000 – £7,500) = £4,500 ÷ 12 = £375 per month. As this is below £625 per month and is below 50% of the total input tax for the year, it is all recoverable. 4,500

	30,000

Practice question 3 *(The answer is in the final chapter of this book)*

Artley

For the year ended 31 March 2004 Artley Ltd had the following transactions.

	£
General sales (standard rate VAT)	120,000
General sales (zero rate VAT)	15,000
Plant sold to another UK trader	5,000
Exempt sales made	100,000
Wages to employees	75,000
New motor car bought for salesman (petrol provided for business use only)	6,500

(None of the above amounts include VAT)

Input tax attributable to:

Taxable supplies	10,000
Exempt supplies	6,500
Overheads	3,000

Required

(a) Compute the total amount of output tax for which Artley Ltd would be required to account, and how much input tax could be deducted therefrom for the year ended 31 March 2004. Assume that the standard method of attribution applies.

(b) State the corporation tax implications of any disallowed input tax.

10 VAT group registration

10.1 Introduction

Two or more companies can elect for a VAT group registration to apply, where they are members of a 51% group or where companies are under common control.

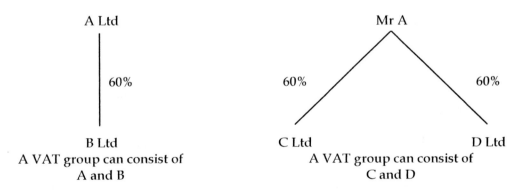

The definition does *not* require effective interest, but all companies must have a fixed establishment in the UK.

Where there is a registration in force, the VAT group appoints a representative member who is responsible for accounting for all input and output VAT by preparing a single VAT return for the group.

The effect can be considered in terms of advantages and disadvantages.

Advantages		*Disadvantages*	
(a)	VAT on intra-group supplies eliminated	(a)	All members remain jointly and severally liable
(b)	Only one VAT return required	(b)	A single return may cause administrative difficulties collecting and collating information
		(c)	The inclusion of a net repayment company (zero-rated supplies) would result in loss of monthly repayments

 Particular care needs to be taken where a company makes exempt supplies, as its inclusion within a VAT group may make the group partially exempt. This may restrict the amount of input tax recoverable by the group as a whole.

10.2 Example

S Ltd, Z Ltd and E Ltd have the following forecast sales and purchases for the year ended 31 March 2004.

	S Ltd £	Z Ltd £	E Ltd £
Taxable supplies	900,000	300,000	–
Exempt supplies	–	–	600,000
Purchases	300,000	100,000	200,000
Overheads	200,000	–	–
Management fee	60,000	20,000	40,000

The purchases, overheads and management fee are all standard rated. The overheads cannot be directly attributed to the sales of any of the three companies. All figures are exclusive of VAT where applicable.

Required

Explain the implications of the following.

(a)   Including E Ltd in the VAT group
(b)   Excluding E Ltd from the VAT group

10.3 Solution

(a)   If E Ltd is included in the VAT group, the group will become partially exempt. The recovery of input tax on the overheads will be limited to:

$$\frac{\text{Taxable supplies}}{\text{Total supplies}} \qquad \frac{1,200,000}{1,800,000} \; 66.67\% \text{ rounded up to } 67\%$$

The amount of input tax recoverable is therefore £200,000 × 17.5% × 67% = £23,450.

The balance of £11,550 (£35,000 – £23,450) is not recoverable.

(b)   If E Ltd is excluded from the VAT group, VAT of £7,000 (£40,000 × 17.5%) will be payable on the intra-group management fee. This is not recoverable as E Ltd makes wholly exempt supplies.

On balance, therefore, it is preferable to exclude E Ltd from the group as the overall liability will be reduced by £4,550 (£11,550 - £7,000).

11 Overseas aspects of VAT

11.1 Overview

Many traders will have transactions with overseas countries. You therefore need to have an outline knowledge of the different VAT treatments which will apply. In particular, there is a need to distinguish between transactions within or outside the European Union.

You need to distinguish the VAT treatment of the following.

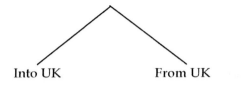

Transactions within the European Union (EU)

Into UK   From UK

Transactions outside the EU

Imports   Exports

11.2 EU transactions

Into UK	Transactions	Accounting for VAT
Supplier and customer registered	Zero rated	(a) VAT paid by customer at the appropriate rate in force in the UK (b) VAT paid then reclaimed as input VAT in the appropriate quarter (c) Known as the destination system
Supplier registered but not customer	VAT charged at supplier's appropriate rate	This is known as the origin system
From UK		
Supplier and customer registered	Zero rated	VAT registration number of customer must be shown on invoice
Supplier registered but not customer	Standard rated	Where supplies to the destination country exceed an EU threshold, the supplier will have to register for VAT in *that* country.

11.3 Non EU transactions

Imports

The importer has to pay VAT at time of entry, and may then recover VAT through the quarterly system.

Exports

All goods and services are zero rated.

11.4   Example

Overseas Ltd, a UK resident company registered for VAT, has the following international transactions.

(a)   Sale of children's toys to a customer in Germany, who is VAT registered in Germany.
(b)   Sale of ladies' handbags to Venezuela.
(c)   Sale of men's ties to an Italian customer, who is not VAT registered.
(d)   Purchase of silk fabric from Hong Kong.

Outline the VAT treatment in each case for Overseas Ltd.

11.5   Solution

(a)   Overseas Ltd will charge VAT at zero rate because it is an EU transaction, and the customer is VAT registered.

(b)   The transaction is zero rated as an export outside EU.

(c)   The transaction must be standard rated as the customer is not VAT registered.

(d)   VAT will be paid at point of entry into UK. Overseas Ltd will then recover VAT through the quarterly system.

12   Summary

Supplies of goods and services are either *taxable supplies* (standard rated or zero rated) or *exempt supplies*. They are standard rated unless they fall into specific categories classified as zero rated or exempt.

Traders *must* register for VAT if their taxable supplies exceed certain thresholds. *Voluntary* registration is also possible and may be advantageous, particularly to traders making zero rated supplies.

Periodic VAT returns, along with VAT payments, must be submitted to Customs.

The cash accounting scheme and the annual accounting scheme are designed to reduce the administration burdens on small businesses.

Penalties and interest are charged to enforce timely and accurate submission of VAT returns and payments.

 Multiple choice questions 1 - 4 *(The answers are in the final chapter of this book)*

Each of the questions below has only one correct answer.

1   Fred Threads Ltd orders a stock of goods on a 'sale or return' basis.

It pays a refundable deposit on 25 May.
The goods are despatched on 3 June.
The company confirms acceptance of the goods on 15 July.
An invoice is issued on 20 July.

What is the tax point for VAT purposes?

A   25 May

B   3 June

C   15 July

D   20 July

2   A customer purchased goods from a retailer for £80 plus VAT.

Which of the following need not be shown on the VAT invoice?

A   The retailer's VAT registration number

B   The rate of VAT

C   A description sufficient to identify the goods supplied

D   An invoice number

3   Spline Ltd makes taxable supplies of £70,000 and exempt supplies of £30,000 in a tax period. In the same period input tax is £5,500 of which £4,125 is attributable to taxable supplies and £875 to exempt supplies.

To what input tax credit is the company entitled?

A   £4,125

B   £4,475

C   £4,625

D   £5,500

4   Fancy Weeds Ltd acquired a car on hire purchase for use in its retail clothes business. About 60% of total annual mileage is for business purposes. The total amount to be paid over the next three years is as follows.

	£
VAT exclusive price	10,000
VAT	1,750
Finance charge	2,115
	13,865

On what amount may capital allowances be claimed?

A   £10,000

B   £11,750

C   £12,115

D   £13,865

CHAPTER 15

Employment income - benefits

EXAM FOCUS

Under the old syllabus, employees' taxation tended to be examined in the optional part of the paper. In the pilot paper for the new syllabus, this topic appears in one of the multiple choice questions and is also an optional question in part C of the paper.

The most likely areas for examination are the calculation of benefits in kind and the employers' compliance requirements.

Before 6 April 2003, income from employment (including pensions and certain social security benefits) was labelled as 'Schedule E' under the time honoured schedular system. In an effort to modernise the tax system, the Schedule E legislation was rewritten by the Income Tax (Earnings and Pensions) Act 2003 with the label 'Schedule E' replaced by 'employment income', 'pension income' and 'social security income' as appropriate. In time the other Schedules will be re-labelled as the relevant parts of the legislation are rewritten in plain English. Although the term 'Schedule E' no longer has any meaning, examiners and others may continue with its use and you should be prepared for that.

LEARNING OUTCOMES

This chapter covers the following learning outcomes of the CIMA syllabus:

> Apply knowledge of the Benefits in Kind (BIK) system for employees

> Identify the rules for different types of employees

> Calculate the total assessable benefits of an employee and explain the effect on code numbers .

In order to cover these learning outcomes the following topics are covered:

> Employment income assessments
> Benefits: all employees
> Benefits assessable on employees earning at least £8,500 a year and directors.

1 Employment income assessments

1.1 Types of income

Employment income assessments are made on all earnings received from an office or employment. Such income includes salaries, wages, bonuses, commissions, directors' fees, tips, general allowances and benefits.

Any pension resulting from an employment is also assessed under the employment income rules.

1.2 Basis of assessment

The basis of assessment for earnings is the receipts basis. This means that income is taxed in the year in which an employee receives it or becomes entitled to the payment, if earlier. (Except for benefits and pensions which are assessable when they arise).

1.3 Allowable expenses

The taxpayer can deduct various expenses he incurs from the assessable amount.

♦ Expenses incurred wholly, exclusively and necessarily in the performance of his duties.

♦ Costs of business travel and subsistence. Business travel includes journeys made in the performance of an employee's duties. It does not include travel between home and the permanent workplace, ie ordinary commuting.

♦ Professional subscriptions.

♦ Amounts donated under the payroll giving scheme. Under this scheme employees can have sums deducted from their salary by their employer and paid directly to charity.

♦ Contributions to company pension schemes.

Here is a proforma employment income computation.

		£
Salary/fees/commission/bonus etc		X
Benefits		X
		X
Less:	Professional subscriptions	(X)
	Donations under payroll giving schemes	(X)
	Company pension contributions	(X)
	Expenses incurred wholly, exclusively and necessarily in the performance of duties	(X)
Assessable employment income		X

1.4 Example

Underwood is employed as an insurance salesman at a monthly salary of £950. In addition to his basic salary he receives a bonus which is paid in May each year and which is related to the sales achieved by Underwood in the year to the previous 31 October. His bonuses are as follows.

Bonus for year to	Paid during	£
31 October 2001	May 2002	1,920
31 October 2002	May 2003	1,260
31 October 2003	May 2004	2,700

Underwood made the following payments in respect of his employment in 2003/04.

	£
Contribution to occupational pension scheme (3% of basic salary)	342
Subscription to Chartered Insurance Institute	100
Payroll deduction scheme (in favour of Oxfam)	200

Required

Compute the assessable employment income for 2003/04.

1.5   Solution

Underwood's emoluments assessable for 2003/04 are as follows.

		£	£
Basic salary (£950 × 12)			11,400
Bonus paid in May 2003			1,260
			12,660
Less:	Allowable expenses		
	Subscription	100	
	Pension scheme	342	
	Payroll deduction scheme	200	(642)
Assessable employment income			12,018

1.6   The overseas element

An individual could be employed in the UK or employed overseas. He could be a foreign national on a short tour of duty in the UK or perhaps a UK national seconded abroad for several years by his UK employer. There are a number of different situations which could arise and the tax rules have been designed to give three main treatments:

1   If an employee is resident and ordinarily resident in the UK (see below for definition) he is taxable in full on his employment income. This is regardless of where he earns the income and whether, if he is paid abroad, he remits the income to the UK. This is a simple treatment which applies to virtually all 'UK based' employees.

2   If an employee is either not UK resident or UK resident but not ordinarily resident in the UK he is taxable on his UK earnings as he receives them (ie receipts basis regardless of whether they are brought to the UK).

3   If the employee is UK resident but not ordinarily resident in the UK, his earnings in respect of duties carried out wholly outside the UK are taxable, but only on the amounts he remits to the UK.

Note that if the individual can avoid UK resident tax status he is not taxable on his overseas earnings.

Residence and ordinary residence are not specifically defined in the Taxes Act.

In practice an individual is resident in the UK for a year of assessment if:

(a)   he spends at least 6 months in the UK in that year or

(b)   he spends some time in the UK in that year and, together with the previous three years he averages at least 3 months per annum in the UK.

An individual is ordinarily resident in the UK if he regards the UK as his home at least for the present. For example, visitors to the UK are regarded as ordinarily resident in the UK if they intend to remain here for at least 3 years.

2 Benefits: all employees

2.1 Classifying benefits

Benefits are split into three categories.

♦ Exempt benefits
♦ Benefits assessable on all directors and all employees
♦ Benefits assessable on directors and employees earning at least £8,500 per annum.

Before we consider the specific benefits here are some general points which are *frequently* examined.

♦ If an employee pays his employer for a benefit, the assessable amount is reduced (except for partial payments for private petrol, covered below).

♦ An employee may be able to claim that a benefit (or part of it) was provided wholly, exclusively and necessarily for business purposes. In such situations you should first calculate the benefit, then claim an expense deduction to clear it.

♦ For most benefits *time apportion* the assessable amount if the benefit was only available for part of the tax year. This should be done in *months* and is a very popular adjustment in exam questions.

2.2 Exempt benefits

These include the following.

♦ Job related accommodation

♦ Subsidised canteen available to all staff provided the level of subsidy is broadly similar for all grades of employees and directors.

♦ Luncheon vouchers up to 15p a day

♦ Removal expenses up to £8,000 for a new employment or if an employee's job is relocated

♦ Personal expenses (eg telephone calls home) paid by the employer whilst the employee is required to stay away on company business (up to £5 per night)

♦ Parking spaces near place of work – for cars, bicycles or motorcycles

♦ Workplace nurseries (crèches)

♦ Contributions by an employer to an approved (occupational) pension scheme

♦ Sport and recreational facilities available generally for the staff, provided that the facilities are not available to the public generally

♦ Air miles, etc obtained through business travel or use of a company credit card

♦ Outplacement counselling services to employees made redundant

♦ Liability insurance

♦ The provision of a mobile telephone

♦ The expenses of work related training borne by the employer

♦ Loans which do not exceed £5,000 at any time during the tax year

♦ The provision of bicycles or cycling safety equipment to enable employees to get to and from work, provided they are available to staff generally

♦ The provision of computer equipment worth up to £2,500 (see later)

♦ Mileage allowances paid up to the Inland Revenue authorised rates for use of the employee's own car, motor bike or bicycle for business (see beyond).

♦ Contributions by an employer towards the additional household costs incurred by an employee working from home instead of at the employer's premises. Only payments above £2 pw require supporting evidence.

♦ The funding of an annual party or similar event (eg Christmas office party or staff Summer outing) up to £150 per attendee per year.

♦ Up to £250 per recipient per tax year of value from a third party received by an employee in connection with his employment (eg hospitality event or Christmas hamper to the purchases manager from a supplier firm).

♦ A long service award of £50 for each year of service.

2.3 Benefits assessable on all employees and directors

The following benefits are assessable on all employees and directors, irrespective of the level of their earnings.

Type of benefit	*Amount assessable*
The gift of an asset convertible into money (eg a suit or a television set)	Cash equivalent (ie the price the employee could obtain if he converted the benefit into cash). However, directors and employees paid over £8,500 pa are assessed on the cost to the employer
The payment by an employer of an employee's liabilities	The amount paid by the employer
Cash vouchers	Redemption value of the voucher
Non–cash vouchers (includes luncheon vouchers over 15p, transport vouchers, cheque vouchers)	Cost of voucher to the employer
Credit cards	Whatever the employee charges to the card (but not interest and annual fee)
Accommodation	See below (parts 1 and 2 only)

2.4 Accommodation

The assessable benefit depends on whether the accommodation is job related or not.

Accommodation is 'job related':

(a)   if necessary for the proper performance of employment duties

(b)   if provided for better performance of duties and it is customary to provide accommodation in such circumstances

(c)   if there is a special security threat and the accommodation is part of the arrangements to counter the threat.

'Job related' therefore includes accommodation provided for caretakers, hotel staff, clergy and certain members of the government.

The calculation of the benefit is split into three parts.

Benefit in kind	Not job related	Job related
1 Basic charge for the provision of the property	Higher of the annual value of the property (ie the gross rateable value) and the rent paid by the employer	No charge
2 Additional charge where the cost of the property and improvement costs was more than £75,000	(Cost - £75,000) × official rate of interest (currently 5%)	No charge
3 Ancillary services – this only applies to employees who earn more than £8,500 per annum		
Use of furniture	20% per annum of market value when first provided	Maximum benefit chargeable for furniture and living expenses is 10% of net remuneration (see below)
Living expenses eg heating/ electricity, decorating (not structural repairs)	Cost to employer	

Net remuneration consists of cash remuneration plus all other assessable benefits, *excluding* the ancillary services being considered, less allowable expenses and professional subscriptions.

2.5 Example

Mr X lives in a furnished company flat that cost his employers £105,000 in June 1999. The annual value (ie gross rateable value) of the flat is £2,500 and Mr X pays his employers rent of £100 a month. The accommodation is not job–related. Furniture costing £6,000 was first provided in June 1999.

The official rate of interest is 5% on 6 April 2003.

Required

Calculate Mr X's assessable benefit for 2003/04.

2.6 Solution

	£
Basic charge – annual value	2,500
Additional charge – (£105,000 – £75,000) = £30,000 × 5%	1,500
Use of furniture 20% × £6,000	1,200
	5,200
Less contribution by employee (£100 × 12)	(1,200)
	4,000

3 Benefits assessable on employees earning at least £8,500 a year and directors

3.1 Scope

The benefits covered in this section apply only to those employees earning at a rate of at least £8,500 a year and to directors, irrespective of their level of earnings.

To decide whether or not an employee should be included in this category, we calculate their earnings including the taxable value of all benefits. The assessable benefits are calculated as if the employee *is* earning at least £8,500. No expenses are deducted for the purpose of this calculation.

Directors are assessed in the same way as employees earning £8,500 a year. The only exception is directors who

♦ work full-time in the business **and**
♦ do not have a material interest in the company (ie more than 5% of the share capital).

3.2 Expenses

Reimbursed expenses are treated as earnings. The employee can then claim a deduction if he shows that they were incurred wholly, exclusively and necessarily in the performance of the duties.

The treatment of entertaining expenses depends on the way in which they are met. Employees cannot claim a deduction for entertaining expenses paid out of their salary, or out of a general allowance. However, a deduction can be claimed for expenses specifically reimbursed by the employer or paid for out of a specific entertaining allowance.

The employer may pay a mileage allowance if an employee uses his own car, motor bike or bicycle for business.

The Inland Revenue specify authorised mileage rates. The tax position is as follows:

♦ If the allowance is paid at the authorised rate, the allowance is not treated as earnings, nor can any deduction be claimed.

♦ If the allowance is paid at a rate in excess of the authorised rate, only the excess is treated as earnings, and is taxable.

♦ If the allowance is paid at a rate less than the authorised rate, none of the allowance is treated as earnings, but a deduction may be claimed for the shortfall.

The rates are 40p per mile for the first 10,000 miles and 25p per mile thereafter for cars. The rate is 24p per mile for motor bikes and 20p per mile for bicycles regardless of mileage. The employer may pay a tax free allowance of 5p per mile for each passenger carried in the employee's car for business purposes, but if no allowance is paid the employee cannot claim a deduction. These rates should be given to you in the examination if required.

3.3 Company cars

When a car is made available for private use, an assessable benefit is deemed to arise as a result of the *private* use of the car.

The benefit is calculated as a percentage of the list price of the car when first registered. (The maximum list price is £80,000.)

List price includes the cost of extras, both those provided with the car and any made available subsequently.

The list price can be reduced by any capital contribution made by the employee, subject to a maximum of £5,000.

Determining the percentage

The minimum percentage is 15% and the maximum is 35%. The percentage depends on the rate at which the car emits carbon dioxide – usually recorded on the car's registration document (and likely to be supplied in the exam).

If the emission rate is no more than 155 grams per kilometre travelled, the minimum percentage of 15% applies. This is increased by 1% for every extra 5 grams emitted. Diesel engine vehicles are surcharged an extra 3% to reflect the additional pollutants compared to petrol engines for the same carbon dioxide level of emission although for both petrol and diesel the maximum percentage is 35%.

To encourage the car industry to produce even cleaner car engines, the base level of emissions will be further reduced to 145g/km in 2004/05 and 140g/km in 2005/06. Thus a car with an emission rate of 172g/km attracts a benefit charge based on 18% of list price in 2003/04 rising to 20% in 2004/05 and 21% in 2005/06.

There are special rules for situations where the emission data is not available but these are not examinable.

Non–availability

Where a car is temporarily unavailable to the employee for 30 days or more during any part of the tax year the benefit is reduced proportionately. Non–availability of less than 30 days is ignored.

A common exam mistake is miscounting the number of months of availability.

Running costs

Running expenses (for example servicing, insurance) are deemed to be included in the benefit figure and do not produce an additional benefit. However, the provision of a chauffeur is counted as an additional benefit valued at the private use portion of the driver's salary costs.

Cars used only for business

Where an employee is specifically forbidden from using his company car for private purposes and, as a matter of fact, does not so use it, there will be no assessable car benefit.

There is also no benefit where there is provision of a company car (and associated services) which is a 'pool' car. This is one which is not exclusively used by any one employee, and which is not available for travel from home to work, being garaged at company premises, and only used for business travel.

3.4 Example

Sue is provided with a 2000 cc petrol driven Rover by her employer. The emission rate shown on the registration document is 221 gms of carbon dioxide per kilometre and list price of the car when new was £16,000. During 2003/04 Sue drove 3,000 business miles and paid her employer £2,000 in respect of her private use of the car.

Required

Calculate the benefit assessable on Sue for 2003/04.

3.5 Solution

The amount of the benefit arising is as follows.

	£
£16,000 × 28%	4,480
Less: Contribution	(2,000)
Benefit	2,480

The benefit is calculated at the rate of 28% being 15% + (220 − 155) × $\frac{1}{5}$.

3.6 Example

Paul is provided with a 2300 cc diesel powered Audi by his employer. The list price of the car when new was £30,000. During 2003/04 Paul drove 20,000 business miles. The emission rating of the car is 211g/km.

Required

Calculate the benefit assessable on Paul for 2003/04.

3.7 Solution

The amount of the benefit arising is as follows.

£30,000 × 29% = £8,700

The benefit is calculated at the rate of 29% (15% + (210 − 155) × $\frac{1}{5}$ + 3% (diesel)). Note that the business mileage driven and the engine size is of no relevance to the calculation.

3.8 Fuel provided for private purposes

In order to counter the provision of tax–free private petrol or diesel for company cars, such provision is the subject of a benefit charge which is in addition to the charge for the provision of the car itself.

The fuel benefit is calculated as £14,400 multiplied by the same percentage used for calculating the car benefit. The figure of £14,400 applies for 2003/04 and will probably be provided in the exam room if you need to use it.

The fuel benefit is nil if either:

♦   the employee has to pay his employer for *all* fuel provided for private use; or
♦   the fuel is only provided for business use.

There is no reduction if the employee only partially reimburses his employer for private fuel. This is a common source of error in exam questions.

If private use fuel is permanently withdrawn during the year the benefit charge is restricted by time apportioning. For example, if a car and private use fuel is provided from 1 August 2003 onwards but the provision of private use fuel is suspended from 1 November 2003 onwards, the fuel charge is only 3/12ths of an annual charge. However, if the employer recommences private fuel provision before 6 April 2003, a full 8/12ths charge will apply. This rule is designed to close a simple loophole of an employer merely providing the fuel on the day the tank needs refilling!

3.9 Example

Joan was employed as sales manager of Wilt Ltd from 1 August 2003 at a salary of £60,000 per annum. From 1 November 2003 the company provided her with an 1,800 cc car, the list price of which was £15,000 and the emission rate was 184 g/km. Up to 5 April 2004 she drove 6,000 miles of which 4,500 were private. The company paid for all running expenses, but initially only business use petrol. From 1 January 2004 the company paid for all petrol use including private use. Joan made a contribution to her employer of £15 per month towards the provision of the petrol for her private use.

Required

Calculate Joan's assessable earnings for 2003/04.

3.10 Solution

	£	£
Salary (£60,000 × $^8/_{12}$)		40,000
Car benefit (£15,000 × 20%)*	3,000	
Less: non–availability ($^7/_{12}$)	(1,750)	
		1,250
Fuel benefit (£14,400 × 20% × $^3/_{12}$)		720
Assessable earnings		41,970

*The percentage is 20% = 15% + (180 – 155) × $^1/_5$.

3.11 Company vans

In the case of a company van with private use, the assessable benefit is as follows.

♦   £500 per annum if the van is under four years old at the end of the tax year.
♦   £350 per annum if the van is over four years old.

There is no additional benefit charge for the provision of private fuel.

3.12 Beneficial loans

Where by reason of employment an employee or a relative is provided with an interest free or cheap loan, the benefit derived from such an arrangement is taxable. There is no charge if the loan(s) did not exceed £5,000 at any time during the tax year.

Where the loan is used for a qualifying purpose, it will not result in a tax charge. A qualifying purpose is where, for example, the employee uses the loan to:

♦   purchase shares in a close company, or
♦   purchase plant and machinery (but not a car) for use in their employment.

The assessable benefit is calculated as follows.

	£
Loan outstanding x the official rate of interest	X
Less: Interest actually paid by the employee	(X)
Assessable benefit	X

The loan outstanding is calculated as follows.

$$\text{Loan outstanding} = \frac{S+E}{2} \times \frac{M}{12}$$

♦ S = Balance on loan at the start of the tax year (or when the loan is first provided, if later).

♦ E = Balance on loan at the end of the tax year (or when fully repaid, if earlier).

♦ M = number of complete tax months in the tax year during which the loan was outstanding.

This is referred to as the average method.

There is an alternative method for calculating the outstanding loan. This is known as the precise method, which calculates the benefit each time the balance or the official interest rate changes.

The average method is used unless either the taxpayer or the Inland Revenue insist on the precise method applying.

The official rate of interest used for the May and November 2004 exams is likely to be 5%.

3.13 Example

Mr Borrow, an employee of Generous Ltd, was given an interest free loan of £20,000 on 6 June 2003. He repaid £5,000 on 5 December 2003.

Required

What is the assessable benefit using the alternative methods?

3.14 Solution

Average method

$$\frac{£20,000 + £15,000}{2} = £17,500 \times {}^{10}\!/_{12} \times 5\% = £729.$$

Precise method

		£
6 June 2003 – 5 December 2003	$£20,000 \times {}^{6}\!/_{12} \times 5\% =$	500
6 December 2003 – 5 April 2004	$£15,000 \times {}^{4}\!/_{12} \times 5\% =$	250
		750

Mr Borrow would therefore not elect for the precise method. The difference between the two results is unlikely to be sufficiently significant for the Revenue to apply the precise method.

3.15 Gifts and use of assets

If an asset (for example, a television) is owned by the company but the employee is allowed to use it privately, the assessable benefit is calculated as 20% of the open market value when first made available (usually 20% of the cost).

In the case of computer equipment, provided the benefit does not exceed £500 it will not be taxable. If the benefit exceeds £500, only the excess is assessable.

If an asset which is new is gifted to the employee, the benefit will be the cost to the company.

If an asset has been used and is then subsequently gifted to an employee, the benefit is the higher of:

♦ market value (MV) at the date of the gift (less the amount paid by employee).

♦ original market value less benefit amounts assessed to date (less the amount paid by the employee).

3.16 Example

A suit costing £300 was purchased for Bill's use by his employer on 6 April 2002. One year later, the suit is purchased by Bill for £20, the then market value being £30.

Required

Calculate the amounts assessable on Bill.

3.17 Solution

The assessable benefits are computed as follows.

2002/03	
Annual value (20% × £300)	£60
2003/04	£
Suit's current market value	30
Less: Price paid by employee	(20)
	10
	£
Suit's original market value	300
Less: Assessed in 2002/03 in respect of use	(60)
	240
Less: Price paid by employee	(20)
	220

Thus the assessable benefit in 2003/04 is £220, being the greater of £10 and £220.

3.18 General charging section

This covers any other benefits not listed above. The assessable benefit will be the marginal cost to the employer of providing the benefit (package holiday, medical insurance etc) even if, thanks to the employer's buying power, this is less than the price an employee would have to pay.

3.19 Collecting the tax on benefits

The tax due on benefits is usually collected by reducing an employee's PAYE code number by the amount of the benefit. This means that the tax is collected on a monthly (or weekly) basis along with the tax due on any cash remuneration.

The operation of PAYE and the calculation of code numbers are dealt with in the following Chapter.

Practice question 1 *(The answer is in the final chapter of this book)*

LA Raider

LA Raider is employed by Coliseum Ltd

The company accounts show the following information.

Year to 30 November	2002 £	2003 £	2004 £
Salary (paid monthly)	47,780	48,500	53,000
Bonus (paid in the following February)	13,000	14,200	12,700

The following information is provided in respect of 2003/04.

♦ The senior employees have been able to use the company yacht moored on the south coast for two weeks each year since its purchase. Raider spent his fortnight on the boat along with his family. The yacht cost the company £42,000 in 1998 (current value £33,000) and running and maintenance expenses amounted to £6,000 during the year.

♦ Raider belongs to a private medical scheme and the company paid the required premium of £1,270 (including £650 for his family).

♦ Raider took meals in the fully subsidised executive canteen, the cost for the year being £335. Another subsidised canteen was available for the other staff.

♦ Raider was paid a round sum expense allowance of £1,870 out of which he paid £800 on entertaining customers and £550 on business travel.

♦ When at the company premises Raider has use of a car owned by the company for business journeys. It had a list price of £62,000 and an emission rating of 248g/km, is 3,500 cc, costs £4,800 a year to run and the chauffeur's salary is £17,500. It is garaged at the company's head office and is used in addition by all the directors.

♦ Raider is also provided with a two year old 3.5 litre Rover (list price of £27,000). However, he prefers to use his own car, a Lotus, and therefore lets his wife use the Rover which is fully expensed by the company. The carbon dioxide emission rate of the Rover is 282 g/km. His business mileage in his own car is 12,000 miles. All cars run on petrol, and the list prices include delivery and number plates.

♦ He pays 3% of his basic salary into the company's occupational pension scheme. His company contributes 7% of his salary.

♦ Raider is provided with a 1% loan from his employer of £20,000 which was granted three years ago to assist with the purchase of his residence. He has no other loans and has paid interest only, on a monthly basis.

Required

Compute Raider's assessable earnings for 2003/04 as far as the above information allows.

Assume the average official rate of interest for 2003/04 is 5%.

The Inland Revenue authorised mileage rate is 40p a mile for the first 10,000 miles and 25p a mile thereafter. The fuel benefit base figure for 2003/04 is £14,400.

4   *Summary*

The basis of assessment for employment income is the receipts basis. The assessment of benefits in kind depends on whether the employee earns at a rate of more than £8,500 a year.

Company cars are the most likely form of benefit to be examined. Employees are taxed on a percentage of the car's list price. The percentage depends on the amount of carbon dioxide emission ranging from 15% to 35% moving up in 1% steps for every 5 gms/kilometre in excess of the 2003/04 base line of 155 g/km.

Multiple choice questions 1 - 5 *(The answers are in the final chapter of this book)*

Each of the questions below has only one correct answer.

1   Norman earns £3,000 per year and the company he works for gives him luncheon vouchers of 90 pence per working day. He also has the use of a one year old 1,300 cc car, all repairs and the insurance being paid for by the company. The car had a list price of £11,400 when new.

On which benefits will Norman be assessed to tax?

A   Neither

B   Luncheon vouchers only

C   Car only

D   Luncheon vouchers and car

2   Gertrude commenced employment with Holidays Ltd on 1 October 2003 and was paid a salary of £1,150 per month on the last day of each month. From 1 November 2003 she was given use of a new 1,800 cc car with a list price of £15,000 with all private petrol paid for by the company. The car has a carbon dioxide emission rating of 158 gms/km.

What was her assessable employment income from Holidays Ltd for 2003/04?

A   £6,900

B   £8,737

C   £9,997

D   £11,310

3   Laura works part-time for Kent Ltd and on 30 April 2004 received a bonus of £6,000 in respect of the company's year ended 31 December 2003.

The amount assessable for 2003/04 will be

A   Nil

B   £4,500

C   £5,500

D   £6,000

4   Peter is a director of Saffron Ltd and he owns 7% of the ordinary share capital.   In 2003/04 he earned £5,000 and was provided with a new 1,000 cc motor car with a list price of £8,000.   The company paid £200 for his private petrol in 2003/04 towards which Peter contributed £10 per month.   Peter's business mileage in 2003/04 was 20,000 and the car has a carbon dioxide emission rating of 202 gms/km.

What is Peter's assessable income from Saffron Ltd in 2003/04?

A   £5,000

B   £6,200

C   £10,256

D   £10,376

5   In 2003/04 Hock, a director of a wine-importing company, is paid £10,000 per annum and is given the use of a new 1,997 cc car list price £16,000 (emission rating: 178 gms/km), plus wine to the value of £1,000.   His 20 year old student daughter, Jane, also works for the company on Saturdays, is paid £15 per day and has the use of a new 1,250 cc car list price £8,000 (186 gms/km rating).   Hock uses £600 of the wine promoting the company's products.   No private petrol is paid for by the company.

The employment income on which Hock will be taxed for 2003/04 is:

A   £13,860
B   £14,400
C   £15,120
D   £15,720

CHAPTER 16

Other aspects of employment taxation

EXAM FOCUS

The new syllabus requires a greater depth of knowledge on all aspects of employee taxation than that required under the previous syllabus. There is a greater emphasis on compliance requirements, in particular. These lend themselves easily to assessment by multiple choice question.

In the lecturers' conference dealing with the new syllabus, the examiner stated that the topic of salary versus benefits might be examined in compulsory Section B. So this chapter ends with a consideration of alternative means of remunerating employees.

LEARNING OUTCOMES

This chapter covers the following learning outcomes of the CIMA syllabus:

> Identify the compliance requirements imposed on employers in relation to employee taxation

> Explain the effect of benefits on code numbers

> Identify methods of minimising employers' National Insurance Contributions (NIC)

> Evaluate the relative tax efficiency of different methods of rewarding employees.

In order to cover these learning outcomes the following topics are included:

> Compliance requirements
> National Insurance Contributions
> Alternative methods of remuneration
> Status issues and IR 35.

---

1 Compliance requirements

1.1 Introduction

Employees settle the majority (if not all) of their income tax and national insurance liabilities through the PAYE system. This is a highly organised and regulated system of procedures and key documents to ensure that income tax and NIC are accurately deducted.

The main examinable areas are as follows.

- ◆ The identification and function of key documents and procedures within PAYE.
- ◆ The operation of the PAYE coding system.

1.2 Key documents

The main documents are described below.

P11

For each employee, the employer is required to operate *a deductions working sheet* (P11). This records the gross pay, income tax and national insurance (both employee and employer contributions), for each payment period (ie weekly or monthly) throughout the relevant tax year. The precise operation is considered further below.

The working sheet will also contain details of the *PAYE code* to be operated for the individual so that the correct tax is deducted each period.

P35

This is a year end summary which the employer completes from the individual P11 sheets recording the *totals* of PAYE and NIC for all employees. The form is due by 19 May following the end of the tax year. If the P35 is submitted late, there is an automatic penalty of £100 per 50 employees for each month of delay.

P14 and P60

The employer must supply each employee with a form P60 at the end of each tax year. This is completed from the details contained on the P11. It records details of gross pay, tax deducted, and the national insurance contributions for both employee and employer. It is part of the P14 pack, which consists of three parts.

♦ Parts one and two are sent to the Inland Revenue, one of which is for National Insurance contribution purposes. These must be sent to the Inland Revenue by 19 May.

♦ Part 3 is the form P60 which, under income tax self assessment, must be provided to employees by 31 May following the tax year.

P9D and P11D

These two returns record the details of expense payments and benefits provided to employees by the employer.

♦ Form P9D shows taxable benefits and expense payments for those earning at a rate of less than £8,500 per annum.

♦ Form P11D shows the cash equivalent of benefits and expense payments for individuals earning at a rate of more than £8,500 per annum, and for all directors (unless they own 5% or less of the shares and work full time in the business with earnings of less than £8,500 pa).

♦ The forms P9D and P11D do not have to show amounts covered by a dispensation or by a PAYE settlement agreement (PSA). A dispensation is an agreement reached with the Inland Revenue which allows an employer to omit details of expenses which are not taxable on the employee. A PSA is a payment made by an employer which covers the tax and NIC on certain benefits and expenses.

♦ The returns must be submitted to the Revenue by 6 July following the tax year together with form P11D(b) (which is used to calculate the Class 1A NIC liability – see beyond). If they are submitted late, there is an automatic penalty of £100 per 50 employees for every month of delay. A copy of the form must be supplied to the employee, so that the relevant details can be entered in their self assessment return.

♦ There is a penalty of up to £3,000 per form if an employer fraudulently or negligently provides incorrect or incomplete information.

P45

This is a four part document to ensure the continued accurate operation of PAYE income tax and NIC during a tax year, when an employee changes employment.

The form records the total pay, tax and NIC to date in the tax year and the PAYE code number in use.

Part 1 is sent to the Inland Revenue. Parts 1A, 2 and 3 are given to the employee. Part 1A is for the employee to retain for their self assessment records. Parts 2 and 3 are for the new employer.

P46

This form is used where a new employee does not produce a form P45. It helps the new employer to establish the individual's PAYE position, so that tax can be accurately calculated.

P46(Car)

Where an employee is provided with a company car, the employer is required to notify the Inland Revenue so that the employee's coding notice can be appropriately amended. This return must be submitted within 28 days of the relevant quarter end. The quarters run to 5 July, 5 October, 5 January and 5 April.

Tax tables

Employers are provided with special tax tables to enable them to accurately compute the tax due. These are tables A – D.

It is important to learn the form numbers and their purpose as you may be asked, for example, the role of a 'P45'.

Practice question 1 *(The answer is in the final chapter of this book)*

Solomon Daisy

Solomon Daisy is a director and the majority shareholder in Tappertit Limited, a small lock manufacturing company. He has approached you as taxation adviser for advice relating to certain matters regarding PAYE (pay as you earn). Extracts from his letter are as follows.

> 'Jim has been employed by me for many years, but has now decided to move to another job much nearer his home. To replace him I have agreed to employ Sally Perkins. I understand that there are certain PAYE formalities and I would be most grateful if you could advise me of these....'

> 'In addition, I understand that I need to complete forms P11D for myself and certain employees. Can you advise me of which employees and directors they should be completed for and the reasons for this procedure....'

Required

Draft notes in preparation for a meeting with Mr Daisy in order to explain these points.

1.3   *The operation of PAYE*

The operation of PAYE depends on the employee's code number.

The PAYE code number

Employees are notified of their code number on form P2. The employer is notified on form P9. The notice of coding sets out the allowances and deductions an employee is entitled to. Any net allowance is deducted before applying tax. It does not apply for NIC.

The following illustration demonstrates how a PAYE notice of coding operates.

Illustration

Ken has been issued with the following coding notice for the tax year 2003/04. He earns £24,000 per annum and is a basic rate taxpayer. He is paid monthly.

Your tax allowances	£	Amounts taken away from your total allowances	£
Personal allowance	4,615	Car benefit	3,200
		Medical insurance	316
Total allowances	4,615	Total deductions	3,516

Your tax-free amount for the year is £1,099 (£4,615 – £3,516) making your tax code 109L.

Note: The personal allowance available for taxpayers for 2003/04 is £4,615. Higher allowances (the age allowances) are available to taxpayers over age 65.

As you can see, the benefits received by Ken have reduced the amount of allowances due to him. Without the benefits, his code number would have been 461L.

The code 109L above is a typical code consisting of numbers followed by a suffix. The code *number* for an individual is the net allowances less the last digit. The suffix L denotes personal allowance only.

The suffix allows the Revenue to tell the employer to increase a code number by a certain amount, for example following the annual budget increase, without the need to reissue codes for all employees. However, a T suffix indicates that the code number can only be changed by the Revenue itself.

Some codes have a *prefix*, the most common being the 'K' prefix. This is used when the deductions exceed the allowances. It is used to collect additional tax, so that the employee does not have further tax liabilities to settle at the end of the tax year.

There are some miscellaneous codes which are relevant:

- BR means that basic rate tax applies to the whole salary
- DO means that higher rate tax applies to the whole salary
- OT means no allowances available
- NT means no tax deducted

The coding notice for 2003/04 is compiled using 2002/03 P11D information. In addition, any underpayments of tax up to £2,000 can be collected through the code number provided the request is made before 30 September following a tax year (usually on the self assessment return). For example, if a higher rate taxpayer (ie paying tax at the marginal rate of 40%) owed £200 of tax for a previous year, his allowance would need to be reduced by £500 to collect the underpayment. This is because £500 × 40% = £200.

Calculating the PAYE

At each pay day, the gross pay of an individual will be entered on form P11, and the total gross pay since 6 April will be ascertained.

Using the employee's PAYE code and the Pay Adjustment tables (Table A), the employer can work out what personal allowance is available to offset against gross pay. This is known as the tax-free pay. The balance of gross pay is taxable.

To find the total tax due to date the employer uses the taxable pay tables (Tables B – D) to look up the tax due. This is then compared to the tax *already deducted* to date, to ascertain the tax due for the current pay period.

Continuing with the above illustration, Ken will be charged to tax, for each monthly paid period, using his code as follows.

	£
Gross pay	2,000
Tax–free pay (£1,099 ÷ 12)	(91)
Taxable pay	1,909

As you can see, the code number is used to spread the allowances evenly over the tax year.

The tax tables will then compute the correct tax to date at 10%, 22% or 40%.

For 2003/04 an individual is taxed at 10% on the first £1,960 of taxable income and at 22% on taxable income between £1,960 and £30,500. Where taxable income exceeds £30,500 the 40% 'higher rate' applies. The PAYE system spreads the tax bands as well as the allowances evenly over the tax year.

In Ken's case the monthly tax will be calculated as follows.

£		£
$\dfrac{1,960}{12} =$ 163 × 10% =		16.30
1,746 × 22% =		384.12
1,909		400.42

The PAYE tax and national insurance is paid over to the Inland Revenue on a monthly basis, 14 days after the end of each *tax* month (ie by the 19th of each month). If the total average monthly amount of PAYE tax and NIC for all the employees does not exceed £1,500 it can be paid quarterly instead of monthly.

Practice question 2 (The answer is in the final chapter of this book)

Alfred

Alfred, aged 45, has a salary of £20,000 per annum. He is provided with a new company car, list price of £17,895, with effect from 6 October 2003. The car's carbon dioxide emission rating is given as 194 gms/km. He also receives medical insurance cover which costs his employer £600 every year. He has received this for several years. He has no other income.

Required

Calculate Alfred's code number for 2003/04.

---

2 National Insurance Contributions

2.1 Primary Class 1 contributions

Class 1 primary contributions are due from all employees aged between 16 and the retirement age (65 for men, 60 for women).

 For the tax year 2003/04 there is an earnings threshold of £89 per week (£4,615 pa) and an upper earnings limit of £595 per week (£30,940 pa). Earnings falling within these limits are charged at a rate of 11% and earnings in excess of the upper earnings limit are charged at the rate of 1%.

Contributions are based on what the employee receives in cash, not on benefits, for an earnings period (eg a week or a month). Contributions can also be charged on vouchers, unless they are exempt for income tax purposes.

Primary contributions are deducted from gross pay and collected through the PAYE system.

A reduced rate (9.4%) applies if the employee is contracted out of the State Second Pension (S2P).

2.2 Secondary Class 1 contributions

 Class 1 secondary contributions at the rate of 12.8% are due from employers. They are paid for all employees who are over 16 and earning more than £89 per week. There is no upper earnings limit for the employer. They are an allowable deduction from the employer's trading profit.

If the employee is contracted out of S2P there is a reduced rate for earnings below the £595 employee upper earnings limit, depending on the form of occupational pension scheme – 'money purchase' or 'final salary'.

2.3 Example

Peter earns £130 a week. Calculate the Class 1 contributions payable by Peter and his employer for 2003/04. (The annual amount should be calculated.)

2.4 Solution

Employee contributions (£130 – £89) × 11% × 52 = £235
Employer contributions (£130 – £89) × 12.8% × 52 = £273

2.5 Example

Clare earns £700 a week. Calculate the Class 1 contributions payable by Clare and her employer for 2003/04. (The annual amount should be calculated.)

2.6 Solution

Employee contributions (£595 – £89) × 11% × 52 = £2,894
(£700 - £595) × 1% × 52 = £55
_____
£2,949
_____

Employer contributions (£700 – £89) × 12.8% × 52 = £4,067

 The employee can take advantage of the upper earnings limit, but not the employer.

2.7   Example

Mr Dexter is an employee who earns a weekly salary of £150 throughout 2003/04. In addition he receives a bonus of £2,000 in the week commencing 3 July 2003. Mr Dexter is not contracted out of the state earnings related pension scheme.

Required

Calculate the primary and secondary Class 1 contributions payable in respect of Mr Dexter in 2003/04.

2.8   Solution

The primary Class 1 contributions (payable by Dexter) will be as follows.

	£
1 week × (£595 – £89) × 11%	56
1 week × (£2,150 - £595) × 1%	16
51 weeks × (£150 – £89) × 11%	342
	——
	414
	——

The secondary Class 1 contributions (payable by the employer) will be as follows.

	£
1 week (£2,150 – £89) × 12.8%	264
51 weeks × (£150 – £89) × 12.8%	398
	——
	662
	——

As you can see from the above example, it is possible to minimise an employee's NIC by paying a bonus. This is because, as there is a maximum weekly earnings limit for national insurance contribution of £595, only £445 (£595 – £150) of the bonus suffers primary Class 1 contributions at the full 11% rate. It is, however, impossible to minimise employer's NIC in this way as there is no upper earnings limit. So, the whole bonus is subject to employer's secondary national insurance contributions.

Note also that directors are assessed to employee's national insurance contributions by reference to an 'annual' period. This means that they cannot avoid NIC by paying themselves a small salary and a large bonus.

Practice question 3 *(The answer is in the final chapter of this book)*

Bella

Bella Ltd has two employees, Fred and George. They receive wages of £6,864 and £32,480 (gross) per annum respectively. In addition, Fred and George received a Christmas bonus of £600 and £2,500 respectively during the week commencing 21 December 2003. Neither Fred nor George is contracted out of the state earnings–related pension scheme.

Required

Calculate the total National Insurance contributions for which Bella Ltd should account to the Inland Revenue for 2003/04.

2.9 Class 1A contributions

Class 1A contributions are payable by employers on any benefits provided to employees, with the exception of childcare. (These contributions are *not* payable by employees.) The contributions are calculated at the full rate of 12.8% on the value of the benefits as calculated under the income tax rules. (Note that benefits provided to employees earning less than £8,500 per annum are exempt from Class 1A NIC.)

Class 1 NIC for employees and employers is paid to the Revenue with PAYE tax. Class 1A NIC on benefits, payable by the employer only, is paid annually by 19 July following the tax year.

2.10 Example

Jill earns £22,000 a year and a new car is made available to her with petrol provided. The list price is £15,500 and the engine capacity is 1,800 cc. The car's carbon dioxide emission rate is 237 gms/km.

What is the Class 1A liability?

2.11 Solution

Only the employer has a Class 1A liability. There is no additional employee NIC for Jill.

Class 1A is 11.8% × the value of the benefit for income tax which is:

		£
Car	£15,500 × 31%*	4,805
Fuel	£14,400 × 31%	4,464
		9,269
	Class 1A liability = £9,269 × 12.8%	£1,186

*15% + (235 – 155) $\frac{1}{5}$ = 31%

2.12 Class 1B contributions

Class 1B contributions are paid by employers only on amounts which have been covered by a PAYE settlement agreement (PSA) and which would have otherwise been subject to Class 1 or Class 1A.

PSAs are used to collect income tax on small or irregular benefits. As mentioned above, PSA benefit payments do not have to be reported on P9Ds or P11Ds.

Class 1B is paid at the rate of 12.8% not just on the amounts that would have attracted Class 1 or Class 1A but on the income tax which the employer pays under the PSA. Class 1B is due on 19 October following the tax year in which the benefits are supplied.

3 Alternative methods of remuneration

3.1 Introduction

The payment of cash remuneration has the following tax and NIC consequences

♦ the employee is liable to pay income tax and primary class 1 NIC
♦ the employer is liable to pay secondary class 1 NIC.

By changing the way in which an employee is remunerated, some of the income tax or NIC charges may be minimised or even avoided altogether.

There are several alternative methods of remuneration which may prove beneficial for either the employee or the employer. For example:

♦   the payment of a bonus
♦   the provision of benefits
♦   payments into a pension scheme
♦   share option schemes
♦   dividend payments.

Each of these will be considered briefly below.

3.2   Bonus v salary

You learned earlier in this chapter that the payment of a bonus may reduce an employee's NIC liability. You can now apply that knowledge in answering the following practice question.

Practice question 4 *(The answer is in the final chapter of this book)*

Janice

Janice is employed at a salary of £18,000 per annum.   Her employer is considering the following pay increases.

(a)   A £5,000 increase in salary plus a year-end bonus of £1,000.
(b)   A £1,000 increase in salary but a year-end bonus of £5,000.

Required

What is the NIC position for Janice in 2003/04 under the alternatives her employer is considering?

3.3   Benefits v salary

The tax consequences of benefits depend on the particular benefits concerned. However, there can be some tax advantages in providing benefits rather than an increase in salary.

♦   Some benefits are exempt from income tax, for example, mobile phones, subsidised canteens, workplace nurseries and home use of computers.

♦   There is usually no employees' NIC on benefits.

Note that Class 1A and 1B NIC are payable by the employer. These are based on the amounts assessed to income tax. So, for example, the payment by an employer of a £300 medical insurance subscription will incur the same NIC charge for the employer as the payment of £300 cash to the employee. However, the employee will incur no NIC on the medical benefit and so would prefer this (on tax grounds) to the payment of salary.

The employer may make a Class 1A NIC saving if the provision of a benefit is cheaper than the provision of salary. For example, the retail price of a television is £300, but the employer can obtain it for £250. In this case, the benefit charge (and hence the Class 1A NIC charge) is based on the cost to the employer, that is £250. It is therefore preferable, for both the employer and the employee, to provide the television rather than give the employee the cash to purchase it.

3.4   *Example*

Ron is a basic rate taxpayer who earns £20,000 per year. His employer has offered him the choice of either (a) a pay increase of £4,000 a year or (b) a company car.

The company car has a list price of £15,000 and a carbon dioxide emission rating of 294 gms/km. Ron will use the car for private purposes only and will have to pay for his own petrol.

Ron's employer is a company, paying corporation tax at the standard rate of 30%.

Required

Outline the tax consequences of the two options for both Ron and his employer.

3.5   *Solution*

(a)   Ron has not yet reached the upper earnings limit for NIC, so all of his increased salary will be liable to Class 1 NIC at the 11% rate. The increased NIC will be £4,000 × 11% = £440. Ron will also be liable to pay basic rate income tax of £4,000 × 22% = £880 on the bonus. This will leave Ron with £2,680 (£4,000 - £440 - £880).

Ron's employer will be liable to pay Class 1 NIC of £512 (£4,000 × 12.8%). However, both the salary and the additional NIC will be deductible in calculating the company's taxable profits. The true cost of the increased salary to the employer is therefore

	£
Salary	4,000
NIC	512
	4,512
Tax relief at 30%	(1,354)
Cost to employer	3,158

(b)   With an emission rating of 294 gms/km (over 255 gms/km) the maximum percentage of 35% applies and the car benefit will be £5,250 (£15,000 × 35%). This will increase his income tax liability by £1,155 (£5,250 × 22%). There are no NIC consequences for Ron.

The employer will have to pay Class 1A NIC of £672 (£5,250 × 12.8%). Tax relief at 30% will reduce this cost to £470 (£672 × 70%). Assuming the company has purchased the car for £15,000, it will qualify for capital allowances of £3,000 per annum. These will save CT of £900 a year (£3,000 × 30%).

There is no clear cut answer as to which option is preferable. The decision depends on a number of unknown factors. For example

♦   Does Ron want a car? If so, would the net salary of £2,680 be sufficient for him to buy one himself (perhaps by leasing)?

♦   Does the company already own the car? If not, how does it propose to finance its purchase?

The decision is also sensitive to changes in tax rates, for both the employer and employee, and the amount of business mileage undertaken by the employee.

3.6 Pension contributions

Another method of remunerating employees is by making contributions into a pension scheme. This is a very tax efficient way of providing for retirement for the following reasons.

♦ Employees get tax relief through the PAYE system for any contributions they make.

♦ Employers get tax relief on their contributions; they are normally deductible in the accounting period of payment.

♦ The employer's contribution is not classed as taxable remuneration. So the employee does not incur income tax or NIC on the contribution. There is no employers' NIC either.

♦ The pension scheme itself is exempt from income tax and capital gains tax, although it cannot recover tax credits on dividend income.

♦ On retirement, up to one and a half times final salary may be taken as a tax–free lump sum.

An employee's contribution to an *occupational pension scheme* is limited to 15% of his or her remuneration. This is subject to an upper limit on remuneration of £99,000 (which means that the maximum contribution is 15% of £99,000 = £14,850).

Employees may make additional voluntary contributions (AVCs) to either the company scheme or a separate 'freestanding' scheme. These are subject to the 15% limit.

The pension payable under an occupational pension scheme is usually based on the employee's final salary although employers have become aware how expensive final salary schemes are likely to be and therefore 'money purchase' schemes are becoming more common.

If there is no occupational pension scheme, contributions can be made to a *personal pension scheme*. An employee is not obliged to use his employer's occupational scheme. If he or she chooses, the employee can opt out of the occupational scheme and take out a PPS. However, this is not normally advisable as it usually means foregoing the advantage of employer contributions.

An employee, whether or not in an occupational pension scheme, can pay up to £3,600 pa into a personal pension scheme. This is paid net of basic rate tax so the net maximum is £2,808 (3,600 × 78%). This does not apply if the employee is in an occupational pension scheme and is either a director controlling 20% of the employer company shares or receives salary (net of occupational pension contributions) of £30,000 pa.

For an employee not in an occupational pension scheme the maximum allowable premium is calculated as a percentage of *net relevant earnings*, or is £3,600 if greater. *Net relevant earnings* are earnings chargeable under the employment income rules (including benefits), less any expenses claimed. Earnings are subject to the same upper limit of £99,000.

The maximum percentages payable under a personal pension scheme depend on the employee's age at the *start* of the tax year, as follows.

Age at start of tax year	%
Up to 35	17 ½
36 – 45	20
46 – 50	25
51 – 55	30
56 – 60	35
61 and over	40

You are likely to be given this information in the exam room if it is needed.

The pension payable under a personal pension scheme depends on the performance of the pension fund.

3.7 *Share scheme incentives*

The provision of shares or share options is becoming an increasingly popular element of remuneration packages from both an employee and an employer perspective. There are numerous different types of scheme; they can be subdivided initially into approved schemes and unapproved schemes.

Unapproved share schemes

Unapproved schemes have the following tax consequences.

♦ There is no income tax charge on the grant of an option to purchase shares, provided the option must be exercised within 10 years. If the option is chargeable, the charge is based on the difference between the market value of the shares at the time of the option and the price payable for the shares at the time the option is exercised.

♦ When the shares are purchased by the employee, the difference between the market value of the shares and the price paid by the employee is assessable under the employment income rules. (Any amount paid for the option may also be deducted as may any amount charged to income tax on the grant of the option.)

♦ If the shares are a readily convertible asset, the employer must charge PAYE tax and NIC at the time the shares are acquired. (Shares are readily convertible assets if they can be sold on the Stock Exchange.)

♦ The employer is required to pay employers' NIC, although the employer can require the employee to meet this cost.

♦ If the employee does not pay for the shares immediately on exercising the option, he is treated as receiving an interest free loan. This may give rise to an employment income charge under the beneficial loan provisions.

♦ Provided the employee bears an income tax charge on the grant or exercise, the employer company is allowed a trading deduction in the AP of exercise equal to the market value of the shares at exercise less any consideration received.

♦ Similarly, if shares are awarded (or bought) and the employee suffers an income tax charge, the employer company is allowed a deduction in the AP of the award equal to the market value of the shares less any consideration received.

You can see from the above list that unapproved schemes offer no real tax advantages for either the employee or the employer. The employee does, however, receive shares which may appreciate in value. He is motivated to contribute to the company's success as the option allows shares to be purchased at a fixed price. The employer can choose which employees and directors can be remunerated in this way without being restricted by the limits and conditions of the Revenue approved schemes.

Approved schemes

Approved schemes have the following advantages.

♦ There is normally no income tax charge on either the initial grant or the exercise of an option to purchase shares.

♦ There will be a capital gains tax charge on the employee when he or she eventually sells the shares but there are exemptions such as taper relief and the annual £7,900 gains exemption. By selling off the shares over several years even substantial holdings can be sold without attracting significant CGT.

♦ The running costs incurred by the employer are deductible in computing Schedule DI profits.

♦ The employer company is allowed a trading deduction in the AP of exercise equal to the market value of the shares at exercise less any consideration received.

♦ Similarly, if shares are awarded (or bought) under a SIP (see below), the employer company is allowed a deduction in the AP of the award equal to the market value of the shares less any consideration received.

There are a number of different types of approved scheme. Each scheme has its own qualifying conditions. These are summarised briefly below.

Save as you earn (SAYE) share option schemes

The employee is granted an option to buy company shares at an agreed price, at a future date. The employee is likely to exercise the option if the market price of the shares exceeds the option price at the date it can be exercised.

♦ The price at which options are granted must be at least 80% of the market value of the shares at that time (ie no more than 20% discount permitted).

♦ There is no income tax charge on either the grant or the exercise of the option, where the cost of the shares is paid out of the proceeds of a SAYE scheme.

♦ Participants pay between £5 and £250 monthly into a SAYE account.

♦ Options can be exercised at the end of three, five, or seven years when the SAYE contract term ends.

♦ All employees, both full-time and part-time, must be eligible to join. Variations are permitted for length of service, etc. Certain exclusions can apply (ie employees with less than five years service or part-time directors).

♦ Directors or employees with a material interest of 25% or more must be excluded.

Company share option plans (CSOPs)

From an income tax perspective, CSOPs are essentially the same as share option schemes. But there are differences in the participating employees and conditions of the schemes.

♦ Key employees can be selected, provided they are not part-time directors. Unequal terms of participation may apply and options can be linked to individual performance.

♦ Employees or directors with a material interest of 25% or more must be excluded.

♦ The price at which options are granted must not be materially less than the market value of the shares at the date of the grant.

♦ The value of unexercised options when granted cannot exceed £30,000.

♦ The option must be exercised between three and ten years of the date it is granted (or earlier than three years where employment ends through injury, disability, redundancy or retirement).

Share incentive plans (SIPs)

These were introduced by the Finance Act 2000. They are intended to replace profit sharing schemes (see below). The plans are operated through a trust. The trustees hold the shares for the employees until they are taken out of the plan or sold.

♦ Employers can give employees up to £3,000 of shares each year free of tax and NIC.

♦ Employees can buy up to £1,500 of 'partnership' shares each year out of their pre-tax salary.

- Employers can match partnership shares by giving up to two free shares for each partnership share the employee buys. These 'matching' shares are also free of IT and NIC at that point.

- Employees cannot normally withdraw shares from the plan for three years.

- Shares are subject to tax on their initial value if taken out of the plan between years three and five.

- Shares held for more than five years are completely free of IT and NIC.

- Any increase in value in the shares while they are in the plan will be free of tax and NIC.

- The plan must be available to all employees. Variations are permitted for length of service, etc.

- Employees or directors with a material interest of 25% or more must be excluded.

Enterprise Management Incentives (EMI)

 This scheme was also introduced by the Finance Act 2000. It allows small high risk companies to reward selected employees with share options worth up to £100,000 each at the date of grant.

- There is normally no tax or NIC on the grant or exercise of the option.

- Employees or directors with a material interest of 30% or more must be excluded.

- The option must be capable of being exercised within 10 years.

- If an employee has both EMI and CSOP options, the EMI maximum (£100,000) is restricted by the value of the CSOP options held.

- The total of EMI options issued must not exceed £3 million.

Profit sharing scheme

This is where the employer provides funds for an employee trust, which uses the funds to buy shares in the company and then allocates them to employees.

- There is no income tax charge under the employment income rules, provided the shares are retained by the trust for at least three years after being allocated to the employee.

- The shares must be held by the trustees for at least two years but if the shares are then sold before the three year retention period has expired, there is an employment income charge. This is the lower of the shares' initial value or their sale proceeds.

- The scheme must be available to all employees, both full-time and part-time. Variations for length of service and remuneration are permitted. Employees with less than five years service may be excluded.

- Directors or employees with a material interest, defined here as 25% or more of the ordinary share capital, *must* be excluded.

- The maximum market value of shares which can be allocated to a participating employee is the greater of

  - £3,000 and
  - 10% of remuneration, subject to an overall maximum of £8,000.

- The relief is being abolished and will not apply to share appropriations made after 31 December 2002. Companies are encouraged instead to provide shares under the SIP arrangements.

Practice question 5 *(The answer is in the final chapter of this book)*

Podsnap

You are the chief accountant of Old Heep Motor Traders plc (OHMT), a large quoted car dealership. You have received the following letter from the finance director. He holds approximately 1% of the 80 million shares in issue, and is a higher rate taxpayer.

M Jaggers Esq
Dickens House
Rochester
Kent

1 May 2004

Dear Mr Jaggers

I am currently preparing my tax return for the year to 5 April 2004 and would like you to explain to me the income tax liabilities which I will have on the following share transactions.

(1)   On 17 March 2001 I was allocated 4,500 ordinary shares in OHMT under the approved profit sharing scheme. Their value at the time was £0.75 per share. On 23 June 2003 I needed some money urgently, and so I asked the trustees to advance the shares to me immediately. I sold them on the same day for £2.08 per share.

(2)   On 11 June 1997 I was granted an option to purchase 8,000 ordinary shares in OHMT for £0.60 per share (their value at the time) under the terms of the approved company share option plan. On 12 July 2003 I exercised options over 4,000 shares, and sold them on the same day for £2.12 per share.

(3)   The company had a good year in 2003, and in place of a bonus the board approved the granting of an option on 13 February 2004 for me to purchase 30,000 shares for £1 each, although they were worth £2.20 each on that day. The options are exercisable at any time until 12 February 2015.

Yours sincerely

John Podsnap

Required

Write a reply to Mr Podsnap explaining the income tax liabilities arising in 2003/04 on the share transactions. (Ignore the CGT implications).

Approach to the question

(1)   This is an approved profit sharing scheme. How long do the trustees need to retain the shares for Mr Podsnap to avoid a tax charge? What happens if they advance the shares to him before that date?

(2)   This is an approved CSOP. How soon can options be exercised under this scheme?

(3)   This is an unapproved scheme. The option price is significantly less than the current market price. There is also a very long period in which the options can be exercised. Do these factors give rise to a tax charge at the time the options are granted?

3.8   *Dividends v salary*

If an employee or director is also a shareholder, it may be possible to pay them a dividend rather than an increased salary. Dividends are not classed as earnings for the purpose of National Insurance and so there is no NIC liability for either the employee or the employer.

There are, however, some drawbacks to consider.

◆   Dividends are not a deductible expense in calculating Schedule DI profits. So the company will receive no tax relief.

◆   Entitlement to some Social Security benefits, for example, the state retirement pension, is dependent on an individual paying a certain amount of Class 1 NIC.

◆   The payment of a pension under an occupational pension scheme often depends on an individual's final salary. Final salary does not include dividends.

◆   The position of other shareholders also needs to be considered.

◆   For an employee and for a director with a contract of employment, it will be necessary to pay sufficient salary to comply with the National Minimum Wage regulations.

3.9   *Example*

Easy Ltd wishes to provide an additional amount of £100,000 net income to its key shareholder and director Mr Difficult, and is unsure whether to provide this as a cash bonus or dividend. Its 'profits' for the year ended 31 March 2003 are likely to be either £350,000 or £590,000 depending on the outcome of a technical dispute with the Inland Revenue as to the deductibility of certain repairs expenditure. Mr Difficult is a higher rate taxpayer whose salary is £50,000. Advise the company as to the relative cost of the proposed alternatives.

3.10   *Solution*

The first point to note is that if the aim is to guarantee Mr Difficult the same net income under either alternative then his *gross* income under each alternative needs to be calculated.

◆   Bonus route — gross bonus of £169,492 (ie £100,000 × $^{100}/_{59}$), less 40% PAYE and 1% NIC deduction £69,492, leaves net income of £100,000. Note the NIC cost to Mr D is 1% of the gross as his earnings already exceed the upper limit.

◆   Dividend route – dividends are taxed at a top rate of 32.5%. So to be left with £100,000, Mr Difficult needs a gross dividend of £148,148 (£100,000 × $^{100}/_{67.5}$). The net dividend receivable will therefore be £133,333 as when grossed up by $^{100}/_{90}$ this will give £148,148. Dividends are not 'earnings' for NIC purposes.

The cost to the company is therefore as follows.

	Bonus route			*Dividend route*	
					Dividend
	£	£			£
Bonus	169,492	169,492	Cash		133,333
'ER's NIC × 12.8%	21,695	21,695	Cost		133,333
	191,187	191,187			
Tax relief thereon					
(i) If 'P' £590,000 × 32.75%	(62,614)				
Net cost	128,573				
(ii) If 'P' £350,000					
£50,000 × 32.75%		(16,375)			
£141,187 × 19%		(26,826)			
Net cost		147,986			

The decision is sensitive to the rate of tax relief obtained on the bonus. If the profits for the year ended 31 March 2004 are £590,000, relief will wholly be obtained at 32.75% as the profits fall within the marginal band. The bonus route is therefore cheaper than the dividend route. However, if the company has profits of £350,000 then only £50,000 is relieved at the marginal rate (ie profits above the lower limit) while the rest is at 19% and the overall cost is higher than for the dividend.

4 Status issues and IR35

4.1 Introduction

An individual who 'works' for a company may be self-employed, or an employee. A self-employed person will work under a 'contract for services', whereby he agrees to carry out certain specific tasks. An employee, on the other hand, works for the company under a 'contract of service' which has the nature of a master/servant relationship.

Being an employee carries certain rights under employment law and also imposes obligations on the employer. In particular, the employer is required to apply PAYE and NIC to the employee and bear the employer's share of NICs.

Whether an individual is an employee or is self-employed is a question of fact; a worker cannot simply declare himself to be self-employed. It is, however, possible to escape employment status by providing services through a personal service company.

Anti-avoidance measures were introduced to limit the tax and NIC lost to the Exchequer by employees providing their services through an intermediary – usually a company but possibly a partnership. The Chancellor singled out the particular abuse of employees who resign on a Friday from their employment but return to the same desk the following Monday under a contract between the "employer" and their own personal service company.

The company invoices for the individual's services (plus VAT, if appropriate) and the "employer" pays gross without having to apply the PAYE regulations nor having to pay a 12.8% Class 1 NIC charge. The intermediary company pays CT at probably only 19% (or less if profits below £50,000) on profits net of any expenses wholly and exclusively incurred for the trade.

The individual is an employee of the company – or better still, a director without a contract of employment thereby side stepping the National Minimum Wage regulations. As an employee there is the risk of being fined under the NMW regs for not paying himself enough or perhaps just not keeping sufficient records to prove it. He then draws sufficient remuneration (or director's fees) to just exceed the lower earnings limit for NIC purposes thereby creating entitlement to benefits but no Class 1 liabilities. He can draw out the rest as dividends as and when he chooses. There is scope for dividing the shareholding with his spouse so that two basic rate bands are utilized before higher rate income tax is payable. In fact income can roll up indefinitely net of a 19% CT charge (or less) so that good and bad years can be evened out and the individual need never pay higher rate tax unless he so chooses.

4.2 The scope of IR35

The rules were enacted in FA 2000 following consultation and first took effect for 2000/01. They are commonly referred to as the 'IR35' rules, IR35 being the number of the Inland Revenue Press Release which first set out the proposed details.

The rules only apply to relevant engagements – ie, contracts between the company and the client which would have been a contract of employment in the absence of the intermediary.

Although the client is a significant beneficiary of the abuse he is not the focus of the provisions. Instead, the "employee's" company has to treat the income from relevant engagements arising in a fiscal year as if it were paid out as salary to the employee and account for the notional income tax and NIC on 19 April following the end of the fiscal year. This notional salary is deemed paid at the end of the tax year.

The notional salary is the income from the relevant engagements but reduced by

♦ Any actual salary and benefits received in the year:

♦ Expenses incurred by the company which would have been deductible under the employment income rules if the individual had incurred them personally (see Chapter 15)

♦ Contributions made by the company to an occupational pension scheme

♦ Employer's NIC paid during the year on actual salary and on the notional salary

♦ 5% of gross payments from relevant engagements as a flat rate deduction to cover overheads and training etc, whether or not the money is spent.

To avoid a double charge to tax the notional salary and NIC is allowable for calculating corporation tax profits. Where dividends are subsequently paid they are ignored as part of the individual's taxable income if the company elects that they should be matched against notional salary. Subsequent drawings of salary cannot, however, be matched against the notional salary.

This explanation assumes that only a single individual is providing his services through a personal service company. There are additional rules where more than one individual operates through the same company or where the intermediary is a partnership of individuals.

5 Summary

You need to be aware of the numbers of the various returns and the dates on which they need to be submitted. The most important forms are listed below.

Form	Purpose	Due date
P35	Year end summary of PAYE and NIC	19 May
P14	Individual record of PAYE and NIC	19 May
P60	Employee's copy of the P14	31 May
P9D	Return of benefits for lower paid employees	6 July
P11D	Return of benefits for employees earning over £8,500	6 July

Class 1 NIC is payable by both employees and employers. It is payable on cash remuneration. Employers are liable to pay class 1A NIC on the benefits provided to employees and Class 1B on amounts covered by a PSA including the income tax thereon.

NIC can sometimes be avoided by using alternative methods to remunerate employees. For example

♦ the payment of a bonus, rather than a salary increase, may minimise the employee's NIC
♦ the provision of benefits in kind, rather than a salary increase, avoids employees' NIC
♦ contributions into a pension scheme avoid both tax and NIC
♦ the payment of a dividend, rather than salary, avoids NIC altogether.

There are several different share schemes that can be used to minimise tax and NIC. Most of these schemes must be offered to all employees. The exception are company share option schemes and the enterprise management incentive schemes. These two schemes allow employers to target key employees.

In order to retain the tax benefits of the various share schemes, it is usually necessary to retain the shares (or delay the exercise of the option) for a minimum period of three years.

Status issues are also important especially the IR 35 anti-avoidance provisions where the worker seeks shelter behind a personal service company in situations which would otherwise be 'employment'.

Multiple choice questions 1 - 4 (The answers are in the final chapter of this book)

Each of the questions below has only one correct answer.

1   Jeremy, who was not contracted out for National Insurance purposes, was assessed under the employment income rules on the following for 2003/04.

	£
Gross salary	12,000
BUPA subscription	515
Contribution towards mortgage (£175 paid each month)	2,100

The secondary Class 1 National Insurance contributions payable by his employer were

A   £1,043

B   £1,214

C   £1,280

D   £1,805

2   The National Insurance contributions which an employer deducts from employees' earnings are

A   Class 1 Primary

B   Class 1 Secondary

C   Class 2

D   Class 4

3   Caroline is a waitress and is paid a salary of £9,300 in 2003/04. Her employer also pays her £700 as her share of tips collected through a service charge. In addition her employer paid £600 to cover her travelling expenses between home and work.

On what amount will Class 1 National Insurance contributions be payable?

A   £9,300

B   £9,900

C   £10,000

D   £10,600

4   Jenny is employed for two days a week by Choral Ltd at an annual salary of £6,720. In addition she is given the choice between having a company car with an original list price of £5,000 and an alternative of £150 a month.

Jenny chooses the car, in which she travels 3,000 business miles in 2003/04 and which has a carbon dioxide emission rating of 192 gms/km.

What is the assessable benefit arising in respect of Jenny's car in 2003/04?

A   Nil

B   £1,100

C   £1,250

D   £1,800

CHAPTER 17

Solutions to practice questions

Chapter 1

Multiple choice questions

1	C			£
		Premium $(20,000 \times 72\%)$		14,400
		Rent $(^{10}/_{12} \times 6,000)$		5,000
				19,400

2	C	Property 1	£	£
		Rents		4,200
		Allowable expenses	649	
		Wear and tear $10\% \times £4,200$	420	
				(1,069)
				3,131
		Property 2		
		Rent		6,000
		Less Expenses		(800)
				8,331

3	B	Year to 31 March 2004:	
			£
		Gain 1	10,000
		Gain 2	22,000
		Loss 1	(18,000)
		Net gains	14,000
		Loss b/f	(14,000)
		Net gains	Nil
		Loss c/f: (15,000 – 14,000)	1,000

4   C   Incorporation does not of itself cause an AP to start. Commencing to trade and acquiring a source of income thereon does and an AP starts on 1.1.04. This ends 12 months later being the longest CAP allowed, ie 31.12.04.

5   A   The amount charged on the accruals basis (£600) is allowable for Schedule D Case I purposes.

Chapter 2

1   Walton

Year ended 31 March 2004	£
Schedule D Case I (W1 and W2)	365,724
Schedule DIII	2,900
Gains	1,538
PCTCT	370,162
CT liability (W3)	81,569

Workings

(W1)   Schedule D Case I

	£
Adjusted profit (W2)	370,524
Less Capital allowances	(4,800)
	365,724

(W2)   Adjustment of profit

	£
Net profit	381,499
Add Disallowable expenses	6,344
Less Debenture interest receivable	(2,900)
UK dividends (net)	(13,365)
Profit on sale of investment	(1,054)
	370,524

(W3)   Corporation tax liability
Step 1
Find 'Profits'

	£
PCTCT	370,162
FII (£13,365 × $\frac{100}{90}$)	14,850
'P'	385,012

Step 2

Calculate liability

♦   The FY03 applies to the year ended 31 March 2004.
♦   'P' is above the lower limit of £300,000; marginal relief applies

	£
PCTCT £370,162 × 30% =	111,049
Less Marginal relief (£1,500,000 - £385,012) × $\frac{370,162}{385,012}$ × $\frac{11}{400}$	(29,480)
CT liability	81,569

2 Shadow Ltd

Year ended 31 March 1999

	£	£
PCTCT £190,000 × 21% =		39,900
ACT paid (£180,000 - £18,000) × 20/80 =	40,500	
Maximum set-off £190,000 × 20% =	38,000	(38,000)
Mainstream CT		1,900
Surplus ACT carried forward	2,500	

Year ended 31 March 2000

	£	£
PCTCT £110,000 × 20% =		22,000
Maximum set-off £110,000 × 20% =	22,000	
Shadow ACT (£90,000 - £27,000) × 20/80 =	15,750	
Maximum set-off of surplus ACT	6,250	
Surplus ACT brought forward		(2,500)
Mainstream CT		19,500

Shadow Ltd has now been able to relieve all of its surplus ACT.

Multiple choice questions

1 B

12m AP ended 31.3.04	£
Schedule D Case I (490,000 – 35,000)	455,000
Gain	60,000
Schedule D Case III	90,000
PCTCT = 'Profits' for SCR	605,000
CT × 30%	181,500
Less Tapering relief $^{11}/_{400}$ (1,500,000 – 605,000)	(24,612)
	156,888

2 C

PCTCT × 20% = maximum set off	£
102,500 × 20% =	20,500
Less Shadow ACT (£22,000 × $^{1}/_{4}$)	(5,500)
Set off available	15,000
Surplus ACT b/f	18,000
Utilised in the year	(15,000)
Surplus ACT c/f	3,000

3 A

CT liability	£
46,500 × 19%	8,835
Less Tapering relief $^{19}/_{400}$ × (50,000 – 46,500)	(166)
CT payable	8,669

4 A

Return period	IT deducted £	IT suffered £	IT paid £
31.3.03	-	220	
30.6.03	-	110	
30.9.03	550	220	
	550	550	Nil (14.10.03)

5 C   IT is payable 14 days after the end of the 'quarter' in which the relevant interest was paid, ie by 14.4.04. Where the company has a non-calendar year end its first 'quarter' will be less than 3 months to take it to the next calendar quarter end.

Chapter 3

1   **Uranus**

1   Running expenses, except for depreciation, are an allowable deduction. The depreciation must be disallowed as this will be replaced by capital allowances. The private use of the car is irrelevant for Schedule DI purposes (but will affect the director's personal tax position – see Chapter 15). Therefore add back £6,000.

2   Disallow all entertaining except staff entertaining. Therefore add back £21,000.

3   The costs of registering a patent are allowable as a trading expense, therefore no adjustment is required.

4   Part of this lease cost will be disallowed as the car is expensive (over £12,000). The portion added back is as follows.

$$\frac{½ (£20,000 - £12,000)}{£20,000} \times £6,000 = £1,200$$

5   This is disallowed as it is a charge on income. Therefore add back £616.

6   The lease payment of £30,000 is disallowed as it is capital. There is, however, an allowable deduction over the life of the lease.

Assessable on landlord: $£30,000 \times \dfrac{51 - 6}{50} = £27,000$

Allowable deduction: £27,000/6 years = £4,500 per annum.

7   No adjustment is required as trading interest is an allowable deduction. (The accruals basis applies).

8   No adjustment is required. This is a specific provision, based on the best information available at the balance sheet date. It is therefore deductible. There will be a credit in the following year's accounts, when the £5,000 is recovered.

9   Repairs to put a dilapidated purchase into a suitable condition for trade use are classed as capital expenditure. Any part of the cost that can be attributed to normal maintenance is allowable. The disallowance is therefore £160,000 - £40,000 = £120,000.

10   The costs are allowable as they relate to employees. Therefore no adjustment is needed.

11   As the warehouse can be put to immediate use in the trade, prior to the repairs being carried out, no adjustment is needed in respect of the cost of the repairs.

Multiple choice questions

1   B   Expenditure incurred on entertaining customers and suppliers is disallowable.

2   B   Donations to political parties and charities are disallowable in computing Schedule DI profits. Small donations to local charities are allowable. Gifts of drink are disallowed.

3   C   The increase in the general provision and the loan to the customer must be added back.

4   B   Renewal expenses of a short lease (ie less than 50 year life) are allowable, as are debt collection expenses. The abortive planning application is, however, related to a capital purpose and is disallowed. (424 + 672) = £1,096.

5   A   Repair to newly acquired machine is capital. New toilet is capital.
Repair to roof, £4,450, allowed.

Chapter 4

1   ENT Ltd

	General pool £	Expensive car £	Allowances £
Year ending 31 December 2002			
Tax WDV b/f	24,000		
Additions (no FYA)			
15 April 2002		12,600	
16 July 2002	9,200		
17 August 2002	9,400		
Disposals			
30 April 2002	(3,200)		
	39,400	12,600	
WDA restricted		(3,000)	3,000
WDA 25%	(9,850)		9,850
	29,550	9,600	12,850
Year ending 31 December 2003			
Disposals	(7,900)	(9,400)	
	21,650	200	
Balancing allowance		(200)	200
WDA 25%	(5,413)		5,413
Tax WDV c/f	16,237	-	5,613

2   RBT Ltd

	General pool £	Expensive car 1 £	Expensive car 2 £	Short-life asset £	Allowances £
Six months to 30 June 2002					
Addition (no FYA)					
1 February 2002	5,750				
WDA 25% × ⁶⁄₁₂	(719)				719
Addition (FYA)					
1 January 2002				10,000	
FYA 40%				(4,000)	4,000
	5,031			6,000	4,719
Year ending 30 June 2003					
Additions (no FYA)					
30 September 2002		12,200			
1 October 2002	6,210				
	11,241	12,200		6,000	
WDA restricted		(3,000)			3,000
WDA 25%	(2,810)			(1,500)	4,310
Addition (FYA)					
1 October 2002	8,478				
FYA 40%	(3,391)				3,391
	13,518	9,200		4,500	10,701
Year ending 30 June 2004					
Addition (no FYA)					
1 February 2004			18,000		
Disposal					
1 June 2004				(4,000)	
(£4,700 × ⁴⁰⁄₄₇)					
	13,518	9,200	18,000	500	
Balancing allowance				(500)	500
WDA restricted			(3,000)		3,000
WDA 25%	(3,380)	(2,300)			5,680
Addition (FYA)					
1 June 2004	16,130				
FYA 100%	(16,130)				16,130
Tax WDV c/f	10,138	6,900	15,000	-	25,310

Multiple choice questions

1.   C   Input tax on cars available for any element of private use non-deductible, ie £2,135.

2.   B

	£
False ceilings not plant	-
Murals are plant	5,000
Pool is plant	45,000
	50,000

3.   B

	General pool £
Cost of car	7,200
WDA (25% × $\frac{9}{12}$)	(1,350) Private use irrelevant
WDV c/f	5,850

4.   B

	General pool £	SLA £	£
WDV b/f		4,230	
Purchase	6,580		
Sale £3,525 × $\frac{40}{47}$		(3,000)	
Balancing allowance		1,230	1,230
WDA × 25%	(1,645)		1,645
	4,935		2,875

5.   C   **Eight months ended 31 March 2004 – capital allowances**

	General pool £	Expensive car £	Total £
Additions	20,000	16,000	
FYA 40%	(8,000)		8,000
Computer FYA 100%			2,000
WDA restricted £3,000 × $\frac{8}{12}$		(2,000)	2,000
WDV c/f	12,000	14,000	12,000

Chapter 5

1   Plummer

(a)   (i)   The warehouse will qualify for IBA as it is a building used to store goods or materials to be used in a manufacturing process.

(ii)   The canteen will qualify for IBA as it is a building provided for the welfare of workers employed in a manufacturing business.

(iii)   No IBA will be due on the office as it is separate from the manufacturing building.

(iv)   IBA will be available as the building is used for the maintenance or repair of goods.

(b)

	Factory £	Extension £	Allowances claimed
Year ended 31 December 1995			
Construction costs (land excluded)	175,000		
WDA £175,000 × 4%	(7,000)		7,000
	168,000		
Years ended 31 December 1996 – 2003			
8 × £7,000	(56,000)		56,000
Addition in year ended 31 December 1998		39,000	
WDA 4% × 6 years		(9,360)	9,360
Tax WDV at 31 December 2003	112,000	29,640	
Allowances claimed			72,360

Explanatory tutorial notes

(1)   Writing down allowances can be claimed provided the factory is in use at 31 December 1995.

(2)   Additions are separate items for IBA purposes.

(3)   Remember WDA is based on cost *not* reducing balance basis as for plant and machinery.

2   Leaden

(a)   Balancing adjustment

On sale the position is as follows.

	£
Allowable cost	115,000
Proceeds are £190,000 but limited to cost	(115,000)
Net cost	Nil

Since the use of the building has not 'cost' the company anything, any allowances given will be clawed back by the Inland Revenue in the form of a balancing charge.

A £55,200 *balancing charge* is made to take back all the IBAs given.

	£
IBAs given (excess allowances)	55,200
IBAs clawed back by balancing charge	(55,200)
Actual tax cost	Nil

(The £75,000 profit on disposal is taxable under the capital gains rules).

(b)   Alternative calculations

		£
(i)	Allowable cost	115,000
	Proceeds	(100,000)
	Net cost	15,000
	Compare net cost with IBAs given	
	Net cost	15,000
	IBAs given	(55,200)
	Excess IBAs given = balancing charge	(40,200)
		£
(ii)	Allowable cost	115,000
	Proceeds	(50,000)
	Net cost	65,000
	Compare net cost with IBAs given	
	Net cost	65,000
	IBAs given	(55,200)
	Shortfall of IBAs given = balancing allowance	9,800

The balancing adjustments are effective in the year ended 31 March 2004.

3   **Brown**

Step 1

Identify qualifying eligible expenditure

Qualifying expenditure

	£
Ground levelling	3,125
Construction of building	351,750
Car park	12,000
Road construction	16,250
Quantity surveyor's fees	5,250
Architect's fees	11,875
	400,250

Notes

(1)   Land does not qualify for IBAs.

(2)   Writing down allowance is only available in respect of a period if the building is in industrial use at the end of a period. So no WDA is available in the year ended 31 December 2002.

Step 2

Claim writing down allowances (excluding year of disposal)

Year ended 31 December 2003	£	*Allowances given* £
Qualifying expenditure	400,250	
WDA (4%)	(16,010)	16,010
Residue before sale	384,240	

Step 3

Disposal procedure

Balancing adjustment year ended 31 December 2004

Find net cost		£
(i)	Cost	400,250
	Sale proceeds (note 1)	(180,000)
	Net cost	220,250
(ii)	Compare with allowances claimed	(16,010)
	Balancing allowance	204,240

Allowances to Smith Ltd for the year to 31 December 2004

$$\text{Annual WDA} = \frac{£384,240 - £204,240}{25 \text{ years} - 1 \text{ year } 1 \text{ month}} = £180,000 \times \frac{12}{287 \text{ months}} \quad £7,526 \text{ per annum}$$

Although the ventilation equipment and central heating system are installed in the building, they are normally treated as plant and machinery for capital allowance purposes. Provided that Brown Ltd is a small or medium sized business, it will be able to claim 40% first year allowances in the year in which the expenditure was incurred (ie the year to 31 December 2002) even though the building was not brought into use until the following period. If Brown Ltd is a large company, it will only be able to claim 25% WDA, again starting in the period of expenditure.

Tutorial notes

(1)   The sale proceeds to be considered must be those which relate to the eligible expenditure (ie matching like with like). The total sale proceeds of £250,000 included items like land and fixtures, which need to be deducted.

(2)   The IBAs for each accounting period for Brown Ltd are as follows.

Year ended 31 December 2003	£16,010
Year ended 31 December 2004	£204,240

These are then deducted from the adjusted trading profit to find the Schedule D Case I profits.

---

4   Mellor

(a)   *Step 1*

Identify the eligible expenditure

	£
Purchase price	335,000
Exclude land	(35,000)
	300,000

Step 2

Writing down allowances

Year ended 30 April 1999	Tax balance £	Allowance claimed £
Cost 1 September 1998	300,000	
WDA 4%	(12,000)	12,000
	288,000	
Year ended 30 April 2000		
Notional WDA	(12,000)	–
Year ended 30 April 2001	276,000	
Notional WDA	(12,000)	–
	264,000	
Year ended 30 April 2002		
WDA 4%	(12,000)	12,000
Residue before sale	252,000	24,000

Step 3

Disposal procedure

Year ended 30 April 2003 – year of disposal (no WDA)

	£
Eligible cost	300,000
Sale proceeds (restricted)	(300,000)
Adjusted net cost	Nil
Balancing charge (= IBAs given)	24,000

Tutorial note. The excess of sale proceeds is a capital profit dealt with under the taxation of capital gains rules.

(b)   **Major Ltd**

   (1)   Find residue after sale

	£
Residue before sale	252,000
Balancing charge	24,000
Residue after sale	276,000

   (2)   Writing down allowance for Major Ltd is then

$$\frac{276,000}{21 \text{ years } 3 \text{ months}} = \text{£12,988}$$

Tax life used 1 September 1998 – 1 June 2002 = 3 years 9 months

   (3)   Year ended 31 August 2002

	£
WDA (per annum)	12,988
(21 years × £12,988 a year)	272,748
Year 22 (balance)	3,252
	276,000

(c)   **Mellor Ltd**

$$\text{Adjusted net cost} = (\text{cost} - \text{sale proceeds}) \times \frac{\text{Period of industrial use}}{\text{Total period of ownership}}$$

$$(\text{£300,000} - \text{£180,000}) \times \frac{25 \text{ months}}{45 \text{ months}} = \text{£66,667}$$

	£
Adjusted net cost	66,667
Less Allowances actually given (see (a) above)	(24,000)
Balancing allowance	42,667

(d)   Major Ltd

	£
Residue before sale (see (a) above)	252,000
Less Balancing allowance	(42,667)
Residue after sale	209,333
Limited to allowable cost	180,000

Major Ltd will get total allowances of £180,000 spread over the remaining industrial life of the building, ie £8,471 per annum (£180,000 ÷ 21.25 years).

---

5   Straw

Corporation tax computation for the year ended 31 January 2004

		£
Schedule D Case I (W1 and W2)		289,400
Schedule D Case III	Building society interest	1,200
	Local Authority stock interest	34,000
Chargeable gain (£49,400 – £2,000)		47,400
		372,000
Less Gift Aid		(2,000)
Profits chargeable to corporation tax		370,000
Corporation tax liability (W3)		79,925
Less IT set-off (W4)		Nil
		79,925

Workings

(W1)   Schedule D Case I

	£
Adjusted trading profit	298,400
Less Capital allowances (W2)	(9,000)
	289,400

(W2)   Capital allowances

		£	Pool £	Expensive car £	Total £
Tax WDV brought forward			12,000		
Addition	Not qualifying for FYA			22,000	
			12,000	22,000	
WDA – 25%			(3,000)	(3,000)*	6,000
Addition	Qualifying for FYA	7,500			
	40%	(3,000)			3,000
			4,500		
Tax WDV carried forward			13,500	19,000	9,000

*Restricted

(W3)   Calculation of liability

Step 1

	£
PCTCT	370,000
FII	–
P	370,000

Step 2

Accounting period is 12 months ending 31 January 2004. Therefore:

	FY 2002 1 February 2003 – 31 March 2003 £	FY 2003 1 April 2003 – 31 January 2004 £
Lower limit	300,000	300,000
Upper limit	1,500,000	1,500,000
Rate	30%	30%
Fraction	$\frac{11}{400}$	$\frac{11}{400}$

Only one corporation tax computation is required as the marginal relief fraction is the same for both financial years.

Step 3

	£
PCTCT £370,000 × 30%	111,000
Less Marginal relief	
(£1,500,000 - £370,000) × $\frac{11}{400}$	(31,075)
Corporation tax liability	79,925

(W4)   IT set-off

Step 1

IT on 'interest'

	£
BSI receipt	Nil
Local Authority Stock receipt	Nil
Debenture interest payment (£10,000 × 20%)	2,000
	2,000

Step 2

IT on 'other investment income' and payments

	£
Income	(Nil)
Payments	
Gift Aid donation (paid gross)	Nil
	Nil

Step 3

There is no IT suffered on income received so no IT to set off.

---

6   Unimaginable

12 months to 31 May 2003

	£
Schedule D Case I (W1 – W3)	297,925
Schedule DIII (£4,760 + £1,250)	6,010
Capital gain	29,000
PCTCT	332,935
Corporation tax liability (W4)	68,915
Less IT set-off (W5)	-
Corporation tax payable	68,915

Workings

(W1)   Schedule D Case I

	£
Adjusted profit	311,000
Add Balancing charge (W3) on factory 2	25,000
Less Capital allowances (W2)	(30,075)
Industrial buildings allowances (W3)	(8,000)
	297,925

(W2) **Capital allowances on plant**

	£	Main pool £	Expensive cars 1 £	Expensive cars 2 £	CA summary £
CAP year to 31 May 2003					
Tax WDV b/fwd		32,500	11,000	–	
Additions		15,000		16,000	
		47,500			
Disposals		(28,000)	(8,000)		
Balancing allowance			3,000		3,000
		19,500			
WDA @ 25% (expensive car restricted)		(4,875)		(3,000)	7,875
Additions qualifying for FYA					
Plant	48,000				
FYA @ 40%	(19,200)				19,200
Total allowances					30,075
		28,800			
Tax WDV c/fwd		43,425	–	13,000	

(W3) **Industrial buildings allowance**

(i) **Factory 1**

	£
Qualifying cost (offices less than 25%)	200,000
WDA @ 4%	8,000

(ii) **Factory 2**

WDA per annum = $\dfrac{£100,000}{20}$ = £5,000

As the factory is sold above cost, all the IBAs claimed will be clawed back as a balancing charge.

Balancing charge £5,000 × 5	£25,000

(W4) *Step 1*

	£
PCTCT	332,935
FII ($£8,437 \times \frac{100}{90}$)	9,374
'P'	342,309

Step 2

Financial years which affect CAP (12 months ending 31 May 2003) are as follows.

	FY02	FY03
	10 months	*2 months (1 April 2003 – 31 May 2003)*
Rates	30%	30%
Fraction	$\frac{11}{400}$	$\frac{11}{400}$

As the rates and the fraction are the same for both years, there is no need to apportion the PCTCT nor perform separate calculations.

Step 3

		£
PCTCT	$£332,935 \times 30\%$	99,880
Less	Marginal relief (FY02 and FY03)	
	$^{11}/_{400} \times (£1,500,000 - £342,309) \times \dfrac{332,935}{342,309}$	(30,965)
		68,915

(W5) **IT suffered or deducted on 'interest'**

	£
Local Authority stock interest received gross	-
Bank (also not applicable)	-
Debenture interest paid ($£4,000 \times 20\%$)	800
IT deducted as 'collected' for Revenue $\therefore$ no IT set-off	(800)

Multiple choice questions

1   D   £

   Planning permission   3,000
   Site clearance   2,500
   Groundwork (including road)   4,000
   Building (including admin office 25% or under)   96,000
                                                                            ————
                                                                            105,500
                                                                            ————

2   D   An estate agent's office is not an industrial structure.

3   A   Second user gets WDA on residue of expenditure spread over balance of 25
            year tax life.

   $$\frac{\text{Residue (lower cost)}}{\text{Tax life remaining (25 – 4)}} = \frac{75,600}{21} = £3,600$$

4   C   Allowances given   £

   y/e 31 December 1986 £90,000 × 25%   22,500
   WDA £90,000 × 4%   3,600
                                                                            ————
                                                                            26,100

   y/e 31 December 1987 to 31 December 2002
     (16 – 2) 14 × 3,600   50,400
                                                                            ————
                                                                            76,500
                                                                            ————

5   D   £

   Drawing office qualifies for IBAs   8,000
   General office, within 25% limit   21,000
   Remainder of building cost   71,000
   Levelling land   3,000
                                                                            ————
   Qualifying cost   103,000
                                                                            ————

Chapter 6

1   JHN

	£
Plant (W1)	1,816
Painting (W2)	(1,000)
Car – exempt	–
Memorabilia (W3)	3,453
Land (W4)	Nil
Total gains	**4,269**

Workings

(W1)   Plant

	£
Proceeds	15,000
Cost	(8,000)
Unindexed gain	7,000
Indexation allowance ($0.648 \times £8,000$)	(5,184)
Chargeable gain	1,816

(W2)   Painting

	£
Proceeds	6,500
Cost	(7,500)
Loss	(1,000)

No indexation is available to increase the loss.

(W3)   Memorabilia

	£
Proceeds	19,000
Cost	(7,000)
Unindexed gain	12,000
Indexation allowance ($1.221 \times £7,000$)	(8,547)
Chargeable gain	3,453

(W4)   Land

	£
Proceeds	25,000
Cost	(15,000)
Unindexed gain	10,000
Indexation allowance (1.278 × £15,000)*	(10,000)
	Nil

*Restricted, because indexation cannot create an allowable loss

---

2   JMY

(i)   The gain with a rebasing election.

| *Sale of holiday cottage* | 31 March 1982 |
	£
Sale proceeds	33,000
31 March 1982 value	(10,000)
Unindexed gain	23,000
Indexation allowance (1.227 × £10,000)	(12,770)
Indexed gain	10,230

(ii)   The gain without a rebasing election

| *Sale of holiday cottage* | Cost | 31 March 1982 value |
	£	£
Sale proceeds	33,000	33,000
Cost	(12,000)	
1982 value		(10,000)
Unindexed gain	21,000	23,000
Indexation allowance 1.277 × £12,000*	(15,324)	(15,324)
Indexed gains	5,676	7,676
Lower gain	5,676	

*Higher of cost and 1982 value.

JMY Ltd should therefore **not** make the rebasing election if there were no other relevant potential disposals to take into account.

---

3   **Time**

(a)   Calculate the gains or losses on individual transactions for the year ended 31 March 2003.

    (i)   *Land (number 1)*

	Cost £	1982 value £
Sale proceeds	25,000	25,000
Cost	(9,800)	
1982 value		(8,500)
	———	———
Unindexed gain	15,200	16,500
Indexation March 2003* – March 1982 ($1.265 \times £9,800$)	(12,397)	(12,397)
	———	———
Indexed gain	2,803	4,103
	———	———

The lower gain is taken: £2,803.

    (ii)   *Land (number 2) – part disposal*

	Cost £	1982 value £
Sale proceeds	25,000	25,000
Cost $\dfrac{25,000}{25,000+16,000} \times £12,000$	(7,317)	
1982 value $\dfrac{25,000}{25,000+16,000} \times £17,000$		(10,366)
	———	———
Unindexed gain	17,683	14,634
Indexation allowance ($1.265 \times £10,366$)	(13,113)	(13,113)
	———	———
Indexed gain	4,570	1,521
	———	———

The lower gain is taken: £1,521.

Year ended 31 March 2004

    (iii)   Land (number 2) remainder

	Cost £	1982 value £
Sale proceeds	28,000	28,000
Cost (£12,000 – £7,317 used)	(4,683)	
1982 value (£17,000 – £10,366)		(6,634)
	———	———
Unindexed gain	23,317	21,366
Indexation December 2003 – March 1982 ($1.302 \times £6,634$)	(8,637)	(8,637)
	———	———
Indexed gain	14,680	12,729
	———	———

The lower gain is taken: £12,729.

Prepare summary

	Year ended 31 March 2003 £	*Year ended 31 March 2004* £
Gain (1)	2,803	12,729
Gain (2)	1,521	
	4,324	12,729

(b)   Calculate corporation tax on gains

In the year ending 31 March 2003 the impact of gains is to increase profits to £204,324 (ie £200,000 + £4,324) which means that the company is charged at FY02 small company rate of 19%. Therefore the CT liability on capital gains is £4,324 at 19% = £822.

In the year ending 31 March 2004 the impact of the gains is to increase profits to £312,729 which means that the company is marginal at FY03 rates.

Tax on profits including gains is as follows.

	£
PCTCT and 'P'	312,729
FY03 (30%)	93,819
Less Marginal relief $\frac{11}{400} \times$ (£1,500,000 – £312,729)	(32,650)
CT liability	61,169

The tax on profits excluding gains is as follows.

	£
PCTCT and 'P'	300,000
This would be at FY03 small rate therefore 19% =	57,000

Therefore tax on gains is £61,169 – £57,000 = £4,169, giving a marginal rate of 32.75%.

---

4   Mangle

Summary of chargeable gains	£
Desk (W1)	1,490
House (W2)	78,416
Antique table (W3)	2,000
Painting (W4)	(1,500)
	80,406

Workings

(W1) **Desk**

	Cost £	31 March 1982 value £
Proceeds	13,000	13,000
Cost	(4,000)	(5,000)
Unindexed gain	9,000	8,000
Indexation allowance £5,000 × (1.302)	(6,510)	(6,510)
Take smaller gain: £1,490	2,490	1,490

Apply $\frac{5}{3}$ rule as chattel sold for more than £6,000 and cost/1982 value is less than £6,000.

(£13,000 – £6,000) × $\frac{5}{3}$ = £11,667, therefore not taken.

(W2) **Property**

		Cost £	31 March 1982 value £
Proceeds		220,000	220,000
Cost	April 1978	(3,000)	–
	October 1979	(1,500)	–
	March 1982 value		(58,000)
	October 1984	(4,000)	(4,000)
Unindexed gain		211,500	158,000
Indexation allowance			
	£58,000 × (1.302)	(75,516)	(75,516)
	£4,000 × (1.017)	(4,068)	(4,068)
Lower gain taken: £78,416		131,916	78,416

(W3) **Antique table**

	£
Proceeds	7,200
Less Cost	(1,000)
Unindexed gain	6,200
Less Indexation allowance £1,000 × (1.053)	(1,053)
	5,147
Apply $\frac{5}{3}$ rule: gain is restricted to $\frac{5}{3}$ (£7,200 – £6,000)	2,000

(W4)   Constable painting

	£
Proceeds – restricted to minimum	6,000
Less Cost	(7,500)
Unindexed loss	(1,500)

Multiple choice questions

1   C

	£
Sale proceeds	7,000
Costs of sale	(100)
Cost	(3,000)
	3,900
Indexation	(1,500)
	2,400
Restricted to ⅔ (7,000 – 6,000)	1,667

2   D   All four of the assets are exempt.

3   C Tangible movable property which is a wasting asset (50 years or less useful life) is an exempt asset, ie greyhound. This does not exempt the lathe as it qualified for capital allowances.

Chapter 7

1   KNN

	£
Sale proceeds	13,000
Cost (W1)	(5,080)
	7,920
Indexation (£9,065 – £5,080)	(3,985)
Chargeable gain	3,935

Workings

1985 pool

		Number of shares	Cost £	Indexed cost £
At 1 April 1985 (provided)		1,800	3,100	3,428
Indexed rise to September 1988	£3,428 × 0.144			494
Acquisition September 1988		3,200	9,600	9,600
		5,000	12,700	13,522
Indexed rise to October 2003	£13,522 × 0.676			9,141
				22,663
Disposal $\frac{2,000}{5,000}$ × £12,700/£22,663		(2,000)	(5,080)	(9,065)
Pool carried forward		3,000	7,620	13,598

2   Spencer

Step 1

Apply the identification rules

Number sold – 14 May 2003				350
(1)	Same day acquisitions			Nil
(2)	Shares acquired in previous nine days			Nil
(3)	1985 pool (1 April 1982 onwards)			
	10 August 1987		100	
	6 May 1998		150	
				250
(4)	1982 pool (pre 31 March 1982)			
	6 May 1972 300 shares, balance only			100
				350

Step 2

Compute the gains on each category

1985 pool

	£
Sale proceeds 250/350 × £14,000	10,000
Cost (W1)	(8,700)
	1,300
Indexation (W2 – W1) £11,606 – £8,700 = £2,906	(1,300)
	Nil

Indexation cannot create a loss.

1982 pool

	Cost £	1982 value £
Sale proceeds 100/350 × £14,000	4,000	4,000
Cost or 1982 value (W3)	(1,583)	(1,700)
Unindexed gain	2,417	2,300
Indexation (1.273 × £1,700)	(2,164)	(2,164)
	253	136

Lower gain applies   136

Workings

(W1 & 2)

1985 pool

	Number	Cost £	Indexed cost £
At 6 April 1985	–	–	–
Purchase 10 August 1987	100	3,000	3,000
Indexed rise to May 1998 £3,000 × 0.601			1,803
Purchase 6 May 1998	150	5,700	5,700
	250	8,700	10,503
Indexed rise to May 2003 £10,503 × 0.105			1,103
	250	8,700	11,606
Disposal 14 May 2003	(250)	(8,700)	(11,606)

(W3)

	Number	Cost £	1982 value £
May 1972 purchase	300	4,750	5,100
Disposal 14 May 2003	(100)		
$\frac{100}{300}$ x £4,750		(1,583)	
$\frac{100}{300}$ x £5,100			(1,700)
Carry forward	200	3,167	3,400

Step 3

Summary – sale of 350 shares

		£
(i)	1985 pool	Nil
(ii)	1982 pool	136
Chargeable gain		136

3   Scarlet

Scarlet Ltd – 1985 pool

		Number	Cost £	Indexed cost £
Balance at 5 May 1986		2,500	3,900	4,385
4 April 1987 Bonus issue 1 for 2		1,250	–	–
		3,750	3,900	4,385
Indexed rise to January 1988	£4,385 × 0.056			246
				4,631
19 January 1988 rights issue 1 for 3 × 140p		1,250	1,750	1,750
		5,000	5,650	6,381
Indexed rise to September 2003	£6,381 × 0.756			4,824
		5,000	5,650	11,205
Cost of sale $\frac{1,500}{5,000}$ × £5,650 / £11,205		(1,500)	(1,695)	(3,361)
Pool		3,500	3,955	7,844

20 September 2003	Sale of 1,500 shares		
	Proceeds		4,725
	Less Pool cost		(1,695)
			3,030
	Less Indexation (£3,361 – £1,695)		(1,666)
	Chargeable gain		1,364

4   Colonel

Step 1

Identification of disposal

			Number	Disposal of 3,500
1985 pool				
Purchase	December 1985	1,000		
Rights issue	April 1987	500		
		1,500	1,500	(1,500)
1982 pool				
December 1975		1,500		
Rights issue April 1987		750		
		2,250	2,250	(2,000)
		C/f	250	

Step 2

Calculation of gain

		£	Summary £
1985 pool			
Sale proceeds 1,500/3,500 × £32,000		13,714	
Cost (W1)		(6,000)	
Unindexed gain		7,714	
Indexation (W2 – W1) (11,188 – 6,000)		(5,188)	
Gain		2,526	2,526

1982 pool	£	£	
Sale proceeds 2,000/3,500 × £32,000	18,286	18,286	
Cost or 1982 value (W3)	(4,000)	(4,667)	
Rights issue (W3)	(2,667)	(2,667)	
Unindexed gain	11,619	10,952	
Indexation			
Higher of cost and 1982 value (1.297 × £4,667)	(6,053)	(6,053)	
On rights issue (0.793 × £2,667)	(2,115)	(2,115)	
Gain	3,451	2,784	
Take the lower gain			2,784
Total gain			5,310

Workings

(W1 & 2)

1985 pool	Number	Unindexed cost £	Indexed cost £
At 6 April 1985	–	–	–
Acquisition December 1985	1,000	4,000	4,000
Indexed rise to April 1987			
£4,000 × 0.060			240
	1,000	4,000	4,240
Rights issue	500	2,000	2,000
	1,500	6,000	6,240
Indexed rise to November 2003			
£6,240 × 0.793			4,948
	1,500	6,000(W1)	11,188 (W2)

(W3)

1982 pool	Number	Cost £	1982 value £	Rights issue
December 1975 (see note)	1,500	4,500	5,250	
April 1987 rights issue	750			3,000
	2,250	4,500	5,250	3,000
Disposal	(2,000)			
$\frac{2,000}{2,250}$ x £4,500		(4,000)		
x £5,250			(4,667)	
x £3,000				(2,667)
Carried forward	250	500	583	333

Note   £3.50 × 1,500 (ie shares actually held at 31 March 1982 fixed value).

No indexation in 1982 pool working.

Multiple choice questions

1   A   Gains on 'loan relationships' are dealt with under Schedule D Case III and not as capital gains.

2   C

		Cost £	Indexed cost £
3.7.85	Issued	11,500	11,500
24.5.86	Indexation update		
	$0.028 \times 11,500$		322
			11,822
	Rights issue $(1,000 \times 130)$	1,300	1,300
		12,800	13,122
10.10.03	Indexation update		
	$0.857 \times 13,122$		11,246
		12,800	24,368
	Indexation on disposal $(24,368 - 12,800)$		11,568

3   C   Indexation runs from the month the expenditure is incurred, ie February 2004.

Chapter 8

1   LKK

The gain on the sale of the first asset is computed as follows.

	£
Sale proceeds	35,000
Less Cost	(20,000)
	15,000
Indexation (based on March 1982 value)	
£25,000 × 0.216	(5,400)
	9,600
Rollover relief	(9,600)
Chargeable gain	Nil

The full gain is rolled over as all of the sale proceeds are reinvested.

The gain on the second disposal is calculated as follows.

	£	£
Sale proceeds		95,000
Cost	40,000	
Rolled over gain £9,600/2 =	(4,800)	(35,200)
Unindexed gain		59,800
Indexation £35,200 × 0.852		(29,990)
Chargeable gain		29,810

2   DRV

(a)   (i)   Sale of original freehold factory (purchased May 1983)

		£
Sale proceeds (December 1987)		130,000
Less	Cost	(65,000)
Unindexed gain		65,000
Less	Indexation allowance (December 1987 – May 1983)	
	0.220 × £65,000	(14,300)
Chargeable gain		50,700
Less	Roll-over relief upon purchase of replacement factory	
	in October 1987	(50,700)
Gain chargeable		Nil

(ii) Sale of replacement factory

	£	£
Sale proceeds (March 2004)		275,000
Cost (October 1987)	190,000	
Less Rolled over gain	(50,700)	
		(139,300)
Unindexed gain		135,700
Less IA (March 2004 – October 1987)		
0.794 × £139,300		(110,604)
Chargeable gain (assuming no other acquisitions within rollover period)		25,096

(b)   (i)   Sale of original factory (purchased May 1983)

	£
Sale proceeds (December 1987)	130,000
Less Cost	(65,000)
Unindexed gain	65,000
Less IA (December 1987 – May 1983) as before per (a) (i)	(14,300)
	50,700
Less Roll-over relief (deemed used in replacement)	(35,700)
Chargeable gain year ended 31 March 1988 (representing proceeds of sales not reinvested: £130,000 – £115,000)	15,000

(ii) Sale of replacement factory

	£	£
Sale proceeds		275,000
Cost	115,000	
Less Rolled over gain	(35,700)	
		79,300
Unindexed gain		195,700
Less IA (March 2004– October 1987) (0.794 × £79,300)		(62,964)
Chargeable gain		132,736

Multiple choice questions

1   C   Reinvestment must be made in the period commencing one year before disposal (1 June 2002) and ending three years after disposal (1 June 2006).

2   C   Shop replacement purchased more than 12 months before disposal does not qualify. Office purchased within three years after disposal does qualify even for a different trade.

3   A

	£	£
Unindexed gain		350,000
Less IA		(70,000)
Indexed gain		280,000
Actual proceeds	800,000	
Qualifying reinvestment	(600,000)	
Chargeable		(200,000)
Eligible for roll over		80,000

4   A

	£
Proceeds	1,200,000
Less Cost	(480,000)
	720,000
Less IA	(73,440)
Indexed gain	646,560

Attributable to qualifying use (two-thirds) = 431,040

	£
Attributable proceeds $\frac{2}{3} \times 1,200,000$	800,000
Reinvested	(720,000)
Cannot be held over	80,000
Rollover relief (431,040 – 80,000)	351,040

5   B   Ships are qualifying assets.

         (A)   Not fixed plant and machinery.

         (C)   Not *used* in claimant's business.

         (D)   Not *occupied* for business purposes.

Chapter 9

1   Alfred Ball

Step 1

CT proformas

	31.12.2001 £	Year ended 31.12.2002 £	31.12.2003 £
Schedule D Case I	42,000	19,000	–
Schedule D Case III	3,000	2,000	1,000
Chargeable gains	4,000	4,000	4,000
	49,000	25,000	5,000
S393A(1)(a) current year relief			(5,000)
	49,000	25,000	–
S393A(1)(b) carry back relief	-	(25,000)	
	49,000	-	
Gift Aid	(10,000)	Wasted	
PCTCT	39,000	Nil	Nil

The Gift Aid of £10,000 paid in the year ended 31 December 2002 is wasted.

Step 2

Loss memorandum

	£
Year ended 31 December 2003	(67,000)
Current year	5,000
Carry back – 12 months to year ended 31 December 2002	25,000
Loss available to carry forward at 31 December 2003	(37,000)

2   Coriander Ltd

Set up CT proformas for all relevant years

	12 m/e 30.6.2001 £	*9 m/e 31.3.2002* £	*12 m/e 31.3.2003* £	*12 m/e 31.3.2004* £
Schedule D Case I profit	27,600	12,450		12,000
S393(1) carry forward relief				(12,000)[3]
Schedule D Case III	1,200	1,300	1,400	1,600
Chargeable gains (£12,000 – £6,000 brought forward)	–	–	–	6,000
	28,800	13,750	1,400	7,600
Current year relief – S393A(1)(a)			(1,400)[1]	
	28,800	13,750	–	7,600
Trade charges	(3,000)	(3,000)	–	-
	25,800	10,750	–	7,600
Carry back relief – S393A(1)(b)	(6,450)[2]	(10,750)[2]		
PCTCT	19,350	–	–	7,600

*Restricted to profits available

Loss memorandum

	£
Year ended 31 March 2003	
Trading loss (£75,000 + £6,550 + £3,000)	(84,550)
(1) Used Current period	1,400
(2) Carry back	
(i) 9 months – period ended 31 March 2002	10,750
(ii) 3 months – year ended 30 June 2001 (see note below)	6,450
12 months	(65,950)
(3) Carry forward against Schedule DI – Year ended 31 March 2004	12,000
At 31 March 2004 to carry forward	(53,950)

Note   This is £25,800 × $\frac{3}{12}$ but £28,800 × $\frac{3}{12}$ would also have been acceptable for exam purposes as trade charges could be relieved against the other 9 months.

3 Unblocked

(a) Corporation tax computations after claiming loss relief

	Year ended 30.06.2001 £	Year ended 30.06.2002 £	3 months 30.09.2002 £	6 months 31.03.2003 £	9 months 31.12.2003 £
Schedule DI (W1)	47,000	156,500	55,000	44,000	–
S393(1) (W3)	(47,000)	(24,000)			
Schedule A	–	1,500			
Capital gain	–	–	10,800		71,100
Less Capital loss b/fwd (W4)			(10,800)		(4,200)
Total profits	–	134,000	55,000	44,000	66,900
S393A(1)(a)				–	(66,900)
S393A(1)(b)		(33,500)	(55,000)	(44,000)	
	–	100,500	–	–	–
Less Gift Aid	–	(1,000)	Wasted	Wasted	Wasted
PCTCT	–	99,500	–	–	–
CT liability (W5)	–	19,651	–	–	–

(b) Tax refunds

	Year ended 30.06.2001 £	Year ended 30.06.2002 £	3 months to 30.09.2002 £	6 months 31.03.2003 £
Original PCTCT				
Total profits	Nil	134,000	55,000	44,000
Less Gift Aid		(1,000)	(1,000)	(1,000)
PCTCT		133,000	54,000	43,000
Step 1 Original CT payable (W6)	Nil	26,267	10,260	8,170
Step 2 Revised CT from part (a)	Nil	19,651	Nil	Nil
Step 3 Tax refunds	Nil	6,616	10,260	8,170

Workings

(W1) Schedule D Case I

	3 months to 30.09.2002 £	6 months to 31.03.2003 £	9 months to 31.12.2003 £
Trading profit/(loss)	61,250	56,500	(268,750)
Less IBAs (W2)	(6,250)	(12,500)	18,750
Schedule DI	55,000	44,000	(250,000)

(W2) **Industrial buildings allowances**

Purchased	New or secondhand	Sold
1 September 2002 (3 months 30 September 2002)	Secondhand	31 December 2003 (9 months to 31 December 2003)

$$\text{Allowance} = \frac{£250,000}{25 \text{ years} - 15 \text{ years} *} = £25,000 \text{ per year}$$

* 1 September 1987 to 1 September 2002

	£	
3 months 30 September 2002	6,250	($£25,000 \times \frac{3}{12}$)
6 months 31 March 2003	12,500	($£25,000 \times \frac{6}{12}$)
Balancing charge	18,750	

> WDA for an *annual* period

(W3) **D1 losses memorandum**

	Brought forward £	9 months to 31 December 2003 £
Trading loss	71,000	268,750
Less Balancing charge		(18,750)
	71,000	250,000
S393(1) – carry forward relief	(47,000)	
	24,000	
S393(1) (9) – carry forward relief	(24,000)	
	Nil	
S393A(1)(a) – current period		(66,900)
		183,100
S393A(1)(b) – carry back 6 months to 31 March 2003		(44,000)
		139,100
S393A(1)(b) – carry back 3 months to 30 September 2002		(55,000)
		84,100
S393A(1)(b) – carry back – $\frac{3}{12} \times £134,000$		(33,500)
		50,600

(W4) **Other losses memorandum**

	y/e 30.6.01
	£
Capital loss	(15,000)
3m to 30.9.02	10,800 gain
9m to 31.12.03	4,200 gain
	Nil

(W5) **CT liability Year ended 30 June 2002 (revised)**

Revised PCTCT and 'P' = £99,500

Therefore the small rate applies: 20% for FY01 and 19% for FY02. The CT liability is as follows.

	£
£99,500 × 20% × $\frac{9}{12}$	14,925
£99,500 × 19% × $\frac{3}{12}$	4,726
	19,651

(W6) **Original CT liability**

	£
Year ended 30 June 2001	Nil
Year ended 30 June 2002	
£133,000 × 19.75% (average rate)	26,267
Three months ended 30 September 2002	
FY02 £54,000 × 19%	10,260

*Small company rate applies because £54,000 is less than $\frac{3}{12}$ × £300,000 = £75,000 but greater than $\frac{3}{12}$ x £50,000 = £12,500.

| *Six months ended 31 March 2003* | |
| FY02 £43,000 × 19%* | 8,170 |

*£43,000 is less than $\frac{6}{12}$ × £300,000 = £150,000 but greater than $\frac{6}{12}$ × £50,000 = £25,000.

Multiple choice questions

1   B   Losses b/f can be set off only against Schedule D Case I profits from the same trade, ie £14,000.

2   C   Losses must first be set off against other income before charges of the same accounting period. Any remaining loss can then be carried back for relief against the profits of the preceding 12 months.

	£	£
Loss 12 m/e 31.12.03		(300,000)
S393A same AP (DIII)	20,000	20,000
Available to c/b		(280,000)
S393A c/b to preceding 12m		
Total profits before non-trading charges £(190,000 + 10,000)	200,000	200,000
Total c/f		(80,000)
Total S393A relief	220,000	

NB: Relief for the Gift Aid paid will be lost.

3   D

	y/e 31.10.02 £	6 m/e 30.4.03 £
Schedule D Case I	12,000	Nil
Gains	-	4,000
Total profits before charges	12,000	4,000
Current AP loss set off S393A		(4,000)
Loss carried back under S393A	(6,000)	
	6,000	
Less Charges	(1,000)	
	5,000	

4   D

	£	£
Schedule D Case I		175,000
Losses b/f	180,000	
S393(1) set-off	(175,000)	(175,000)
Losses c/f	5,000	-
Schedule D Case III		30,000
Gains	20,000	
Capital losses b/f	(30,000)	Nil
Capital losses c/f	(10,000)	
Charges		(10,000)
		20,000

5   A   The loss bought forward must be set off against the next available trading profits *from the same trade*, ie the manufacturing trade only, ie £56,000.

Chapter 10

1   Zeus

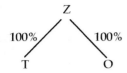

♦   Three associates

♦   ZOT are a 75% group

	Small companies' rate	*Starting rate*
♦ Upper and lower limits are	$\frac{£1,500,000}{3} = £500,000$	$\frac{£1,500,000}{3} = £16,667$
	$\frac{£300,000}{3} = £100,000$	$\frac{£300,000}{3} = £3,333$

Calculate the PCTCT and 'P'

	Zeus Ltd £	*Thor Ltd* £	*Odin Ltd* £
Schedule DI (165,000 – 34,000)	640,000	131,000	
Schedule A			24,000
PCTCT before group relief	640,000	131,000	24,000
Group relief (see below)	(31,600)	(43,400)	
PCTCT	608,400	87,600	24,000
FII (£11,160 × $\frac{100}{90}$)		12,400	
Profit for small company purposes	608,400	100,000	24,000

Odin's loss: 99,000 – 34,000 + 10,000 = 75,000

Determine the best way to utilise Odin Ltd trading loss

	Z	T	O
Category	30%	32.75%	19%
Priority	(2)	(1)	(3)
	£		
Allocate loss to Thor	43,400		
Balance to Zeus	31,600		
	75,000		

You need to give £43,400 to Thor Ltd, not £31,000, due to FII.

The loss brought forward *cannot* be group relieved, but only set against Odin's 'trading profits'. As there are none this must be carried forward.

Calculate CT payable

	Z £	T £	O £
PCTCT × 19% =		16,644	4,560
PCTCT × 30% =	182,520		
Trading loss c/fwd			18,000

The royalty of £34,000 is a trading expense paid by Thor Ltd, and taxable trading income in the hands of Odin Ltd. Odin Ltd has written off part of the cost of acquiring the patent for accounting purposes and is allowed to set this off as a debit under Schedule D I.

The marginal corporation tax rate for each of the three companies, before group relief, is Zeus Ltd 30%, Thor Ltd 32.75%, and Odin Ltd 19%. £43,400 of Odin Ltd's loss has therefore been surrendered to Thor Ltd in order to bring its profits down to the lower limit, with the balance being surrendered to Zeus Ltd. A claim under S393A(1)(a) by Odin Ltd against its own income would have only saved corporation tax at the rate of 19%.

2   Pears

Explanation of capital transactions

Group structure

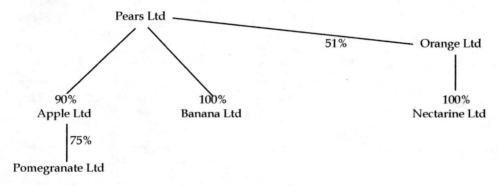

For capital gains purposes, a group of companies consists of a principal company – in this case Pears Ltd – and all its 75% subsidiaries, but not including any company that is not an effective 51% subsidiary of the principal company. Apple Ltd and Banana Ltd are both 75% subsidiaries, and Pomegranate Ltd is a 90% × 75% = 67.5% subsidiary, and these companies are therefore all members of the Pears capital gains group.

Orange Ltd is not a 75% subsidiary of Pears Ltd and therefore neither it nor its subsidiary, Nectarine Ltd, are members of the Pears capital gains group, even though Nectarine is an effective 51% subsidiary of Pears Ltd. However, Orange and Nectarine are themselves a capital gains group.

(1)   Proposed sale of properties to Banana Ltd

The proposal is for members of the Pears group to sell investment assets at full market value to Banana, which can then sell the assets outside the group and set off the gains and losses.

The sale of assets to Banana by members of the Pears capital gains group – that is, by Pears, Apple, and Pomegranate – would be on a no gain/no loss basis. Therefore there will be gains on the sale of the assets by Banana against which the losses of Banana should be available for set off.

Although this would have the desired effect of allowing gains to be netted off against Banana's losses, it is not actually necessary for the intra-group sales to take place. Both Banana and the other group member(s) concerned can make an election stating that Banana is to be treated as having made the disposal outside the group.

Sales by Orange and Nectarine to Banana will not be covered by the no gain/no loss group rules. Instead, they will be treated as being at market value, as Orange and Nectarine are connected persons with Banana. Any transaction will therefore realise actual gains in Orange and Nectarine, thus defeating the object of the exercise. No election can be made as they are not in the same capital gains group as Banana.

(2)   **Proposed sale of investments by Pomegranate Ltd**

The sale of the investments by Pomegranate to Pears Ltd will be at no gain/no loss as both are members of the same capital gains group. There will be no capital gain (or loss) until the shares are sold outside the capital gains group.

---

3   Zoo plc

(a)   There are seven associates (excluding Zoo plc). Upper and lower limits are therefore

$$£187,500 \left\{ \frac{£1,500,000}{8} \right\} \text{ and } £37,500 \left\{ \frac{£300,000}{8} \right\} \text{ respectively.}$$

The starting rate thresholds are similarly

$$£6,250 \left\{ \frac{50,000}{8} \right\} \text{ and } £1,250 \left\{ \frac{10,000}{8} \right\}$$

The definition of an associate includes overseas resident companies (Elk Ltd) and companies only associated for part of the period (Bat and Cod) but excludes dormant companies (Dog Ltd). Zoo plc does not have control over Fox and Gnu Ltd. The associates are as follows.

Ibex, Ant, Hog, Bat, Cod, Elk, Jay.

Note. Gnu, Kea and Lion form a separate 51% group with three associates.

(b)   The main 75% group consists of:

Zoo plc, Ant Ltd (82%), Bat Ltd (90%). Elk Ltd (90%) and Jay Ltd (90% × 100%).

Bat Ltd became part of the group on 1 December 2003. Dog Ltd (85%) qualifies although not yet trading. At 31 March 2004 Cod Ltd no longer qualifies as it has left the group, although it would qualify up to 30 November 2003. Hog Ltd does not qualify (82% × 78% = 63.96% effective interest only) nor does Ibex Ltd (82% × 78% × 70% = 44.77% + 10% = 54.77%). Elk Ltd and Jay Ltd qualify even though Elk Ltd is resident overseas.

(c)   If only a 51% level of control is required then both Hog and Ibex would qualify as well. The 51% group = Zoo, Ant, Bat, Dog, Hog, Ibex, Elk and Jay at 31 March 2004.

(d)   Gnu Ltd qualifies as a consortium company with Zoo, Volt and Watt as the investing members.

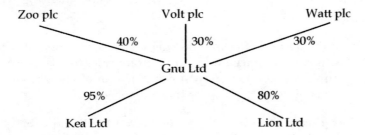

Kea Ltd also qualifies as a consortium company, as it is a 90% trading subsidiary of Gnu Ltd. Lion Ltd does not as the shareholding is less than 90%..

Fox Ltd does *not* qualify as a consortium company as the diagram below demonstrates.

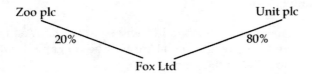

Fox and Unit plc form their own 75% group.

---

4   A Ltd group

(a)   The associated companies for small companies' rate purposes together with the applicable upper and lower thresholds are as follows.

A Ltd, B Ltd, C Ltd, D Ltd, O Inc, E Ltd

Small companies' rate

The upper limit is $\dfrac{£1,500,000}{6}$ = £250,000

The lower limit is $\dfrac{£300,000}{6}$ = £50,000

Starting rate

The upper limit is $\dfrac{£50,000}{6}$ = £8,333

The lower limit is $\dfrac{£10,000}{6}$ = £1,667

B Ltd, C Ltd, D Ltd, O Inc and E Ltd are all under A Ltd's 'control' and hence 'associated' for this purpose.

X Ltd is a single company (ie not associated) and therefore has upper and lower limits of £1,500,000 and £300,000 respectively for small company's rate purposes and limits of £50,000 and £10,000 for starting rate purposes.

(b)   For group and consortium relief purposes:

- ◆   A Ltd, C Ltd, D Ltd and O Inc are a group
- ◆   D Ltd and E Ltd are a group
- ◆   X Ltd and A Ltd are members of a consortium owning B Ltd

Note that although O Inc is in a group with A Ltd, C Ltd and D Ltd, it cannot claim or surrender losses as it is not UK resident. However, if O Inc had traded through a permanent establishment in the UK, its profits or losses of the UK activity could have been group relieved or surrendered respectively.

(c)   MCT payable is as follows.

	B Ltd £	A Ltd £		D Ltd £
PCTCT	80,000	103,000		35,000
Consortium relief from X Ltd	(12,000)			
Group relief from C Ltd	(7,000)	(53,000)	Group relief from E Ltd	(8,000)
Revised PCTCT	61,000	50,000		27,000
CT @ 30%	18,300			
Less marginal relief				
$(£250,000 - £61,000) \times \frac{11}{400}$	(5,197)			
CT @ 19%		9,500		5,130
	13,103	9,500		5,130

C Ltd loss memo

	£
A Ltd	53,000
B Ltd	7,000
	60,000

O Inc   MCT nil, no group relief surrender as overseas company.

E Ltd   MCT nil, £8,000 loss surrendered to D Ltd

X Ltd   MCT nil, £12,000 of £40,000 loss surrendered as consortium relief for B Ltd (maximum 15% × £80,000). Balance of loss (£28,000) carried forward against X Ltd's future trading profits.

Members of a consortium may surrender their losses to the consortium company up to a maximum of their share of the consortium company's profits. C Ltd's loss can 'flow through' A Ltd, the 'link' company. Losses are allocated to save tax at the highest marginal rate.

(d)   There are two main weaknesses in the existing structure from a tax point of view, as follows.

♦   As A Ltd only owns 65% of B Ltd there is a restriction on the group losses that can be surrendered between B Ltd and members of the A Ltd group (A Ltd, C Ltd and D Ltd). Only 65% of B Ltd's profits or losses can participate. Such group relief claims and surrenders would not be restricted if A Ltd held 75% of B Ltd.

♦   The holding in E Ltd is only 72%. Thus, for group relief purposes, E Ltd is not part of A Ltd's group and no claims or surrenders can be made between E Ltd and A Ltd or C Ltd. If A Ltd's effective holding in E Ltd increased to 75% via D Ltd, such group relief claims and surrenders would be allowed.

Multiple choice questions

1   C   Companies are associated even though controlled for part only of the relevant AP. Yellow, Green and Blue are associated with Rainbow. Four associated in total.

2   C   Available loss (8,000)
Available profit (12,000 – (5,000) b/f loss) = 7,000
Group relief maximum is £7,000

3   B   Losses can be surrendered between Mat and Powys (90%)
Losses can be surrendered between Powys and Quorn (80%)
However, losses cannot be surrendered between Mat and Quorn (72%)

4   B   Claims for loss relief

    (1)   Surrender £115,000 to Sub for relief at marginal rate
(lower limit FY 2003 £150,000)

    (2)   Carry back exactly £9,000 for relief at marginal rate
(lower limit FY 2002 £150,000)

Leaves Sub Ltd's PCTCT year ended 31 March 2004 = £150,000

5   D   Cat plc to Dog Ltd – no gain/no loss (75% group)

Dog Ltd to Rabbit Ltd – not in same 75% group

	£
MV of transfer	20,000
Less Cost (to Cat)	(10,000)
Gain before IA of Dog Ltd	10,000

6   C   Sail leaves the group with the asset received via a no gain/no loss intra-group transfer within six years. Gain computed as if the asset was bought and sold for its MV at the time of the no gain/no loss transfer.

	£
MV when transferred	6,000
Less Cost	(2,000)
Gain assessed on Sail on 1 April 2003, ie beginning of AP in which company leaves the group	4,000

(Note that Sail's acquisition cost is now £6,000)

Chapter 11

1   Chinny

	Year ended 30 September 2003 £	3 months to 31 December 2003 £
Schedule D Case I (W1)	186,550	44,182
Schedule D Case III	4,420	780
Schedule A (W2)	8,000	2,000
Chargeable gains	–	55,000
PCTCT	198,970	101,962
CT liability (W3)	37,804	23,080

Workings

(W1)   Schedule D Case I

	Year ended 30 September 2003 £	3 months to 31 December 2003 £
Trading profits time apportioned (12:3)	200,000	50,000
Less Capital allowances	(13,450)	(5,818)
Schedule D Case I	186,550	44,182

(W2)   Schedule A

Rent receivable for 15 months: 8,000 – 3,000 + 5,000 = £10,000

	Year ended 30 September 2003 £	3 months to 31 December 2003 £
Time apportioned (12 : 3)	8,000	2,000

(W3)   Corporation tax liabilities

			Year ended 30 September 2003	3 months ended 31 December 2003
1	PCTCT and 'P' (as there are no dividends)		£198,970	£101,962
2	Financial years		FY02 FY03	FY03
			6m 6m	3m
	Lower limit	Annual	£300,000	
		Three months		£75,000
				More than lower limit
	Upper limit, three months only			
	(£1,500,000 × ³⁄₁₂)			£375,000
			small	marginal
3	Apply rates		FY02	FY03
			19%	30%
			FY03	
			19%	

4   Calculate liabilities

	Year ended 30 September 2003		3 months to 31 December 2003
PCTCT	£198,970		£101,962
	£		£
£198,970 × 19% =	37,804	At 30% =	30,589
		Less $^{11}/_{400}$ (£375,000 – £101,962)	(7,509)
			23,080

Multiple choice questions

			£	£
1	A			
	12 months ended 30 June 2003 b/f		18,000	
	WDA 25%		(4,500)	4,500
			13,500	
	3 months ended 30 September 2003			
	Purchase		9,000	
			22,500	
	WDA 25% × ³⁄₁₂		(1,406)	1,406
				5,906
			21,094	

			General pool
			£
2	A	Year ended 31.3.04	
		Bal b/f	3,500
		Additions	7,500
		Sales	(4,500)
			6,500
		WDA 25%	(1,625)
			4,875
		3 m/e 30.6.04	
		WDA 25% × $\frac{3}{12}$	(305)
		Balance c/f	4,570

			£
3	A	CT computation 3 m/e 30.6.04	
		Schedule D Case I ($\frac{3}{15}$ × 30,000)	6,000
		Schedule D Case VI royalties ($\frac{3}{12}$ × 2,000)	500
		Chargeable gain (1.2.04)	-
		PCTCT	6,500

			£
4	D	12 months ended 31 December 2003 b/f	11,000
		Disposal	(4,500)
			6,500
		WDA 25%	(1,625)
			4,875
		4 months ended 30 April 2004	
		Purchase 3 March 2004	7,485
			12,360
		WDA 25% × $\frac{4}{12}$	(1,030)
		WDV c/f at 30 April 2004	11,330

5	C	**Loan outstanding on 1 January 2005**	
		(£30,000 - £5,000) = £25,000 x 25%	£6,250
		Loan repaid in year to 31 March 2005	
		1 December 2004 - £5,000 but not taxed originally as repaid before 1 January 2005	Nil

Chapter 12

1   Oxo

Year ended 31 March 2004

	£
Schedule D Case I	8,000
Schedule D Case V (W1)	28,682
	36,682
Less Gift Aid paid	(5,000)
PCTCT	31,682
Corporation tax @ 19% (W4)	6,020
Less DTR (W3)	(3,830)
CT payable	2,190

Workings

(W1)   Schedule D Case V

	Mercia DV_1 £	Polia DV_2 £	Total £
Net income received	7,990	16,200	
Add Withholding tax ($\frac{15}{85}$; $\frac{10}{90}$)	1,410	1,800	
	9,400	18,000	
Underlying tax ($\frac{12}{88}$)	1,282	N/A*	
Schedule DV	10,682	18,000	28,682
Overseas tax	2,692	1,800	

*Rental income

(W2)   Analysis of PCTCT

	UK £	Mercia DV_1 £	Polia DV_2 £	Total £
Schedule DI	8,000			8,000
Schedule DV (W1)		10,682	18,000	28,682
Less Charges	(5,000)			(5,000)
PCTCT	3,000	10,682	18,000	31,682

(W3)   Use of overseas tax

		Mercia DV_1 £	Polia DV_2 £	Total £
Schedule D V		10,682	18,000	
UK CT @ 19%	(A)	2,030	3,420	
Overseas tax	(B)	2,692	1,800	
DTR Lower of (A) and (B)		2,030	1,800	3,830

Excess foreign tax is £662 (£2,692 - £2,030)

(W4)   Corporation tax rate

	£
PCTCT	31,682
FII	Nil

Lower limit £150,000 for small company rate and upper limit of £25,000 for starting rate marginal relief – one associate (UK resident subsidiary). M Inc does not rank as an associate as Oxo Ltd does not own more than 50% of the shares. Therefore 19% small company rate applies.

---

2   Columbus

(a)   Corporation tax computation – year ended 31 March 2004

	(i) Rowindan branch £		*(ii)* Rowindan 100% subsidiary £	
Schedule DI	1,200,000		1,200,000	
Schedule DV (Note 1)	200,000		50,000	(Note 2)
	1,400,000		1,250,000	
Less S393A relief	(430,000)		(430,000)	
PCTCT and 'P'	970,000		820,000	
Lower limit	300,000	(2 associated	150,000	
Upper limit	1,500,000	companies)	750,000	
Corporation tax @ 30%	291,000		246,000	
Taper relief $(1,500 - 970) \times \dfrac{11}{400}$	(14,575)		–	
	276,425		246,000	
Double tax relief (W1)	(12,000)		(4,410)	
MCT	264,425		241,590	

Notes

(1)   If it is set up as a branch, all the profits of the branch, irrespective of the amount remitted to UK, will be liable to UK tax under Schedule DV (as the branch is controlled from Rowinda).

(2)   If it is set up as a subsidiary, then remittances become dividends and only the dividends received by Columbus will be taxable.

Since Columbus owns more than 10% of the share capital, relief for underlying tax is available as well as withholding tax.

	£	Dividend £
Profit of subsidiary	200,000	
Tax at 6%	(12,000)	
	188,000	
Dividend 25%	(47,000)	47,000
Retained	141,000	
Underlying tax 25% × £12,000		3,000
Schedule DV assessable		50,000
Amount received (£47,000 × 97%)		45,590
Overseas tax (ie ULT £3,000 + WHT of £1,410)		4,410

Workings

(W1)   DTR

			Branch £	Subsidiary £
(i)	UK tax			
	(a)	DV - £200,000 (branch) = $\frac{£200,000}{£970,000} \times £276,425$	56,995	
	(b)	subsidiary £50,000 × 30%		15,000
(ii)	Overseas tax		12,000	4,410
	Lower		12,000	4,410

(Note 2)

(b)   **Controlled foreign company (CFC)**

These are companies which the Inland Revenue regard as being set up principally to divert income overseas (to a low tax country) from the UK.

This is happening in this case, since previously the income from the sale of tractors in Rowinda was part of UK trading income.

Rowinda is a low tax country since the level of taxation is less than three quarters of the corresponding UK tax rate and it is not an 'excluded country'. The Rowindan establishment is also controlled (100%) by UK residents (exclusively by Columbus Ltd here).

The subsidiary is therefore a controlled foreign company unless any of the following apply.

(i)   It is quoted on a recognised Stock Exchange.

(ii)   Its profits chargeable to tax are less than £50,000 for the accounting period.

(iii) It has an acceptable distribution policy ≥ 90% of income to UK residents for a trading company).

(iv)   It is engaged in exempt activities - autonomous trading activity in country which is not 'non-qualifying'. Non-qualifying business activity includes dealing mainly in goods received from a connected person.

(v)   Motive test is satisfied - tax saving is not main purpose of operation.

None of these are satisfied it would appear and therefore the only way it will not be classified as a CFC is to distribute 90% or more of its distributable profit. The consequence of being a CFC would be for the subsidiary's whole profits to be treated as distributed and these would be assessed on Columbus. Relief would be available for overseas tax on the profits.

(c)   (i)   **Branch**

If goods are invoiced at cost this would reduce DI profits and increase DV profits of Columbus.

This would have no effect on the profits chargeable to corporation tax.

(ii)   **Subsidiary**

If goods are invoiced at cost, DI profits of Columbus would be reduced and the profits of the subsidiary would be increased.

As the subsidiary is non-UK resident, the transfer pricing legislation could be applied. This means that market price would be substituted for cost in computing UK taxable profits (market price = arms length price). No corresponding adjustment would necessarily be made by the Rowindan tax authorities when taxing the subsidiary.

---

3   Mitch

Corporation tax payable for the year ended 31 March 2004

	£
Schedule D Case I	180,000
Schedule D Case V (W1)	120,000
Chargeable gain	68,000
	368,000
Less Charges on income	(5,000)
Profits chargeable to corporation tax	363,000

		£
Corporation tax on PCTCT (£363,000 × 30%)		108,900
Less Marginal relief		
$\frac{11}{400}$ × (£1,500,000 – £363,000)		(31,267)
		77,633
Less DTR (W2)		(25,664)
Corporation tax payable		51,969

Excess foreign tax = £3,136 (£28,800 - £25,604)

Workings

(W1)   Schedule D Case V

As Mitch Ltd controls 10% or more of the voting rights of the Danish corporation, the underlying tax attributable to the foreign dividend must be included.

The gross foreign income is arrived at by grossing up the dividend received from the Danish company, first for the 5% withholding tax and then for the underlying tax of 20%.

(a)   Gross up for withholding tax: £91,200 × $\frac{100}{95}$ = £96,000

(b)   Gross up for underlying tax:

The underlying tax can be calculated as follows.

$$\frac{\text{Dividend} + \text{w / h tax}}{\text{Distributable profits}} \times \text{Tax paid} = \frac{£96,000}{£800,000} \times £200,000 = £24,000$$

Gross dividend is therefore: £96,000 + £24,000 = £120,000.

Foreign tax = £120,000 - £91,200 = £28,800

(W2)   Double taxation relief (DTR)

		UK profits £	Overseas profits £	Total £
Profits		248,000	120,000	368,000
Less	Charges (Note)	(5,000)	–	(5,000)
		243,000	120,000	363,000
Corporation tax @ 21.3865% (W3)		51,969	25,664	77,633
Less	Double tax relief			
Lower of				
(B)	UK corporation tax on foreign profits (£25,664)			
(A)	Foreign tax suffered (£28,800)		(25,664)	(25,664)
	Corporation tax payable	51,969	Nil	51,969

Note. The Gift Aid is set primarily against UK profits in preference to foreign profits, in order to maximise the UK corporation tax attributable to the overseas profits.

(W3)   UK Corporation tax rate

$$\frac{£77,633}{£363,000} \times \frac{100}{1} = 21.3865\%$$

Chapter 13

1   Space

Step 1

	Year ended 31 March 2004
'Profits'	£2,000,000
FY	2003
Rate	30%
CT liability	£600,000

Step 2

The accounting period will be subject to self assessment and to the quarterly system of instalments as the company is large and was large in the previous year.

The liability for the year ended 31 March 2004 should be settled by four equal instalments of £150,000 (£600,000 ÷ 4).

		£
Instalment 1	14 October 2003	150,000
Instalment 2	14 January 2004	150,000
Instalment 3	14 April 2004	150,000
Instalment 4	14 July 2004	150,000
		600,000

Step 3

(1)   A return, including statutory accounts and computations, must be submitted within 12 months of the accounting period end otherwise penalties will be exacted.

(2)   Late payments of tax will give rise to interest charges, which will be deductible under DIII.

Multiple choice questions

1   B   Correcting an error on a CT return may be done within one year following the filing date, ie by 30.9.2004.

2   C   The Revenue can 'repair' a return within nine months of the date on which the return is actually filed.

3   D   21 years following the accounting date.

4   D   Six years after the end of accounting period (unless an enquiry is still in progress) ie until 31 December 2008.

5   D   Notice must be given within 12 months of the quarter date (31 January, 30 April, 31 July or 31 October) immediately following the actual filing date as the return was filed late (normally the notice must be within 12 months of the statutory filing date), ie by 30.4.2005.

Chapter 14

1   NCH

VAT account

	£		£
Input VAT on purchases £9,600 × 7.5%	1,680	Output VAT on sales £16,500 × 17.5%	2,887
Input VAT on expenses £2,400 × 17.5%	420	Understatement of output VAT on previous return £3,000 × 17.5%	525
	2,100	Car fuel charge £300 × $^{7}/_{47}$	45
Input VAT on returns to suppliers £300 × 17.5%	(53)		
	2,047		3,457
VAT payable carried down	1,252	Output VAT on returns from customers £900 × 17.5%	(158)
	3,299		3,299

£1,252 VAT is due for payment by 30 June 2003, 30 days after the quarter end.

Notes

There is no bad debt relief yet as the debt must be six months old from the due date of payment. As it is only three months old, the claim cannot be made until the following quarter.

The car fuel scale charge is VAT inclusive, therefore the VAT element is $\frac{17.5}{117.5}$. This is commonly shortened to $^{7}/_{47}$.

---

2   Tee Total

(a)   Cash accounting scheme

♦   This scheme is open to businesses with a taxable turnover of less than £600,000.

♦   Businesses opting for the scheme still have to issue tax invoices as before, but do not have to account for VAT until they have been paid by their customers and are not able to reclaim VAT until they have paid their suppliers. Thus the scheme provides automatic bad debt relief.

Annual accounting scheme

♦   The annual accounting scheme is available to all businesses which regularly pay tax, having been registered for at least one year and which have a taxable turnover of less than £600,000.

♦   Users have to be approved by Customs and agree an annual assessment of their expected VAT liability based on their previous year's VAT payments. The business then makes nine months' payments of 10% of that assessment (by direct debit) commencing in the fourth month of the annual cycle. The tenth payment, which accompanies the annual return, represents the balance which is due for the year. This must be submitted within two months of the year end. Thus users of the scheme have an extra month in which to pay their VAT liability.

♦   Traders with an annual turnover not exceeding £150,000 can join the scheme without waiting a year from registration.

♦ Traders can request Customs to make quarterly rather than monthly payments in which case they make three quarterly payments each of 25% of the previous year's net VAT liability.

Flat rate scheme

♦ Traders can apply to join a special flat rate scheme if their VAT exclusive annual taxable turnover does not exceed £150,000 and their total turnover (including zero rated and exempt supplies) does not exceed £187,500.

♦ The net tax due to Customs for a return period is then calculated as a flat rate percentage of the total turnover. This includes standard rated and reduced rate standard rated supplies at their tax inclusive amount and zero rated and exempt supplies. Actual amounts of output tax and input tax are irrelevant.

♦ The flat rate percentage depends on the trade sector of the business (and will be provided in the exam room if required). Flat rate traders are still required to issue normal VAT invoices to their VAT registered customers but there are less records for the trader to maintain so there are administrative advantages.

(b) **Default surcharge**

The return for 31 May 2003 should have been returned within 30 days, ie by 30 June. The late filing of returns precipitates a default surcharge period. Customs will issue a default surcharge notice. There is no penalty on this first late filing of the return but, once a surcharge notice is issued, any further late returns for the next four quarters will give rise to a penalty.

Total Ltd needs to ensure that its VAT returns to 31 August 2003, 30 November 2003, 29 February 2004 and 31 May 2004 are submitted in time, otherwise penalties will be charged as a percentage of the VAT due for a return period as follows.

♦ First default in surcharge period – 2%
♦ Second default in surcharge period – 5%
♦ Increasing to 10% on the third and 15% on the fourth and subsequent defaults.

Serious misdeclaration penalty

The return submitted is also inaccurate and may trigger a serious misdeclaration penalty of 15% of the VAT involved in the error.

A misdeclaration occurs where there is a mistake in a VAT return which either understates the trader's tax liability or lays claim to a repayment which is not due. This is considered serious where the error equals or exceeds either £1,000,000 or 30% of the gross tax for the period. The gross tax is the total of input and output tax.

In Total Ltd's case the error is serious, as the error exceeds 30% of the gross tax $(8,500/(24,000 + 4,000 = 28,000) = 30.36\%)$. To avoid a penalty, the company should inform Customs immediately of the error.

3   **Artley**

(a)   **Output tax and input tax for the year ended 31 March 2004**

Outputs chargeable at standard rate	£	£
Sales		120,000
Plant sold to UK trader		5,000
		125,000
Outputs chargeable at zero rate		
Sales		
		15,000
Total taxable outputs		140,000
Exempt sales		100,000
Total outputs		240,000
Output tax on taxable outputs (£125,000 × 17.5%)		21,875
Input tax attributable to taxable supplies	10,000	
Input tax attributable to overheads		
Allowable proportion $\dfrac{(£140,000 - £5,000)}{(£240,000 - £5,000)} = 58\% \times £3,000$	1,740	
(Supplies of capital goods must be excluded)		(11,740)
Net payment to Customs for year		10,135

The *de minimis* exception does not apply as the 'exempt' input VAT of £6,500 + £1,260 = £7,760 exceeds £625 per month on average.

(b)   **Irrecoverable input tax**

The irrecoverable input tax of £7,760 will be treated as an allowable expense in computing Artley Ltd's Schedule DI profit. The input tax on the purchased car is specifically not deductible since it is not used wholly for business purposes, but it forms part of the allowable cost of the car for the purposes of capital allowances.

If the car had been leased then, despite private use by the salesman, 50% of the input tax on the lease rentals would have been recoverable.

Multiple choice questions

1   **D**   The basic tax point is amended in the case of 'sale or return' goods to the earlier of

(i)	adoption of the goods	15 July
(ii)	12 months after the date of despatch	3 June next year

However, since an invoice is issued within 14 days after 15 July, that invoice date becomes the tax point.

Therefore the tax point is 20 July.

2   D   Provided that the tax-inclusive consideration does not exceed £100 (including VAT), retailers may provide a less detailed invoice with only the following particulars.

(a)   Name, address and registration number of the retailer
(b)   Date of supply
(c)   Description sufficient to identify the goods or services supplied
(d)   Total amount payable including tax
(e)   Rate of tax

An invoice number need not be shown.

3   D   The *de minimis* limits, below which exempt input tax is not subject to the partial exemption rules, is £625 per month.

	£	£
Directly attributable exempt input tax		875
Indirectly attributable, ie non attributable	500	
Less $500 \times \dfrac{70,000}{100,000}$ (70%)	(350)	
		150
		1,025

Monthly average = $\dfrac{1,025}{(3)}$ = 342, ie below 625

The exempt input tax is below the *de minimis* limit and is not more than 50% of the VAT on all purchases. The whole £5,500 is therefore allowed.

4   B   VAT cannot be recovered on the purchase of motor cars if there is any element of private use, so capital allowances are claimable on the VAT-inclusive price of £11,750. The finance charge is an allowable trading expense.

Chapter 15

1   LA Raider

Step 1

Calculate the employment income assessable.

A receipts basis is applied to both the salary and the bonus.

			£	£
Salary	(1.4.03 – 30.11.03)	$\frac{8}{12} \times 48{,}500$	32,333	
	(1.12.03 – 31.3.04)	$\frac{4}{12} \times 53{,}000$	17,667	
			_____	
				50,000
Bonus	Paid February 2004			14,200
				_____
				64,200

Step 2

Calculate the assessable benefits.

♦   Use of yacht – 20% × market value when first made available

	£
$20\% \times £42{,}000 \times \frac{2}{52}$	323
Running expenses – $£6{,}000 \times \frac{2}{52}$	231
	____
	554

♦   Medical insurance – premium paid   1,270

♦   Assuming canteen facilities are available to all staff on a similar basis, there is no assessable benefit.

♦   Round sum expense allowance – when entertaining expenses are paid out of a round sum allowance, the allowance is taxable on the employee. A claim can be made for the business travel.   £1,870

♦   Car benefit charge – a genuine pool car does not give rise to an assessable benefit.

The chauffeur's salary is not charged as a benefit since the chauffeur's services are only used on business journeys.

The provision of the Rover will give rise to a benefit calculated as follows.

35% × £17,000   £5,950

The percentage is restricted to 35% (compared to 40% (15% + (280 – 155) × $\frac{1}{5}$)).

♦   Fuel benefit –£14,400 × 35%   £5,040

◆   Beneficial loan

		£
Home loan – $\dfrac{£20,000 + £20,000}{2} \times 5\%$		1,000
Less Interest paid £20,000 × 1%		(200)
		800

In addition Raider can claim for the 12,000 business miles travelled in his own car. The Inland Revenue authorised rate is 40p a mile for the first 10,000 miles and 25p a mile thereafter.

Expense claim :	10,000 × 40p	4,000
	2,000 × 25p	500
		4,500

Step 3

Summary

		£
Salary		50,000
Less Pension contribution 3%		(1,500)
		48,500
Bonus		14,200
Use of yacht		554
Medical insurance		1,270
Round sum allowance		1,870
Car benefit		5,950
Fuel benefit		5,040
Beneficial loan		800
		78,184
Less Expenses		
Business travel		(550)
Mileage claim		(4,500)
		73,134

Multiple choice questions

1   B   LVs only assessable. Car not assessed as earnings below £8,500.

2   B

	£	£
Salary 6 × £1,150		6,900
Car benefit (15,000 × 15%*)	2,250	
Less Non available $\frac{7}{12}$	(1,313)	
	937	
Fuel (14,400 × 15% × $\frac{5}{12}$)	900	
		1,837
		8,737

*Less than 160 gms/km

3   A   Bonus payments are assessed on a received basis. The bonus was received in 2004/05, therefore there is nil assessable in 2003/04.

4   D

	£
Car benefit (8,000 × 24%*)	1,920
Fuel (£14,400 × 24%)	3,456
	5,376
Earnings	5,000
Assessable (£8,500 would be irrelevant, as director)	10,376

*15% + (200 – 155) × $\frac{1}{5}$ = 24%

5   C

	£
Salary	10,000
Own car (16,000 × 19% = 15% + (175 – 155) × $\frac{1}{5}$)	3,040
Jane's car (8,000 × 21% = 15% + (185 – 155) × $\frac{1}{5}$)	1,680
Benefit – wine (1,000 – 600)	400
	15,120

Jane's car is not assessable on her because she is not 'higher paid'. It is deemed supplied by reason of her father's employment and is thus assessable on him.

Chapter 16

1   Solomon Daisy

When a person leaves his employment, his employer will complete a four part form P45. This shows the total pay to date, the tax deducted and the code number that must be applied to find the tax.

The first part is sent to the Inland Revenue. Jim will take the three bottom copies. Two are for his new employer who will use them to prepare his wages records. The other copy is for Jim to retain for his tax records.

If Jim needs to complete a self assessment return, then the information will be essential to enable him to fulfil his statutory obligations. Penalties can be levied on you as an employer for failing to provide this document.

When Sally joins, she will produce the bottom two copies of her P45. As mentioned above one copy will be used by you to prepare her deduction records. The other copy will be completed by you and sent to your PAYE office.

If Sally was previously unemployed, a P45 will be issued to her from the benefit office. If she cannot produce a P45, a form P46 must be completed and submitted to the tax office.

A form P11D is a return of benefits and reimbursed expenses received by directors and certain employees. This form must be completed for all the employees and directors earning at the rate of £8,500 per year, unless they receive no benefits or expenses.

It will not be necessary to submit a P11D for a director provided:

♦   he earns less than £8,500 a year, and
♦   he works full time for the company, and
♦   he does not own more than 5% of the ordinary share capital of the company.

To find whether a person has reached the £8,500 threshold all emoluments (valuing benefits as though they were received by P11D employees) must be aggregated. No expenses can be deducted for this purpose, other than contributions to an employer's pension scheme.

---

2   Alfred

Alfred's tax code will be shown as follows on form P2.

Your tax allowances		*Amounts taken away from your total allowances*	
	£		£
Personal allowance	4,615	*Car benefit (17,895 × 22% × 6/12)*	1,968
		Medical insurance	600
Total allowances	4,615	*Total deductions*	2,568

Your tax-free amount for the year is £2,047 (£4,615 – £2,568) making your tax code 204L.

Note. The car benefit percentage is 22%, 15% + (190 – 155) × $\frac{1}{5}$.

---

3   Bella

Step 1

Calculate the employees' Class 1 contributions.

Fred – for 51 weeks of the year Fred earns £132 per week. For one week of the year Fred earns £132 + £600 = £732. For the week in which the bonus is paid the upper earnings limit of £595 applies.

George – his pay is above the upper earnings limit of £30,940 (£595 × 52) so he will pay NIC at 1% on his bonus.

Step 2

Calculate the employer's Class 1 contributions.

There is no upper earnings limit for the employer and therefore NIC must be paid on all employee's earnings above the earnings threshold.

Employee's NICs

		£	£
Fred	(£132 – £89) × 51 weeks × 11%	241	
	(£595 – £89) × 1 week × 11%	56	
	(£732 - £595) × 1 week × 1%	1	
			298
George	(£30,940 - £4,615) × 11%	2,896	
	(£32,480 + £2,500 - £30,940) × 1%	40	
			2,936
Total payable in respect of employee's liability			3,234

Employer's NICs

		£	£
Fred	(£132 – £89) × 51 weeks × 12.8%	280	
	(£732 – £89) × 1 week × 12.8%	82	
		362	
George	(£32,480 + £2,500 - £4,615) × 12.8%	3,887	
			4,249
			7,483

4   Janice

Although the two packages offer the same cash remuneration (and therefore there is no tax difference within a tax year) the NIC position is different because there is a maximum NIC position per month and her earnings period for NIC appears to be monthly based.

Earnings threshold	£4,615/12	=	£385
Upper earnings limit	£30,940/12	=	£2,578

Alternative (a)   *Alternative (b)*

Monthly salary £23,000/12 = £1,917   £19,000/12 = £1,583

(£1,917 – £385) × 11% = £168.52   (£1,583 – £385) × 11% = £131.78

For the year this is £168.52 × 12 = £2,022.24   For the year £131.78 × 12 = £1,581.36

Alternative (a)   *Alternative (b)*

Bonus £1,000 month 12.   Bonus £5,000 month 12.

	£		£
Maximum earnings for NIC at 11%	2,578.00	Maximum earnings for NIC at 11%	2,578.00
Less salary	(1,917.00)	Less salary	(1,583.00)
	661.00		995.00
11% on bonus of £661	72.71	11% on £995	109.45
1% on £339 (£1,000 - £661)	3.39	1% on £4,005	40.05
	76.10		149.50

		£			£
Total NIC	Salary	2,022.24	Total NIC	Salary	1,581.36
	Bonus	76.10		Bonus	149.50
		2,098.34			1,730.86

Saving in employee's NIC
367.48

Therefore Janice would save £367.48 NIC under the second alternative, although there is a 'time' value of money to take into account.

5   **Podsnap**

M Jaggers Esq
Dickens House
Rochester
Kent

8 May 2004

Dear Mr Podsnap

Thank you for your letter dated 1 May 2004. The tax implications of your share transactions are as follows.

(1)   **Approved profit sharing scheme**

In normal circumstances, there is a charge to both income tax and NIC when an employee receives shares from his employer free of charge. However, if the shares are allocated under the terms of an approved profit sharing scheme, there is no charge provided that the conditions for exemption are met.

One of the conditions for approval of such a scheme by the Inland Revenue is that, upon allocation to the employee, the shares must be held by the trustees of the scheme on his behalf for at least two years. After three years the trustees will advance the shares unconditionally to the employee, and this advance will be free of tax. Between two and three years after allocation the employee may demand that the trustees advance the shares to him, but there will be an income tax charge based upon the value of the shares at the time of the initial allocation or the sale proceeds, if lower.

In your case you received the shares two years and three months after allocation, and so will pay income tax on the initial value, as follows.

$$£0.75 \times 4{,}500 = £3{,}375 \times 40\% \qquad = \qquad £1{,}350$$

(2)   **Approved company share option plan**

When options to purchase shares are granted under the terms of an Inland Revenue approved scheme, there is normally no income tax charge, either on grant or upon exercise of the option.

One of the conditions for the income tax exemption is that there must be a period of at least three years between the grant of an option and its exercise.

This means that there is no income tax charge upon the exercise in July 2003, as this was more than three years after grant.

(3)   **Special option in lieu of bonus**

This option is not within the terms of the company's approved share option plan, as the option price is at a discount of over 54% on the current market value. The tax treatment is therefore that of an unapproved scheme.

If the options can be exercised more than ten years after grant, which is the case here, there is an immediate income tax charge based upon the difference between the 'offer' price and the market value at the time of the grant, as follows.

	£
Market value £2.20 × 30,000 =	66,000
Offer price £1.00 × 30,000 =	(30,000)
Difference	36,000
Income tax @ 40% =	14,400

When you exercise the options there will be a further income tax charge based upon the difference between the market value at the time of exercise and the offer price. However, to avoid double taxation, you will be entitled to deduct the amount charged of £36,000, as mentioned above, from the amount chargeable on the exercise.

As the shares are quoted on the Stock Exchange, they are classed as readily convertible assets. There is therefore liability to both employers' and employees' class 1 NIC at the time the options are exercised. OHMT may ask you to pay the employers' NIC as well as the employees. If you have not agreed to pay the employer's NIC you cannot be forced to do so.

I hope that this answers all your questions. Please let me know if you require any further help.

Yours sincerely

M Jaggers

Multiple choice questions

1   B

	£
Gross salary	12,000
Mortgage contribution	2,100
	14,100
Less earnings threshold	(4,615)
	9,485 × 12.8% = £1,214

NIC on BUPA subscription is collected under Class 1A.

2   A   Class 1 primary NICs are deducted from an employee's earnings.

3   D   Tips paid direct by customers or distributed by a nominated employee (eg the head waitress acting as a 'troncmaster' avoid NIC, but have to be 'NICed' if paid through the employer.

So earnings for NIC = £10,600.

There are no allowable deductions.

4   B   The higher of the cash alternative (150 × 12 = 1,800) and the car benefit (22%* × 5,000 = 1,100) is added to salary to see if Jenny earns at a rate in excess of £8,500 per annum.

	£
Salary	6,720
Cash alternative	1,800
	8,520

Therefore Jenny is taxable on the car benefit calculated as follows:

$(5,000 \times 22\%) = £1,100)$

$*15\% + (190 - 155) \times \frac{1}{5} = 22\%$

Index

Exam Text Review Form

CIMA PAPER 5 TEXT – BUSINESS TAXATION – FINANCE ACT 2003

We hope that you have found this Text stimulating and useful and that you now feel confident and well-prepared for your examinations.

We would be grateful if you could take a few moments to complete the questionnaire below, so we can assess how well our material meets your needs. There's a prize for four lucky students who fill in one of these forms from across the Syllabus range and are lucky enough to be selected!

	Excellent	*Adequate*	*Poor*
Depth and breadth of technical coverage			
Appropriateness of coverage to examination			
Presentation			
Level of accuracy			

Did you spot any errors or ambiguities? Please let us have the details below.

Page	Error

Thank you for your feedback.

Please return this form to:

The Financial Training Company Limited
Block 2, Unit 2, Wincombe Conference Centre
Wincombe Business Park
Shaftesbury
Dorset SP7 9QJ

Student's name: ....

Address: ....

....

....

CIMA Publications Student Order Form

THE
FINANCIAL TRAINING
COMPANY
PUBLICATIONS DIVISION

To order your books, please indicate quantity required in the relevant order box, calculate the amount(s) in the column provided, and add postage to determine the amount due. Please then clearly fill in your details plus method of payment in the boxes provided and return your completed form with payment attached to:

THE FINANCIAL TRAINING COMPANY, 22J WINCOMBE BUSINESS PARK, SHAFTESBURY, DORSET SP7 9QJ

OR FAX YOUR ORDER TO 01747 858821 OR TELEPHONE 01747 854302

For examinations in May 03 ☐ Nov 03 ☐ May 04 ☐ Nov 04 ☐ (please tick)

FOUNDATION

PAPER	TITLE	TEXT ORDER	PRICE £	EXAM KIT ORDER	PRICE £	FOCUS NOTES ORDER	PRICE £	AMOUNT £
1	Financial Accounting Fundamentals		21.00		11.00		6.00	
2	Management Accounting Fundamentals		21.00		11.00		6.00	
3a	Economics for Business		21.00		11.00		6.00	
3b	Business Law		21.00		11.00		6.00	
3c	Business Mathematics		21.00		11.00		6.00	

INTERMEDIATE

PAPER	TITLE	TEXT ORDER	PRICE £	EXAM KIT ORDER	PRICE £	FOCUS NOTES ORDER	PRICE £	AMOUNT £
4	Finance		21.00		11.00		6.00	
5	Business Taxation [FA 2002] (May & Nov 2003)		21.00		11.00		6.00	
	Business Taxation [FA 2003] (May & Nov 2004)		21.00	Available Feb 04	11.00	Available Feb 04	6.00	
6a	Financial Accounting (UK Standards)		21.00		11.00		6.00	
7a	Financial Reporting (UK Standards)		21.00		11.00		6.00	
8	Management Accounting - Performance Management		21.00		11.00		6.00	
9	Management Accounting - Decision Making		21.00		11.00		6.00	
10	Systems & Project Management		21.00		11.00		6.00	
11	Organisational Management		21.00		11.00		6.00	

FINAL

PAPER	TITLE	TEXT ORDER	PRICE £	EXAM KIT ORDER	PRICE £	FOCUS NOTES ORDER	PRICE £	AMOUNT £
12	Management Accounting - Business Strategy		21.00		11.00		6.00	
13	Management Accounting - Financial Strategy		21.00		11.00		6.00	
14	Management Accounting - Information Strategy		21.00		11.00		6.00	
15	Management Accounting - Case Study		21.00					

Sub Total	£		

Postage and packing – please note a signature is required on delivery

UK & NI	£5 for up to 10 books		£
	If only Focus Notes are ordered, £1 each (max £5)		
	First book	**Each additional book**	
Europe	£25	£3	
Rest of World	£40	£4	

TOTAL PAYMENT	£	

The following section **must be filled in clearly** so that your order can be despatched without delay.

TO PAY FOR YOUR ORDER TICK AN OPTION BELOW

A. I WISH TO PAY BY   MASTERCARD ☐   VISA ☐   DELTA ☐   SWITCH ☐

CARD NO. ☐☐☐☐ ☐☐☐☐☐☐☐ ☐☐☐☐ ☐☐☐☐   (Some cards don't need all boxes)

EXPIRY DATE ☐☐☐☐   ISSUE No. ☐☐☐ (Switch only)   All cards - last 3 digits on signature strip ☐☐☐

Cardholder's Signature _____

Cardholder's Name & Address: _____

Cardholder's Tel. No. (Day): _____

B. I WISH TO PAY BY CHEQUE ☐ Cheques should be made payable to _The Financial Training Company Ltd_ and must be attached to your order form. **Personal cheques cannot be accepted without a valid Banker's Card number written on the back of the cheque.**

STUDENT NAME:	
DELIVERY ADDRESS: (Must be the same as cardholder's address. Please contact us if you wish to discuss an alternative delivery address).	
POST CODE:	TEL. NO. (Day):

April 2003 (This order form replaces any previous order forms.)

April 2003 (This order form replaces any previous order forms.)